WHEN THE STARS CAME OUT

The Story of the Mississippi River Festival

Book written by Mark Pierce with Lyle Ward and Jack Twesten
Cover and book layout by Rosanna Cerutti
Editing by Rebekah Icenesse, Sophie Ma, and Astrid Zeppenfeld
Cover photos courtesy of *Alton Telegraph*, Rick Pass, and Rick Stankoven

Manufactured in the United States of America.

PUBLISHING CONCEPTS LLC

For more information, please contact:
Publishing Concepts LLC
6590 Scanlan Avenue
St. Louis MO 63139
www.PublishingConceptsLLC.com

PAPERBACK ISBN: 978-1-957307-14-5
EBOOK (PDF) ISBN: 978-1-957307-15-2

MUSIC

1 2 3 4 5 6 7 8 9 10

To my B. Brother with
Love, Sis.
I hope you enjoy it!
5/23

To Sara and Maddie—
the brightest stars in my sky.

WHEN THE STARS CAME OUT
The Story of the Mississippi River Festival

MARK PIERCE
with
Lyle Ward and Jack Twesten

Mississippi River Festival

CONTENTS

THE MISSISSIPPI RIVER FESTIVAL

THE ONCE WORLD-RENOWNED CONCERT VENUE MISSISSIPPI RIVER FESTIVAL ("MRF") BEGAN AS A PIONEERING EXPERIMENT IN REGIONAL COOPERATION BETWEEN SOUTHERN ILLINOIS UNIVERSITY EDWARDSVILLE AND THE ST. LOUIS SYMPHONY. THE SYMPHONY WAS INVITED TO ESTABLISH RESIDENCE ON THE UNIVERSITY CAMPUS AND OFFER A SUMMER SERIES OF CONCERTS AND CULTURAL PROGRAMS IN AN OUTDOOR AMPHITHEATRE CONSTRUCTED ON THIS SITE. FROM JUNE 1969 THROUGH AUGUST 1980, NEARLY 1.5 MILLION PEOPLE ATTENDED CONCERTS HERE PERFORMED BY SOME OF THE BEST ARTISTS OF THE DAY, INCLUDING: THE WHO, ELTON JOHN, JUDY COLLINS, BOB HOPE, B.B. KING, TINA TURNER, THE ALLMAN BROTHERS, JAMES TAYLOR, THE ST. LOUIS SYMPHONY ORCHESTRA, THE BEACH BOYS, HENRY MANCINI, GORDON LIGHTFOOT, THE GRATEFUL DEAD, THE NATIONAL DANCE TROUPE OF ZAMBIA, JEAN LUC PONTY, THE CHICAGO SYMPHONY ORCHESTRA, CHICAGO, CHICK COREA, JONI MITCHELL, BARRY MANILOW, BOB DYLAN, EMMYLOU HARRIS, SMOKEY ROBINSON, STANLEY CLARKE, PETE SEEGER, ARLO GUTHRIE, THE DUKE ELLINGTON ORCHESTRA, ELLA FITZGERALD, YES, ITZHAK PERLMAN, VAN CLIBURN, WILLIE NELSON, AND THE EAGLES. CROWDS FOUND THEIR SEATS ON THE GRASS OR SAT BENEATH THE SPACIOUS "MRF" TENT. THE EXCELLENCE OF THE PERFORMANCES, THE UNIQUE CHARM OF THE SETTING, AND THE ENJOYMENT SHARED BY THE DIVERSITY OF THE ATTENDEES ELEVATED THE MRF TO LEGENDARY STATUS AMONG ARTISTS AND FANS.

SIU-EDWARDSVILLE ALSO UTILIZED THIS SITE FROM 1963 TO 1982 FOR COMMENCEMENT EXERCISES, INVOLVING NEARLY 35,000 SIUE GRADUATES, WHO, ALONG WITH THEIR FAMILY AND FRIENDS, EXPERIENCED AN EVENT HERE BEARING POWERFUL PERSONAL HISTORICAL SIGNIFICANCE.

SPONSORED BY
THE SIUE ALUMNI ASSOCIATION, THE SIUE FOUNDATION,
THE MRF COMMEMORATIVE COMMITTEE, AND THE ILLINOIS STATE HISTORICAL SOCIETY.
JUNE 2009

Mississippi
River
Festival

INTRODUCTION

"The Mississippi River Festival."

Just mention that phrase to St. Louis area residents of a certain age and you're liable to get some amazing stories. You're just as likely to hear laughter, followed by a response such as, "Oh yeah, I went to the MRF. But I don't remember much about it!"

Chalk it up to the fog of time. Certainly, recollections fade over the course of four or five decades. In some cases, partaking in various legal (and maybe a few illegal) substances as part of an evening's revelry can leave a gauzy haze over one's festival recollections.

That said, memories do remain. And they bring to life a brief moment in time when Edwardsville, Illinois—and the campus of Southern Illinois University at Edwardsville—was one of the nation's musical and entertainment meccas. Between June 20, 1969, and August 23, 1980, the Mississippi River Festival held a mirror to our changing society while entertaining more than 1.5 million attendees.

The America of June 1969 saw Richard Nixon in the White House, the Vietnam War tearing the nation apart, and man preparing to set foot on the moon. Through Watergate, the Energy Crisis, the Bicentennial, and the dawn of Disco, the festival endured. The MRF's final show came as Americans were being held hostage in Iran, and a few months before Ronald Reagan was elected president and John Lennon was assassinated.

From Janis Joplin to the Wilson sisters of Heart; the Paul Butterfield Blues Band to ZZ Top; Arlo Guthrie to Harry Chapin; Smokey Robinson to Donna Summer (and that's just popular music!), the magic of the MRF lies in its musical diversity. Fans could enjoy classical, jazz, rock, dance, barbershop, theater, and bluegrass over the course of a single summer. How many music series could attract Henry Mancini *and* Alice Cooper? Bob Hope *and* Richard Pryor? The St. Louis Symphony Orchestra *and* the Ozark Mountain Daredevils? Sir Michael Redgrave *and* Julie Harris?

In all, more than 350 festival events were held over 12 summers, and a few of those shows stand out above the rest. Bob Dylan came out of seclusion and made a surprise appearance with his pals in the Band in 1969. The Who attracted a crowd of more than thirty-two thousand in 1971 (although we'll never know exactly how many fans were there). The Eagles and Chicago each made multiple trips to SIUE, attracting huge crowds each time. The Grateful Dead played under the tent in 1970 and again ten years later. Jackson Browne came to town and recorded songs for his biggest-selling album in the Edwardsville Holiday Inn. Harry Chapin appeared five times and became a beloved figure in the community.

The list goes on and on. MRF headliners won Oscars, Grammys, Emmys, and Tonys. They were bestowed with Presidential Medals, Knighthoods, and inductions into countless halls of fame.

Despite that level of star power, the Mississippi River Festival always seemed to be on life support. Financial issues plagued the festival for most of its existence. It was only the hard work and dedication of university administrators, St. Louis Symphony officials, local leaders, and a ragtag collection of student workers and volunteers that kept the festival alive for twelve summers. When the end inevitably came—complete with a high-powered, well-heeled villain from the East Coast—fans were left with only the memories. But those memories are rich and deep, and they still bring smiles fifty years later.

For each story you read in this book, understand that there are many more floating around throughout the community. I wish there was a way to capture each and every one of them. Likely, they will live on by being passed down from one generation to the next within families; old chestnuts that get carted out every so often, making everyone laugh like they're hearing them for the first time.

That's exactly where my Mississippi River Festival fascination began. I had just turned twelve when the final festival concert was held, so I never had the chance to set foot on the festival site while the MRF was living and breathing. But my uncle, Jim Muffo, turned me on to much of the music I still listen to and love today, and he would captivate me with tales of his experiences during the festival's early years. A few of those stories are included in the pages that follow. During the summer of 1986, just before I began my own SIUE career, he and I ventured through the weeds to see what remained of the MRF site. The seeds for this book were planted that day.

The Mississippi River Festival is a part of history now, but it remains a beloved piece of nostalgia for thousands of St. Louis area residents. And now, for the first time, the complete story is being told—by the artists who played, the fans who cheered, and the dedicated folks who made it all possible.

This is the story of what happened when the stars came out.

"I can remember seeing the sea of white lights coming off of 157 after a concert. It was unbelievable. Just car after car, so you knew that the concert had just ended. You wondered who played that night, you know? Some of those big ones, the traffic jam would take hours to get out of campus. It was just unbelievable how many cars came out of there!"

—John Jarvis, Fan

Mississippi River Festival

SECTION 1
BEGINNINGS

Like most groundbreaking innovations that evolve from a partnership between two unrelated entities, the Mississippi River Festival (MRF) was designed to create mutual benefit.

The fledgling Southern Illinois University (SIU) campus in Edwardsville, Illinois, was opened in 1965 as an extension of the university's hub in Carbondale, some one hundred miles to the south. Residence centers in Alton and East St. Louis had been functioning well since 1957, but growing enrollment was now exceeding available space. Wishing to establish a stronger presence in the growing St. Louis metropolitan area, SIU President Delyte Morris drove the purchase of 2,660 acres of prime Illinois farmland and the creation of Southern Illinois University at Edwardsville (SIUE).

Tasked with launching this new venture was a group of SIU administrators who packed up their families and moved north to Edwardsville. The man chosen by Morris to lead the tightknit team was Chancellor John Rendleman.

"In 1968, our family moved to Edwardsville because it was going to be a more independent campus rather than just an appendage of SIU Carbondale," remembers John S. Rendleman, the chancellor's son. "As a nine-year-old kid, I didn't pay a lot of attention to the things my dad was doing at the university. But it was a good time for education. There was a lot of construction and programming going on, and there was quite a lot of excitement about SIU Edwardsville in the area."

The band of educators and their families stuck closely together in their new environs, creating a lasting bond. "A lot of administrators moved to Edwardsville to get the campus going, and in those days, the administrators were all pretty tight, and their families were pretty tight," Rendleman says. "It was an easy reach for us to be friends because the university was growing and succeeding, and people were happy to be a part of that."

J'Deanna (Hudgens) Twesten was seven years old when her father, VP of Business Affairs Bill Hudgens, was assigned to the new university. She and her family also moved to Edwardsville. "Both the Rendlemans and our family stayed at the Holiday Inn for about a month while waiting to move into our homes," she recalls. "Mr. Rendleman was always a prankster, and, while visiting us, he handed me an envelope with a dead mouse inside, which made me laugh."

John S. Rendleman wasn't aware of that story. "I don't remember my father being such a joker. I know my mom would not have approved of that little trick."

The new Edwardsville campus enjoyed accessibility via nearby highways to downtown St. Louis, which sits just 20 miles away, as well as the booming population centers of Madison and St. Clair Counties in Illinois. High on the bluffs outside the university's main entrance, on a clear day, the Gateway Arch and other medium-sized skyscrapers that carve out the St. Louis skyline are clearly visible. Morris had a shiny new toy. Now, he needed a way to entice St. Louisans to come over and check it out.

But in those days, many Missouri residents viewed the eastern side of the river as a foreign land. There was a disconnect between the states much greater than the width of the Mighty Mississippi. "Back then, if they would even say Edwardsville on TV, we'd go, 'Oh, they said Edwardsville!' If you grew up there, you didn't grow up in St. Louis—you grew up in Edwardsville," remembers John Klobnak, an SIUE student and festival worker from 1969 to 1973.

The other half of the MRF creation narrative is the St. Louis Symphony Organization (SLSO). Founded in 1880, the symphony is one of the oldest in the nation, delighting classical music fans for decades through acclaimed live concerts and award-winning recordings. But by 1968, the SLSO—along with many other major symphonies throughout the nation—was facing a crossroads. Labor costs were rising, forcing some orchestras to consider mergers or other drastic moves to stay alive. In St. Louis, the local symphony was looking at an $85,000 deficit for the upcoming 1968-69 season, if it happened at all. One week before the scheduled opening concert, the Symphony Society and Local 2 of the American Federation of

Musicians were locked in a labor stalemate. Money was a major sticking point, but so was season length—in turning down an offer of a thirty-nine-week season, the musicians countered by asking for forty-five weeks. Following a four-week strike, a deal was done, and it included a forty-four-week season beginning in 1969. The union had been successful in adding six weeks to the SLSO season. How? A summer music festival on the SIUE campus.

"The vision was to put SIU—just three years after it opened—on the map quickly, knowing that it would take something of this scope to bring people across the river to physically see the campus and know what was in store for this community," says Lyle Ward, an SIUE student turned administrator who would play a fundamental role in the MRF's history. "It also developed because the St Louis Symphony had signed their first twelve-month contract with their musicians, and they had to find twelve-month employment, which they had never done before. It wasn't really a marriage. I always call it an affair between the two organizations because they had mutual interest and attractions to each other. The SLSO needed employment and a vehicle for it. The university wanted exposure."

Festival worker Bob Gill remembered the pioneering aspect of the endeavor. "SIUE was an experiment in higher education. Nobody had ever gone out in the middle of the country and just built a university from scratch. Almost all colleges in the country had been there for a long time, and they were surrounded by a population. Nobody had ever tried this with a four-year university. But to make it work, people had to see this beautiful place, and what better way to do it than to hold concerts and have people come out here and experience the campus."

The connection between SIU and the symphony actually went back a few years, with the SLSO having performed at university-sponsored events in the Metro East towns of Wood River and Collinsville. The idea of a summer concert series on the Edwardsville campus had been discussed before, but it was the contentious 1968 labor negotiations with the musicians' union that ultimately led to an agreement.

Financial details between the university and the SLSO were not disclosed publicly, but according to university Archivist Stephen Kerber, the agreement stated the university would pay the musicians' salaries for a six-week summer series, up to an estimated $133,335. The symphony would pay its conductors, soloists, stagehands, travel, and shipping, plus an additional $15,000 for promotional activities. At the box office, SIUE agreed to pay the SLSO fifty percent of the first $50,000 of gross receipts, plus twenty-five percent of additional box office income, up to a total maximum of $188,835.[1]

Beyond attracting people to visit the burgeoning campus, Delyte Morris intended for the festival to create numerous educational benefits for students. Pointing to a recent campus chorale-SLSO joint performance of Prokofiev's *Ivan the Terrible* as a prime example, Morris said the symphony's presence on campus "should be an important asset to the university's music program. It will bring music students and the symphony closer together."[2]

Ward adds, "The university had a wonderful fine arts division already, but it wanted to create a summer residency for the St. Louis Symphony to teach classes in conducting and give undergraduate students a remarkable opportunity to have that kind of experience. The concept was huge: to use the university as a vehicle to present cultural and entertainment programs for the larger community—not just for the university, but for a fifty-mile radius at the very least. And that took some real vision that early in the institution's existence."

University officials, including Morris, Rendleman, and Hudgens, worked with symphony representatives Peter Pastreich and Stanley Goodman to begin creating this new summer music series. Fortunately, templates existed elsewhere, as similar festivals were popping up in cities such as New York, Chicago, and Cleveland. At the request of Rendleman, Dr. William Tarwater, Chair of SIUE's Department of Music, toured these events and brought his findings back to Edwardsville. "The Mississippi River Festival would not have started without Bill Tarwater," Ward says. "He was a remarkable man, highly respected both academically and administratively. When he came back, he essentially wrote a book of operations with everything he had learned. I looked through it again the other day and it's just remarkable the information that he collected—estimated attendances of different kinds of groups, expenses, the whole thing. He started working with our faculty, the symphony, and our SIUE student committee on desirable concert programs, guest artists, and educational opportunities for students. Bill became a very good friend and mentor."

Following in the footsteps of these other festivals meant the SLSO would not be the only musical entity to perform. Friday and Saturday evenings at the SIUE series would be reserved for symphony concerts, while lighter "pops" concerts featuring the SLSO were targeted for Sunday evenings. But folk and pop artists were being slotted in for weeknight shows. The symphony would be sharing the bill with performers in other genres. "We grew because of the broader programming that we did," Ward says. "When we considered including top contemporary entertainers, there was great sensitivity, particularly in the beginning, that they were truly talented musicians."

That said, no one could yet imagine the legendary artists who would make the trip to Edwardsville over the next decade.

Now, where to hold these concerts? There were plenty of spaces on campus to choose from, but touring officials from the university and the symphony—as well as structural and sound engineers—narrowed the search to two sites. One near the center core of the campus was flagged as a possible future permanent site. But for now, all were dazzled by a tree-adorned, natural amphitheater that sat empty near Bluff Road, on the university's northwestern edge. "We hope to have the symphony concerts out of doors in a beautiful setting on the bluffs," Morris said.[3]

SIUE photographer Charlie Cox witnessed the efforts that transformed the land into a proper concert setting. "The university's physical plant people came in and developed the site a little bit," he said. "They did some grading, changed a few of the humps in the ground, and sewed some grass. That site had been used for commencement ceremonies, so it already had the feel for possible use for this festival."

Student Jim Muffo, a freshman in the fall of 1968, remembers the scene. "It was natural, it was grass, and what SIU did with that, and the way they maintained it and set it up, was beautiful."

"I remember dad taking me out to the proposed concert site for a tour," adds J'Deanna Twesten. "We walked through the front entrance area, which was one of the few times I didn't go through the back entrance, and I saw for the first time the natural hillside where concerts were to be held."

Festival planners connected with the U.S. Tent and Awning company of Sarasota, Florida, which steered them to a tent master named Roy "Skip" Manley. The eccentric, globetrotting, and mildly obsessive keeper of the tent quickly became one of the most colorful, memorable characters in the MRF tale. Manley told local media he was "married to a girl in Edwardsville" for the summer of 1969, and promptly moved into a trailer on the festival site.[4] Much more on Skip to come.

Upon arrival, the festival's iconic tent (well, the first of four iconic tents) was an impressive site—140 feet in length, 170 feet wide, and 65 feet high. Nearly two miles of duck canvas was needed to construct the soil-resistant, water-repellent, and flame-retardant tent, as well as a minimum of four to five miles of galvanized airplane cable and nearly twenty miles of linen thread.

Under the tent, the stage was approximately 60 feet wide—large enough for a ninety-piece orchestra and a 100-voice chorus—with a specially designed acoustic shell located behind. And, to bring much-needed relief to the performers on hot summer nights, an air conditioning system was placed beneath the stage to pump cool air up through the floor.

Before the stage sat approximately 1,900 color-coded director's chairs. Longtime student worker Greg Drexelius has a collection of MRF memorabilia, including original diagrams of the tent area. "There are two different accounts of this," he says. "Some have said there were 1,900 seats. Well, everything I find in my literature and diagrams says it was either 1,877 or 1,878. We were told it was 1,877 back in 1974. One of those two numbers is probably most accurate."

Thousands more could enjoy an unobstructed view from the sloping lawn area beyond the tent. Parking was directed to a nearby soccer field lot, with plans for a new parking lot near the concert site. In addition, shuttle buses would bring attendees from more remote campus lots, if necessary. Speakers were placed on the lawn, but not under the tent. Food service and refreshment stations were set up in a nearby pavilion, with options ranging from sandwiches to full buffet dinners. Picnic tables, toilets, public phones—all taken care of, thanks to the tireless efforts of SIUE's physical plant employees.

Meanwhile, in the shadows, plans for a permanent site began. "It was easier to start the process with a temporary site that was over 18 acres, including the performance and seating area, dining area, lawn area, backstage, the tent, and the front entrance area," Ward says.

By March 1969, festival officials were ready to give this exciting new endeavor a name—the Mississippi River Festival. The moniker aligned with the stated goal to bridge the Illinois and Missouri sides of the community. The accompanying logo, designed by A.B. Mifflin, Coordinator of University Graphics, was a simple but memorable one featuring the MRF name, two wavy lines to represent the nearby river, and a round dot for the moon. The logo would remain unchanged for the duration of the festival's existence.

Local newspapers were catching Festival Fever. Music Critic Frank Peters of the *St. Louis Post-Dispatch* described the new venture as "dramatic. A radical departure from past Symphony Society behavior." He also teased the initial list of pop, rock, and folk acts heading to Edwardsville later that summer—Buffy St. Marie, the Paul Butterfield Blues Band, Janis Joplin, Iron Butterfly, the Band, Joan Baez, Arlo Guthrie, and Joni Mitchell, among others. This is on top of notable SLSO guests such as pianist Van Cliburn and violinist Itzhak Perlman. "If the experiment flops, it will not be for want of trying or failure to look the realities of orchestra economics 1969 in the eye. The St. Louis Symphony is taking the high road… if it wins, the Mississippi River Festival will be a real festival, and the whole St. Louis region, not just the Symphony, will be its beneficiary."[5]

The *Alton Telegraph* also weighed in with an editorial, stating, "President Delyte Morris of SIU merits public commendation (and support) for his foresight in aligning his campus with this great musical organization, which now appears to be really headed upward after some disappointing and frustrating years."[6]

Within the home of Chancellor Rendleman, the list of popular music acts heading to town raised eyebrows. "I know at one time we entertained (St. Louis Symphony Conductor) Walter Susskind at our house, and our dad explained that this was going to be part of the cultural programming for SIUE," John S. Rendleman says. "But it didn't mean anything until we started hearing about some of these rock & roll acts that were coming. I thought, 'Well, that's interesting.' It still was kind of off in the distance, but as it began to happen, we became a lot more aware of famous rock & roll bands coming to Edwardsville, Illinois."

Now it was time to begin selling tickets, and a group of local citizens and volunteer groups took the lead. As this was 1969—with the spirit of peace, love, and brotherhood wafting through the air—tickets for all concerts were kept low, ranging from $1.00 to $5.50.

"It was really a period of optimism and idealism," Ward says. "It had very little to do with any concept of making money. Our goal had always been to try to create an organization that could maintain itself. Our prices were unheard of anywhere, and we maintained them for nine years."

By early May, individual tickets were also on sale at most area Famous-Barr and Stix-Baer & Fuller department stores, Powell Symphony Hall, SIUE, and retail locations throughout the area. In addition, coupon books were available for $20, containing $25 worth of coupons that could be exchanged for reserved seats under the tent or general lawn seats for any show.

As one of the festival's principal aims was to expose the SIUE campus to Missouri residents, traffic studies were conducted to provide an indication of which roads would most likely be used by attendees. Interstate 270 was expected to be the main pathway from Missouri, with Illinois Routes 157, 159, and 143 carrying most East Side fans. SIU traffic police advised attendees to arrive early to avoid the rush and speculated that, if all went as expected, the site would be fully-cleared in under an hour. This timeframe would be challenged numerous times over the ensuing years.

To make attending events easier for area residents who didn't want to deal with traffic, Bi-State Transit System scheduled buses for all MRF concerts, with pickups in downtown St. Louis, at sites in North and West St. Louis County, and throughout the Metro East.

The *St. Louis Post-Dispatch* was buying what MRF officials were selling, calling the effort "easily the most ambitious bi-state enterprise of its kind ever attempted," and adding, "it deserves widespread community support." Noting "the new highways" and relatively short drives from Florissant (20 minutes), Clayton (33 minutes), and downtown St. Louis (25 minutes)—plus the advantage of Missouri motorists having the evening sun at their backs—the editorial concluded, "There is no reason why the Mississippi River Festival should not be popular. The organization, the attractions, and the physical facilities are outstanding. The endeavor is a highly constructive one that merits an enthusiastic response."[7]

Area newspapers ran full-page spreads with schedules of the festival's pop/rock/folk acts, as well as a detailed rundown of each SLSO program, complete with soloists and guests. A map showing how to reach the site from across the St. Louis area (and estimated drive times from seven cities) was accompanied by bus schedules, ticket information, and a summary of what fans could expect from this new entertainment series.

Walter Susskind sat for an interview with Lois Caplan of the *St. Louis Jewish Light* and her "Women's World" section. "We are so delighted with the fine facilities provided by SIU," Susskind said, adding that the symphony's summer concerts would be, "essentially the same as winter music, but we will leave out the experimental stuff." Caplan exhibited a bit of the generation gap pervasive in society that year when she added that the pop and rock events would include "Joan Baez, the New Christy Minstrels, and the Iron Butterfly—not a sculpture, Silly, but an acid rock group. Just ask your teenage son or daughter, who, by the way, will probably want to make all 12 of these happenings, and at these prices, why not?"[8]

In so many ways, the Mississippi River Festival was a unifying force. Missouri and Illinois. Classical and Rock. Young and Old. The festival was building connections. "We're bridging the generation gap with our varied musical program," said MRF Board President John L. Gillis, Senior Vice President of Monsanto Company. "But, even more importantly, we're bridging the river gap. Our aim with this great festival is to bring together 110,000 people on both sides of the Mississippi River in a memorable six-week musical event."[9]

St. Louis Symphony Society President Stanley Goodman, also president of the May Company, went a step further, calling the MRF "the biggest single community effort involving people on both sides of the Mississippi ever undertaken."[10]

In the days leading up to the June 20 opening symphony concert, the festival was even garnering attention from the Metropolis five hours to the north that typically dominated the Land of Lincoln's news cycle. "Times do change," wrote *Chicago Tribune's* Thomas Willis. "Remember when you were taking a trip down Route 66, and now it's I-55? Or when you could honestly expect the St. Louis Symphony orchestra to be playing most of its concerts in St. Louis, or at least in Missouri? Or when universities had only one campus, so it was safe to say, 'at Southern Illinois University,' or the like . . . The foregoing observations resulted from a first look at the prospectus for the Mississippi River Festival, which begins Friday."[11]

Before the initial SLSO concert, a picnic was held on the SIUE campus. For $7.50 a person, the public enjoyed a cold buffet in French picnic baskets, the music of the Barcelona Brass, and local rock group The Guise. Attendees—some of whom traveled from Powell Symphony Hall by bus—were encouraged to wear casual, colorful attire as jugglers, sidewalk artists, and organ grinders mingled.

Signs with the MRF logo were set up at the exits of interstates 270, 70, and 55, as well as Illinois route 143, and at 2,000-foot intervals throughout campus—all to ensure those from outside the Edwardsville area found their way to the concert site safely. Student workers were on hand, directing traffic into the parking lots.

The tent was up. The symphony was in place. Finally, it was time to let the music play.

Milestones
1969-71

"It is more than we'd ever hoped for"
Opening Night with the St. Louis Symphony Orchestra

As Jan Walter Susskind emerged from the MRF wings and strode to his position leading the St. Louis Symphony Orchestra on Friday, June 20, 1969, he was making history. But in looking more closely at his life and career in total, launching the Mississippi River Festival was just one more entry on a legendary resume.

Born in Czechoslovakia in 1913, Susskind was surrounded by music—his father an Austrian music critic and his mother a Czech piano teacher. With this background, Susskind soon found himself studying under composer Josef Suk (son-in-law of the legendary Antonín Dvořák) at the State Conservatorium. At age twenty-six, Susskind was named assistant to George Szell at the German Opera in Prague. But historic events would soon change his life forever.

In early 1939, Hitler's forces were descending on Prague. Two days prior to their invasion, Susskind fled to Britain as a refugee with the aid of a British journalist and consular officials. Susskind promptly resumed his music career in his new surroundings, forming and playing piano for a chamber ensemble called the Czech Trio and conducting the Carl Rosa Opera Company.

Following World War II, Susskind was named musical director of the Scottish Orchestra. He served as conductor of the Melbourne Symphony Orchestra and spent time in Israel and South America before being named head of the Toronto Symphony Orchestra in 1956. He joined the SLSO in 1968.

On opening night of the Mississippi River Festival, Susskind and the St. Louis Symphony Orchestra kicked off the show, appropriately enough, with "The Star-Spangled Banner" and went into Purcell's "Trumpet Voluntary."

With assistance from the Cosmopolitan Singers (a St. Louis chorus founded in the 1950s) and a quartet of soloists, the SLSO filled the early-summer air with Beethoven's "Ninth Symphony" and Schubert's "Eighth (Unfinished) Symphony."

Reviews were glowing. The *St. Louis Post-Dispatch* placed its MRF coverage on page one, with Peters calling the concert "a success," citing the "better than foreseen" performance of the tent and outstanding acoustics.[12] Orchestra manager Peter Pastreich agreed, saying the acoustics were "equal to or better than those at any outdoor facility in existence . . . It is possible to hear with no amplification from any part of the entire lawn. You can hear beautifully back to the entrance. It is more than we'd ever hoped for."[13] Tent master Skip Manley must have been proud.

Robert C. Schaub in the *Edwardsville Intelligencer* singled out Susskind and the symphony for playing the "Trumpet Voluntary" "as it was meant to be played—with verve and enthusiasm and discipline. This told us that the St. Louis Symphony had come to play." In critiquing Beethoven's Ninth, Schaub described Susskind colorfully. "For the first time in the evening, several locks of Susskind's hair shook loose from their appointed places and waved in the air. At times, Susskind's face almost matched his electric red evening jacket."[14] Over the next seven years, Susskind conducted the SLSO, taught classes at SIUE, and made 45 appearances at the Mississippi River Festival.

A crowd of 1,545 were present for the MRF's historic opening night. Officials had gone to great lengths to create a compelling evening for concertgoers at every touchpoint of the experience. "Festival guests had a remarkable environment to attend these performances," Ward says. "As they got out of their cars in the parking lot and walked to the front entrance, there was the box office, where they met our students, got their tickets, and went through this wonderful area of huge yellow and orange canvas sails above their heads that led into the site. That theme continued as they went into shaded areas for the dining spaces and snack bar areas. And then, of course, you became immediately aware of the tent—that was the centerpiece. So, here we are, outdoors under a suspended tent with the walls raised so that fans could see the performance from the natural amphitheater on the lawn. What a great environment that was."

Unlike many popular performers who would grace the MRF stage in the years to come, symphony musicians didn't seem very interested in self-promotion. For them, the music was all that mattered. "The St. Louis Symphony didn't like photographers," Charlie Cox said. "They claimed that they could hear the snap of a camera from a half mile away. Whether that was true or not, I don't know. But they didn't like photographers and they would glare at me when I was photographing them from in front of the stage."

The formal nature of the SLSO's musical approach belied the fact that orchestra musicians also knew how to have a good time. Maybe it wasn't the same kind of good time that Janis Joplin and her contemporaries enjoyed, but it was fun nonetheless. Tom Webb, who spent considerable time backstage during the '69 season as a reporter for SIUE Broadcast Services, witnessed this firsthand.

"I knew quite a few folks in the symphony, and one Sunday night, I went backstage and saw a symphony director go into the dressing room and shut the door," Webb recalls. "I walked back there, said hello to a couple of folks I knew, and then someone said, 'Excuse me, I have to get to the game.' I looked into one of the trailers, which was configured as a break room. There were a couple of tables set up, and the cards were flying. It was a big card game going on during intermission."

"They usually had a poker game going in one of the rooms backstage," Cox added. "When it came time for them to play, they would leave all their cards on the table. But at intermission, they would race down the ramp from the stage with their expensive instruments in their hands and see who could be the first one back to the poker table."

Jim Grandone served as a festival Artist Host Coordinator for a time, requiring him to cater to a headliner's every need. "I had to take care of the guest conductors when they came in, but the orchestra members all knew each other very well," he says. "Between rehearsals and the concert, you had better stay out of the way of the backstage door because they would come in like horses back to their dressing room to play poker. Those games were legendary. They were classically trained musicians, but they were real people.

"While they were doing that, (SLSO Conductor) Leonard Slatkin would hold court on the ramp in the production area, telling jokes. He was a very funny guy. Fabulous guy. This was in contrast to Walter Susskind, whom you were to call 'maestro', if you addressed him at all. And here was Leonard Slatkin, this young guy who was just hilarious, down to earth, and enjoyable to be around, telling jokes to the staff backstage."

"Lenny Slatkin—it's Leonard now, but we called him Lenny at the time—was just a loose, curly-haired guy," Greg Drexelius adds. "He was a great man. Not too many years back, I took a book about the MRF down to the symphony when he was there. My son works at the symphony, and he went back and got him to sign it. Lenny had the most fun showing pictures to the other musicians. In one photo, he was wearing a shirt with musical notes on it, and they asked him if that was during a rehearsal. He said, 'No, that was a concert!' The MRF was different."

As Night One of the Mississippi River Festival faded into history, SIU President Delyte Morris had no idea what lied ahead. But he was encouraged enough by what had transpired to tell a reporter that the festival could develop beyond his expectations.[15]

"It was a very emotional experience"
An Evening with Janis Joplin

The calendar turned to July 1969, and the world anxiously awaited the launch of Apollo 11 and the prospect of man walking on the moon. On a local level, the MRF took a giant leap of its own on July 1 when a raspy-voiced, whiskey-drinking singer from Port Arthur, Texas, came to Edwardsville.

Janis Joplin first gained national attention during the 1967 Monterey Pop Festival as lead singer of Big Brother and the Holding Company. The band's second album, *Cheap Thrills*, hit No. 1 on the Billboard album chart. In 1968, *Time* magazine called Joplin "probably the most powerful singer to emerge from the white rock movement."

Jim Muffo, about to begin his sophomore year at SIUE, remembers seeing *Cheap Thrills* on sale in the university store. "They had record albums right there in the front," he recalls. "She wasn't that well known—she hadn't done 'Bobby McGee' yet—but my friends and I had that album, and that was a really good album. Big Brother and the Holding Company just picked her up not knowing what they had. They were kind of turned off by the fact that she got popular and not them, but they were like a garage band."

Joplin left Big Brother in 1969 and formed the Kozmic Blues Band, a backing group that provided more of an R&B/soul style. Joplin and her new band graced the MRF stage two months before their *Kozmic Blues* album was released to mixed reviews. But by all indications, the response to Joplin's festival appearance was far from mixed.

After Chicago-based acid rock band Aorta opened the show, Joplin took charge before 12,000 fans. In the *St. Louis Post-Dispatch*, Harper Barnes wrote that Joplin "flings herself into every song, her voice scooping up notes and slamming them down, her body moving like a bawdy majorette. At one point, she looked out at the audience with the grin of a naughty child and said, 'Now do you know what rock & roll is all about?'"[16]

Wearing reddish-purple slacks and a light pink blouse, Joplin lit up the stage with her energy and sheer force of will. She seemed to be enjoying herself, announcing, "We've been to England and San Francisco, and I can tell you people are looking good!"[17]

The large crowd was blown away. After finishing her set and leaving the stage, Joplin was summoned back by a long, loud standing ovation. She smiled and shouted, "OK, but you better keep standing or I'll . . ." before launching into a raucous rendition of "Piece of My Heart" that had fans dancing in the aisles and surging forward. Joplin made sure to shake a few hands from the stage before finally ending this unforgettable night.[18]

In his role with SIUE Broadcast Services, Tom Webb had the opportunity to interview Joplin that night. But . . .

"She was just blotto," Webb reflects. "She was just out of it. Normally, I would go back during intermission and approach one of their handlers and say, 'I'd like to interview' whoever the performer was. That night, the guy said, 'OK, you can try.' That told me right there that this was going to be weird, and it was."

Webb chuckles as he recalls the scene. "She had a funny little cigarette in one hand and about half a bottle of Southern Comfort in the other. If you had asked, 'What day is it and where are you,' she wouldn't have known. I recognize, sometimes performers have strange habits, and if you took away her little cigarette and her bottle of Southern Comfort, she probably wouldn't know what to sing. When she was whacked out, she probably was better."

Did Webb get anything he could use? "No," he laughs. "I went back and told my boss (John Moorman) about it, and he said, 'Well, you know, sometimes you bite the bear, sometimes the bear bites you, and sometimes you both go away hungry.' So, this was one of those hungry times."

Charlie Cox was also on hand, as he was for nearly every MRF concert over 12 summers. "One of the first concerts that was exciting for me was Janis Joplin," he remembered. "She had a short career, but a great career. One of the first great rock artists. She had a whiskey voice, and she wore outlandish costumes. You could really see the torment in her face."

Cox's son, Doug, was about to begin his senior year at Edwardsville High School that summer. Courtesy of his father's connection to the university and the festival, he was on the lawn for most MRF shows. But for the Janis Joplin show, he took things a step further. "Dad got two free tickets to every show. They were lawn tickets—a whopping two dollars," he says with a laugh. "Dad would be like, 'Oh, you want these tickets?' So, yeah, of course I usually took them. I think I got good parking too. But for Janis Joplin, I took a date and sprung for tent seats. But I was such a nerd, I wore a coat and tie to see Janis Joplin! I don't know what I was thinking."

Doug Cox would be a festival regular until transferring from SIUE to the University of Southern California film school in 1972. The move would pay off, as Cox has enjoyed a long career in Hollywood as an actor and Emmy-nominated writer. He has fond memories of the MRF and his father's involvement. "He would have to be there for every show and for rehearsals during the day, so it took up a lot of his time. Sometimes it had to be a pain for him, going to work during the day and then coming home for dinner and then going back out there. But dad knew a big part of his job was getting the name of the university out in the media. I would see him walking around taking pictures, and you could tell he was excited to be there. He knew the MRF was big."

Six weeks after her SIUE performance, Janis Joplin would perform at the legendary Woodstock Music and Art Fair in Bethel, New York. But she wouldn't be the only 1969 MRF performer to do so.

"The Woodstock of the Midwest"
Butterfield, Joplin, Guthrie, The Band, Havens & Baez
Warm Up at the MRF

Certainly, the late 1960s were an era ripe with music festivals. Building on the success of California's Monterey International Pop Festival two years before, Woodstock would go down in history as the biggest, most celebrated of all. More than four hundred thousand fans came together for three days in August 1969 to experience some of popular music's biggest names.

In all, 32 artists or bands played Woodstock—and nearly half of them also played the Mississippi River Festival during its run. In fact, six artists—Janis Joplin, Arlo Guthrie, Joan Baez, Richie Havens, the Paul Butterfield Blues Band, and The Band—performed on the SIUE campus in the weeks before they headed east to Woodstock. Of course, in June-July 1969, Woodstock did not yet exist as a cultural touchpoint. It is only in retrospect that the MRF serving as a warm-up for the nation's premier music event takes on an air of significance.

Butterfield played under the tent five nights before Joplin, attracting a crowd of nearly thirty-five hundred with his brand of electric Chicago blues. A master of the harmonica, Butterfield made his bones as a youth jamming with Muddy Waters, Howlin' Wolf and other Windy City legends. Formed in 1963, Butterfield's band faced numerous challenges during its lone Edwardsville trip. After arriving an hour behind schedule, reportedly due to a late plane, band members went straight from car to stage without the benefit of a sound check. In addition, the concert was marred by high winds that required those in charge of the tent to keep the front flap tied down. With less of the stage visible to the cheap seats, lawn fans were forced to congregate tightly into one small area in order to see. For those under the tent, the lack of breeze turned up the heat

Butterfield's appearance spawned the first (but not last) sub-par MRF reviews. An unbalanced sound mix (the brass section overpowered the rest of the band, save for Butterfield's harmonica) set the tone, and the band's performance couldn't make up for the technical limitations. Under an *Edwardsville Intelligencer* headline calling the show "Boring," Dick Norrish described the evening as "loud without let-up" and "putting us to sleep." One fan added, "I don't know what's wrong. You should hear one of their albums. They're much better."[19]

Regardless of the performance quality, the Butterfield show holds a special place in the heart of John S. Rendleman, as it was his first concert. "I have an older brother, and I kind of worshiped him," he recalls. "He and I both discovered KSHE radio around 1969, and that introduced me to music other than the popular stuff that was being played on KXOK, which was kind of bubble gum music. So, when Matthew said let's go out to the MRF and listen to Paul Butterfield, I didn't know exactly who he was, but I said okay. I remember the music was loud enough that it caused my sister to cry. So, that was my introduction to the rock & roll lineup at the MRF."

The twin bill of Guthrie and Joni Mitchell followed on July 7. Son of fabled American singer, writer, and artist Woody Guthrie, 22-year-old Arlo had assimilated the works of his father's contemporaries—including future festival co-star Pete Seeger—to create his own style. He kicked off the show with a one-hour set, singing six songs and mixing in his unique brand of counterculture wit and satire. On this night, observations touched on the Los Angeles Police Department, the coming apocalypse, and a popular topic of the times, marijuana.

Mitchell delivered a more straightforward set, letting her stellar songwriting and exceptional vocal stylings take center stage. The 25-year-old Canadian had been performing in a Florida club in 1965, when she was discovered by David Crosby of the Byrds and brought to Los Angeles. Through Crosby, Mitchell made the connections that launched her career. Her second album, *Clouds*, was released in April 1969 and contained such classics as "Chelsea Morning" and "Both Sides Now."

Before the show, Mitchell spent time with Charlie Cox, roaming the festival landscape. "She was an amateur photographer, and she had brought her camera with her to record some of the sites at which she was performing," Cox said. "She walked around the perimeter of the site with me, taking pictures and asking me about cameras and exposures. We took several pictures together, had a little conversation, and enjoyed our time together."

The Guthrie-Mitchell MRF concert was recorded and later aired by the National Educational Television Network, the forerunner of the Public Broadcasting System (PBS). Tom Webb and a pair of his colleagues from SIUE Broadcast Services were asked to work stage cameras as members of the production crew.

"PBS came in and said they were going to tape the show," Webb says. "John (Moorman) was the point of contact and they asked him to rustle up a crew to run camera, pull cable, etc."

"We spent the day at the site once cameras were in and went through some checking of camera angles, shot pick-off angles and such," Moorman recalls. "The students had never had 'big boy' cameras to mess with. So much of their time was getting a feel for the gear and how to use it. The production staff was both seasoned and tolerant of the 'locals' who became part of the crew. That was a blessing."

Webb was positioned stage left. "It was kind of scary because we were right on the edge of the stage and I had this horrible nightmare of not watching where I was going and, boom, we'd put a camera right into the front row of the audience. I warned the guy that was pulling cable for me, 'You stay between the edge of the stage and the camera whenever possible, just to act as a blocker.' It was kind of fun that we had a chance to be that up close and personal."

Moorman remembers chatting with the artists before the show. "Arlo was focused and not overmanaged. He liked to tell stories about his father and Pete Seeger. I didn't have much time with Joni. Not that she was aloof; she wasn't. She was a couple of years older than Arlo and had more road experience. Like many performers, she had a pre-show routine and liked to stay pretty much inside her bubble."

Webb interviewed the singers later in the evening. "I just said 'Hi,' and asked what they thought of the venue. Joni Mitchell thought it was really great. She said, 'This is gonna be a great place to perform.' So, I got the impression she wanted to come back—same with Guthrie." Both would indeed return to the MRF multiple times.

While only Arlo would play Woodstock, Mitchell definitely made her presence felt, as well. Having been advised by her manager that it would be a better career move to stay in New York City and appear on *The Dick Cavett Show*, Mitchell watched from afar and penned the song "Woodstock" from her hotel room. The song would become a classic for Crosby, Stills, Nash & Young, released as the lead single from their 1970 album, *Déjà Vu*.

The July 14 concert by The Band would long be remembered in Mississippi River Festival lore for something else (stay tuned), but this was yet another act playing under the tent before heading to Woodstock. That summer of 1969, the group consisting of four Canadians and an Arkansas native was earning its status as one of the hottest acts on the rock scene. The Band's debut album, *Music from Big Pink*, had been released to rave reviews, and the quintet had just begun touring the country in support.

Though The Band was new to the scene, these musicians had been working together for more than a decade when they came to the MRF for the first time. Between 1958 and 1964, drummer Levon Helm, bassist Rick Danko, pianist Richard Manuel, guitarist Robbie Robertson, and keyboardist Garth Hudson, assembled one by one as Canadian rockabilly singer Ronnie Hawkins's backing group, The Hawks. For their initial festival show, they brought along a friend. (Again, stay tuned . . .)

Woodstock's opening set, captured for posterity in the subsequent documentary film, was turned in by singer/guitarist Richie Havens. A Brooklyn, New York, native, Havens began singing in neighborhood doo-wop groups as a teen in the 1950s before entering the Greenwich Village folk scene. By his July 22 MRF appearance, Havens had released eight albums, with his 1968 LP *Something Else Again* being his first to crack the Billboard chart.

Havens' MRF show served as a warm-up for his three-hour Woodstock set, which is best remembered for Havens' sweat-soaked orange dashiki, repeated encores (the artists scheduled to follow him had not yet arrived due to traffic congestion), and his improvised performance of "Freedom" based on the spiritual "Motherless Child."

At SIUE, Havens mixed in some hippie-flavored banter, telling fans, "All those statues living around us are going to tell everything. Just because they haven't said anything doesn't mean they won't talk later." On the ecology— today more commonly referred to as environmental sustainability—Havens added, "Don't abuse your coffee cups or empty glasses. You may think it's glass, but the scientists really know."[20]

Political and social messaging was front and center on July 23 when Joan Baez came to town. Five months pregnant with her son, Gabriel, the folk singer discussed the case of her husband, anti-Vietnam War activist David Harris, with the crowd of eleven thousand. Harris had just begun serving a three-year sentence in Texas for refusing military induction. "If he's a good boy, he may get out in less than three years, but I don't expect him to be," Baez said. "He has work to do in prison and I have work to do outside."[21]

After a "soaring" a cappella performance of "Swing Low, Sweet Chariot," Baez led the crowd in the social justice anthem "We Shall Overcome." She was congratulated backstage after the concert by Walter Susskind, who said he was pleased so many young people had come to hear a vocalist "who has taste, talent, and can sing quietly."[22]

Baez, who waived her $10,000 fee and asked that no ticket price exceed two dollars, also earned praise from the *St. Louis Post-Dispatch*. "Miss Baez was magnificent. She has always possessed a clear, pure voice that can pierce to the bone . . . she projects a sense of naturalness and honesty that adds much to her performances."[23]

Other Woodstock performers (The Who, Mountain, Sha Na Na, etc.) would arrive in later years. But this group of six artists would long be remembered for giving Edwardsville fans a small taste of history yet to come and for establishing the Mississippi River Festival as, in the words of John McEuen of the Nitty Gritty Dirt Band, "The Woodstock of the Midwest."

"It was like Woodstock, and I think people looked at it like Woodstock," says Jim Muffo. "They were all there—before they played Woodstock, they played the Mississippi River Festival that summer."

Audio pioneer and MRF mainstay Bob Heil had the opportunity to work many American festivals over the years, but he insists the one at SIUE was special. "You look at how the MRF stacked up with everything else that was going on. Richie Havens, Janis Joplin, all these great artists that appeared at Woodstock—they appeared at the Mississippi River Festival first. So, when you think about that for a little bit, it's like, 'Well, wait a minute.' They were here. Yes, they were here before Woodstock. And I can guarantee you, they were a lot more comfortable playing the Mississippi River Festival than they were doing that Mudfest in New York."

Speaking of Bob Heil, his entrance onto the Mississippi River Festival scene is a fascinating story—and it started with a bang!

"They came in and blew up all my Bozaks!"
Iron Butterfly and the Arrival of Bob Heil

Rock fans—as well as disc jockeys who needed a bathroom or smoke break—fell in love with the strangely psychedelic, yet heavy, 17-minute epic "In-A-Gadda-Da-Vida" when it was released in 1968 by San Diego quartet Iron Butterfly. An edited version of the song had been a Top Thirty-hit that year, propelling the *In-A-Gadda-Da-Vida* album to sell more than thirty million copies worldwide. And on July 10, 1969, more than twelve thousand fans—including a busload of teens from downstate Carbondale—turned out to experience the band's unique style firsthand. Many attendees dealt with challenging traffic conditions as heavy rain caused the university to close the large grass parking lots for fear of cars turning them into mud pits.

In describing his band's sound, 19-year-old singer/organist Doug Ingle said, "We didn't copy anyone, nor were we influenced by anyone. We had an idea about a sound and how it should be expressed."[24] Joined by teenage guitarist Erik Braunn, bassist Lee Dorman, and drummer Ron Bushy, Iron Butterfly attracted the largest and youngest crowd to date at the MRF.

Lyle Ward said this night was eye-opening for him and other festival officials. "When more than ten thousand persons showed up for Iron

Butterfly, we were complete aghast," he recalled. "Outdoor music festivals were such a new thing in 1969. It was the start of the Woodstock era. We didn't think we'd ever have such large crowds."[25]

After an opening set by Florida's Blues Image (whose lone hit, "Ride Captain Ride," would climb to No. 4 on the charts) and a long intermission, Iron Butterfly finally took the stage almost two hours after the concert began. The *St. Louis Post-Dispatch* described what came next as "near-deafening and, at its best, hypnotic."[26]

Of course, the moment (or nearly 30 minutes) everyone had come for arrived at the end, as the band offered up a loud, distorted version of "In-A-Gadda-Da-Vida" that mesmerized the crowd before culminating in a minute-long burst of electronic noise. Excited fans rushed the stage, but SIUE student ushers—dressed in sporty blue and white outfits—stood on the stage apron and held out their hands to motion for the crowd to halt. They did, as local police watched silently from the wings.[27]

"Iron Butterfly was the first concert I ever went to in my life," Jim Muffo says. "Oh, it was heavy, and it was so loud. That was a huge crowd. I was fascinated because I'd never been to a concert before. I was so proud of the fact that I'd gone to Iron Butterfly. I had their album, you know? This was awesome!

"The thing that got me was the next day when I got to SIUE. When you walked down the steps from the first floor of the University Center and went down to the cafeteria, directly across from those steps, there was a big planter that kind of separated the two dining rooms. People sat all around that planter all the time. That's where the freaks congregated. If you had short hair, you didn't want to go try to sit down there because you'd be chastised. That was their place. And I remember hearing people say what a crappy concert that was. And I thought it was great, you know? I guess it's always been that way with music, where certain camps will decide what they think is 'cool' music. So, I guess the 'Crosby, Stills & Nash' camps looked at Iron Butterfly as being too 'out there.'"

Days later, the so-called "generation gap" was again on full display, with Ron Walters writing in the *Alton Telegraph*, "Remember when young men combed their hair and went as gentlemen to hear a band concert? Times, boys, and haircuts have changed. So have the concerts. Crowds of hippies or hippie-like youngsters swarmed to the SIU campus last week to 'dig' the scintillating phrases of the 'Iron Butterfly,' a modern rock-roll, or whatever it's called, orchestra."[28]

What few realized is that the concert almost didn't take place at all. Ron Bushy had awakened from a pre-show nap in tremendous pain, a contact lens adhered to his eye. As Iron Butterfly's drummer was rushed away to receive emergency treatment, Bob Handy—the University Center Director tasked with artist booking for the 1969 season—was told by band management that the concert was off. But, through the magic of modern medicine (i.e., painkillers), Bushy was behind his kit at showtime, and the concert went on as planned. After the final encore, the drummer collapsed to the stage. Handy rushed over. Bushy opened his damaged eye and said, "Told you so, Handy! We wowed 'em!"

Iron Butterfly's audio assault on the SIUE campus had a direct impact on the festival's future, opening the door for a true legend to emerge. He never played an instrument or sang a note on a platinum album. Yet, he was the subject of an exhibit in the Rock & Roll Hall of Fame. He wasn't a household name like Pete Townshend or Jerry Garcia. But without his talents and expertise, those stars and many others wouldn't have sounded as good as they did.

Bob Heil grew up in Marissa, Illinois, playing the organ at the Fox Theater in St. Louis as a teen. It was there that his love of all things 'audio' flourished. In 1966, Heil opened a music shop in his hometown. Heil Sound designed and installed sound systems for venues throughout the St. Louis area, and eventually ventured into the live rock concert business, including a longtime partnership with the Grateful Dead.

Heil was friends with Bob Shaw, sound man for the St. Louis Symphony, who had designed a state-of-the-art audio system for the MRF site. "Their sound system was exquisite," Heil says. "He had put in Bozaks, which are beautiful speakers. They were hi-fi speakers, and for the symphony, that was great."

That was until Iron Butterfly came to town. "I got a call from Bob, and he was almost frantic," Heil recalled. "He said, 'Hey, aren't you doing all those rocker guys?' And I said, 'Well, yeah, we've been out with the Grateful Dead and all that.' He said, 'I'm doing the Mississippi River Festival, and we built this place and it's really great. Well, we thought we'd bring in something for the kiddies, and we brought in Iron Butterfly. They came in and blew up all my Bozaks!'"

Shaw had seen—and heard—enough. "He said, 'I'm gonna give you that contract. I never want to see any of those guys again. They played totally too loud!' And he was just going off about this. I felt sorry for him because, you know, those were very high-end speakers, and he got them all blown out that night," Heil adds.

Heil Sound would operate audio at the Mississippi River Festival for the next seven years, with Ed Drone, an engineer with McDonnell Douglas, playing a pivotal role. "When we started planning what to do, I called in one of my good chums, Ed Drone," Heil remembers. "Ed was really into audio, and he had been on the road with me for a while. He was out with Joe Walsh and the James Gang, and he didn't want to travel as much. So, I said, 'Hey, Ed, I think I've got the perfect deal for you.' He was the master of that whole audio system at the MRF. A lot of people talk about Heil Sound, and they will give me the credit. I appreciate that, but Ed was there every night. He was great at mixing and a great person."

The layout of the site proved to be a major asset when Heil and Drone began designing their plan for the MRF's audio. "One of the great aspects that helped us was that this wasn't just a hill—it was an indentation in a hillside, kind of an amphitheater type thing," Heil says. "At the bottom of that was the tent. Whoever did the original placement was a genius. They probably didn't really think about it, but they were when it came to audio because it just covered everything so well. That amphitheater became a natural acoustic horn; it was wonderful. And you could sit in the back of the grass area and see everybody on stage under that tent. What a cool deal that was."

But that doesn't mean Heil could simply move his equipment into place and start pumping sound throughout the site. He and Drone had to figure out how to compensate for the distance between the stage and the back of the lawn. "The major innovation of the MRF was the delay," Heil says.

"Sound travels 1,120 feet per second. So, we had to delay those speakers out on the lawn to meet that. We had an electronic delay that held back that amount of time, and that hadn't been done in those days. Bob Shaw had built one for the symphony, but we had to really tweak it for the rock stuff and the louder things. Ed was constantly tweaking that because it was very important. You never went to the MRF and said, 'Oh, I gotta sit in this spot because the sound is better.' We wanted to cover that whole grass area, and I think we did a very, very good job at that."

One veteran of dozens of festival shows agrees. "The sound at the MRF was great," says John S. Rendleman. "You could feel it in your chest, which was good for rock & roll. I wasn't sophisticated enough to know the technical specs or anything, but you knew that the equipment that was piled up on stage was not your typical schoolhouse play or concert. Just as a kid, I knew that was serious, serious rock & roll sound. And I think the bands knew it. You can tell when a performer recognizes that he or she is pleasing the audience because they kind of turn it up a little bit. That happened a lot at the MRF. It may have been because of the good sound production. It may have been because of the alignment of the planets. Who knows? But there were a lot of really good nights of music."

Then there was the soundboard, designed by Heil Sound, which made its way from the Mississippi River Festival to the Rock & Roll Hall of Fame in Cleveland, Ohio. "The console that Ed Drone used in just about every show during the time we worked on the MRF is in the Hall of Fame, and it states, 'This is from the Mississippi River Festival,'" Heil says. "I was very honored to have that display. It's on the same floor with Les Paul's stuff and Elvis' Sun Studio stuff."

Rick Haydon went from SIUE student/MRF fan to Professor Emeritus and accomplished jazz guitarist. He's a man who knows a thing or two about audio. "Bob Heil has to be, without a doubt, the man who created live sound," Haydon says. "When you go to a concert now, that sound comes from Bob Heil's genius. The guy was designing this stuff way ahead of everyone else. He was taking studio recording concepts and putting them on stage, so it was better for the audience and better for the guys on stage as well. He was doing time-aligned sound before anybody was doing it. He was building his own portable consoles that worked much like the ones in recording studios. I knew Bob before the MRF because I would go over and buy PA stuff for my band at his place in Marissa. Once he hooked up with Pete Townshend and the Grateful Dead and people like that, he started really developing some great stuff."

"Hey man, don't go. Bob Dylan's here!"
The Festival's Biggest Surprise

As previously mentioned, the Band was flying high in the summer of 1969 behind their debut album, *Music from Big Pink*. A unique combination of rock, country, folk, R&B, and traditional American music, the album grabbed attention as an alternative to the harder-edged-rock of the times.

After backing Ronnie Hawkins, the musicians that formed the Band were asked by Bob Dylan to join his 1965 U.S. tour and a world tour the following year. This was the era in which Dylan was shedding his folk skin and embracing the electric guitar—a move that was highly controversial—and that led to Dylan being labeled "Judas" by folk devotees. Shaken by the negative response, Levon Helm lasted only a few weeks on the '65 tour before leaving to work on an oil rig and sitting out the tour in 1966.

Asked in 1969 about the Band's association with Dylan, Robbie Robertson said he didn't recall how it began. "I think we were playing in Atlantic City at the time. Dylan had heard about us, I guess. And we'd heard about him, but we weren't into that kind of music, and I didn't really know who he was or that he was that famous. I didn't think we could play with each other at all. Then we jammed together, and a lot of things happened. We've had a great effect on each other. Dylan brought us into a whole new thing, and I guess he got something from us."[29]

In July 1966, Dylan was injured in a motorcycle accident and retreated into seclusion at his home in Woodstock, New York. His backing band continued to tour before being summoned to Woodstock by Dylan in early 1967. Renting a nearby large pink house ("Big Pink"), the musicians (with Helm back in the fold) set about recording a set of demos later released as *The Basement Tapes*. This work was the foundation for *Music from Big Pink*, which contained the classic song, "The Weight."

More than four thousand fans came to SIUE on July 14, 1969, to see The Band, not knowing that a legend was waiting in the wings. In the three years since his accident, Dylan had performed in public only once, at a Woody Guthrie Memorial Concert in New York the prior fall. But he was planning a big comeback, having asked The Band to accompany him to England in August for the Isle of Wight Festival. For the MRF, The Band and their former leader organized a surprise rehearsal.

In a 1980 interview with the *St. Louis Post-Dispatch*, Robertson relayed the conversation that set the stage for the Edwardsville reunion. "We were in Woodstock, and we told him we were going to play the Mississippi— what was it, Mississippi River Festival? And he said, 'Maybe I'll go along.' And we said, 'Well, sure, love to have you.'"[30]

Most university and festival officials were not tipped off as to what the musicians had up their sleeves. But one was. "When they arrived in Edwardsville at the good old Holiday Inn, The Band's manager called Bob Handy and asked him to come to the hotel and meet with them," Ward says. "He didn't even tell me about it. He went over and they explained what they were going to do and talked about how we were going to handle it. He met Bob Dylan and the members of The Band. One of them told him, 'Got a surprise for you. Bob's doing the encore if conditions are right for him.'"

So, the evening began, The Band took the stage, and virtually no one in the audience had a clue of what lied ahead. Although one fan may have caught a brief glimpse on the lawn.

"My brother, Steve, and his friend were walking up on the hillside," remembers Mike Reinhardt. "They came back to where we were and Steve said, 'You know, that guy standing up there on the hillside looks like Bob Dylan.' And his friend replied, 'What the hell would Bob Dylan be doing in Edwardsville, Illinois?!'"

Mike laughs at the memory. "My brother said, 'Yeah, I guess you're right.'"

The Band played the first half of its set and then headed backstage for a brief intermission. Ten-year-old John S. Rendleman was charged with serving drinks to the musicians. "Once in a while, I'd do little jobs around the site," he recalls. "Somehow or another, that night, I was carrying a tray of Coca-Colas back to The Band at intermission. From the corner, Bob Dylan looked over at me and said, 'Give me one of those Cokes.' Even then, I knew who he was, and I was very happy to give him a Coke. I didn't realize that this was going to be a big dramatic entrance or anything. I just knew he was backstage and wanted a Coke. We didn't have a conversation or anything. It's just I served Bob Dylan a Coke. There's my brush with greatness."

Robertson, being interviewed by the *Post-Dispatch* alongside actors Jodie Foster and Gary Busey to promote their movie, *Carny*, set the scene for his co-stars. "We played and he stayed backstage. That place was beautiful. It was under a tent, and most of the audience sat on the grass in an open amphitheater. The sound system was perfect—it was timed so people sitting all the way in the back heard the same sound the people in the front did.

"It was so pretty that night that Bob said, 'Maybe I'll go out and play a few songs.' So, I went out after our concert and said, 'Well, a friend of mine came along, and he would like to play,' and so forth. When he came out, the audience rushed the stage. We played 'Slippin' and Slidin'' and something real old and classic, a spiritual ('Got No Home in This World Anymore') and, I think, 'Like a Rolling Stone.' What a beautiful place that was."[31]

In his book, *This Wheel's On Fire*, Helm shared his memories of the night: "Instead of the encore, Bob came back out with us, unannounced, in a brown shirt, pants, and boots. His hair was cut short, and no one recognized him . . . When we finally came back to do 'Slippin' and Slidin',' Bob Dylan sang on the chorus, waved merrily, and split. 'See ya next month,' he said to me."[32]

Harper Barnes described the delirious reaction of the crowd, as well as the limitations of a sound system that wasn't set up for an extra voice, in a front-page *St. Louis Post-Dispatch* review of the concert. "It was difficult to hear the music much of the time. It did not seem to matter much. The excitement generated by Dylan's presence was enough to keep the crowd applauding for more." [33]

Tom Webb was in the house that night, but he didn't have a clear view when Dylan emerged. "I wasn't in the immediate area of the stage," he remembers. "Everybody started screaming and yelling, going nuts. I thought, 'Jeez, something's wrong down there.' So I went down to the audio booth, and I said, 'What's going on?' And they said, 'It's Bob Dylan!' I went, 'Oh, really?!' Dylan did a little set and walked off stage. I hustled backstage, thinking maybe I could catch him, but he was gone in a hurry."

Ward also heard the response but didn't see the historic moment. "I didn't even know it had happened until well into it, and that was through word of mouth from the people who were so excited about it. That very first year, my job was to handle everything up top with all of the ticket sales and ticket collection, so I never left my spot, and I didn't see the show."

That summer of 1969, a sophomore Mass Communications student named Rich Dalton was a constant presence at MRF shows. Through his work at campus radio station WSIE and the friendships he cultivated with student workers, Dalton enjoyed free passage throughout the festival site. "I had a 'park anywhere' sticker that I made for myself while working in the sign shop," he recalls with a laugh, "so I would walk in through the back and watch the show from the side or out on the lawn. I would just wander around because I knew everyone. Things were so loose back then. I don't even recall having like a pass or anything. But I knew enough to stay out of the way of the people who were working and just watch."

Had Dalton been lurking backstage on the night of the Band concert, he may have made contact with Dylan. But . . . "I was off to the side, outside the tent, so I didn't know anything about him being there," Dalton says. "The Band did their set and people started leaving. Then, you heard the music again, and there was this unmistakable voice. All of a sudden, you could see people running back down."

One of the shocked and dazzled fans in the crowd for this historic moment was Michael "Supe" Granda, who would go on to perform under the tent as a member of the Ozark Mountain Daredevils. "The most magical moment was when Dylan played with The Band," he recalls. "The Band was my favorite. I just wanted to hear Levon sing and play the drums, you know? And then, all of a sudden, they announce, 'We've got a special guest.'

Oh, who? Joe Blow? No, Bob Dylan. Oh, magic! The greatest concert I ever saw at the River Festival."

Alton High School student Jim Grandone was also there, having hitchhiked to Edwardsville with friends to sneak onto the lawn and avoid paying a couple of bucks for a ticket. "We didn't have a dollar," Grandone remembers. "We didn't have any money. We weren't working or anything, so we couldn't really afford to buy tickets, even though they were so cheap. It was more fun to sneak in anyway, and I never got caught."

Quick side note: There was no fence guarding the lawn in 1969. "I remember fighting against the fence in the beginning, saying it wasn't the environment we wanted at the festival," Ward says. "But after that first season, I told officials, 'We need to put up a fence.' From the very first day, people were sneaking in."

Over the next eight years, Grandone would serve as an MRF volunteer, Artist Host Coordinator, Production Supervisor, and board member. And from time to time, he encountered fence jumpers from a different perspective. "Years later, it was my job to keep those guys out," he laughs.

From his unpaid spot on the lawn, Grandone became aware of a growing buzz. "We heard rumors circulating about Bob Dylan showing up to play with The Band, and everybody said, 'He's not going to do that.' So, we're sitting there watching, and he walks on stage. The crowd went crazy, to the point where you couldn't hear him for the first few seconds that he was singing."

"It seemed to me that his microphone wasn't working at the very beginning, because you would otherwise automatically recognize that voice," Reinhardt adds. "The fans up front started going crazy and rushing the stage. But we were at the back of the tent and couldn't hear him. I said, 'Hey, there are five guys out there instead of four. There's a little guy in the middle.' Then I looked closer, and said, 'I think that's Bob Dylan!'"

J'Deanna Twesten recalls, "I knew who Bob Dylan was from his folk singer days and 'Blowin' in the Wind,' but I didn't know about his association with The Band. I remember hearing talk about him possibly being there that night. I was on the side of the stage where I always stood, and the Band was very good, all excellent musicians. But when Dylan walked out, it got even better."

Like Bob Handy, SIUE photographer Charlie Cox knew Dylan was coming, and he had been asked to perform a very important task. "The PR man for the symphony had made arrangements with *Newsweek* magazine to publish a picture of him if he showed up. I was directed to have a fresh roll of film in my camera and be ready to shoot a picture of Dylan if he got on stage, and then immediately give that roll of film to this gentleman who was going to take it to the airport and give it to the pilot of a plane that was flying to New York that night. That way, it could be picked up by somebody from *Newsweek* for that week's edition. Well, there was a huge crowd for the performance, and Bob Dylan did come out on stage. Everybody was standing and shouting in the tent so I couldn't see him. I had to stand on a chair to get my picture; people were jostling all around me. I finally got the picture, pulled the roll of film out of the camera, and rushed backstage to give it to the man from the symphony. The courier took it to the airport and the picture did show up in *Newsweek*. But the university did not get credit for it."

Unfortunately, not everyone enjoyed the same memorable experience—some fans left for home or the local watering hole early, not knowing what lied ahead. "I went with a group of guys to see the Band because *Music from Big Pink* was an album that really influenced us," Jim Muffo says. "We were on the lawn—always on the lawn. I never sat in a seat there until the day I graduated. The Band was so good, they walked off, everybody's cheering and stuff, and we got up to leave. There was a freak sitting there next to us. I had no idea who he was. I mean, he was a typical head case, you know? And he says, 'Hey man, don't go, Bob Dylan's here!' And we all just looked at him. We go, 'Oh yeah, yeah, sure he is, yeah right!' Well, this guy swore up and down that Dylan was there. And we were Band fans. Bob Dylan was kind of like from the middle sixties and stuff like that. He had the folk thing, and we weren't really into that. That said, I would've loved to have seen Bob Dylan if I really had known he was there. So anyway, we ended up leaving, and he did come up for an encore. We drove home and you know, that was it. We didn't hear anything until the next day when it came out in the news. And at that point, I kept thinking of that freak, and I'm thinking, 'I bet he's laughing now. If he can remember the fact that we had that conversation, I'm sure he's laughing his butt off.'"

Muffo continues. "I mean, we weren't the only ones who got up and walked out. There were quite a few people leaving, but I'm honest about the fact that I didn't stay. I don't say, 'Oh yeah, I was there.' Most people would probably lie. I was bummed after that because we had a chance to see music history right there with Bob Dylan at this little tent, you know?"

News of Dylan's surprise appearance quickly spread from coast to coast and around the world. For the first time, but not the last, the Mississippi River Festival had burst from the friendly confines of Edwardsville and gone global. Basking in the afterglow, the MRF's executive committee announced that it was so encouraged by the public interest shown in the festival's early weeks, it would be approaching the SIU board of trustees to request continued joint sponsorship with the SLSO for a 1970 season. In the committee's eyes, attendance had been good despite rain impacting some dates, with a parking lot check of license plates indicating attendance from 40 states and Canada.

Two days after Dylan's appearance, the crew of Neil Armstrong, Buzz Aldrin, and Michael Collins blasted off from the Kennedy Space Center in Florida, headed for the moon.

"We watched on a television at the ticket collection area"
Man Walks on the Moon

The world's attention may have been focused on the fate of Apollo 11, but in Edwardsville, the bands played on. The schedule set in the spring was maintained throughout the moon saga, even if a few shows saw meager crowds. After all, who could make the case that the proceedings playing out on television sets in July 1969 were less captivating than a standard music concert?

The St. Louis Symphony Orchestra and soprano Jodanna Rogers dutifully took the stage on the evening of July 20, knowing that even if they delivered the greatest performance of their lives, it would be a mere footnote. It seems amazing that nearly eight hundred people came out for a show that coincided with Neil Armstrong and his colleagues exploring the surface of the moon (especially in the days before VCRs and DVRs).

To be fair, festival officials weren't paying much attention to the evening's concert either. "One of the most memorable times of that year actually had nothing to do with music—it had to do with the fact that we had a television at the ticket collection area, and we watched the first man walk on the moon," Ward says. "That was an exciting time during the middle of a concert at the festival."

The next evening, more than five thousand seven-hundred fans—no doubt beaming with pride in the aftermath of America's momentous achievement—traveled out to see the New Christy Minstrels, an American folk group whose career spanned nearly fifty years. The clean-cut nature of the ensemble stood in stark contrast to earlier headliners such as Joplin and Iron Butterfly. Minstrels' leader Gary Evans told the crowd his group did not sing protest songs "because we're not mad at anybody and don't think you have to riot and wear dirty clothes to show you want peace in the world." The concert ended with "This Land is Your Land," dedicated to the moon landing. [34]

As Apollo 11 was beginning its long trek back to earth on July 22, Richie Havens performed under the tent. But the moon landing wasn't far from his mind, as Tom Webb recalls. "Ironically, that evening, there was a clear sky and a full moon," he says. "(Havens) stopped and talked about it, about how there were guys actually up there. He pointed up at the full moon and said, 'This is gonna be kind of weird, but here we go.' And he went into 'Here Comes the Sun.'"

But not every MRF performer was enthralled by what was occurring. While in town for her July 23 concert, Joan Baez held a press conference and denounced the moon mission, saying the Apollo 11 endeavor "makes [her] sick," and that money spent on space exploration would be better used to address domestic problems. "America is a technological giant and a spiritual midget," she added. [35]

The folk star and her band also had much to say about the year's other major topic of national conversation—the war in Vietnam.

"Everything fell apart"
Vietnam, Kent State and the Departure of Delyte Morris

Over the Mississippi River Festival's first several seasons, the university community—and the nation at large—were entangled in turmoil caused by the Vietnam War. That strife permeated every aspect of the college experience for millions of young people.

"They would play KSHE-95 in the University Center and that song ("One Fine Morning" by Lighthouse) would come on and they'd say 'KSHE news,'" Jim Muffo says. "They would give the body counts. 'Last week, the United States lost 2,468 of our military, and the North Vietnamese lost 50,000.' I mean, come on, it wasn't that lopsided. But that's what was announced. Every time I hear that song, that's exactly what I think of—walking through those doors, sitting there, and listening to KSHE. We were all in the age range of people going over there."

America's involvement in Southeast Asia had begun on a small scale in the 1950s and steadily escalated throughout the next decade. By 1969, the country was deeply divided. Demonstrations and protests were becoming more and more common, and musicians were often on the front lines. During her July MRF show, a member of Joan Baez's band instructed the crowd, "If there are any spare draft cards floating around out there, send them back where they came from." As some in the crowd reacted with applause and laughter, he added, "No, I mean that seriously. You young men out there—if it wasn't for your cooperation, there wouldn't be a war in Vietnam."[36]

As the festival's second season approached, the nation's discord reached a flashpoint. On May 4, 1970, four students at Kent State University were shot and killed by Ohio National Guard troops during an anti-war rally. The tragedy's repercussions would echo across the nation, and that included the SIU campuses in Edwardsville and Carbondale.

Anti-war demonstrations turned violent on the SIUC grounds, with a crowd of between four thousand and six thousand students damaging university buildings and demonstrating on the lawn of SIU President Delyte Morris' home. In response, Morris closed the campus and asked

Gov. Richard B. Oglivie to send in the National Guard; one thousand troops soon arrived in Carbondale.

"When Kent State happened, everything fell apart," Muffo remembers. "There were demonstrations in Edwardsville. There was a group that tried to take down the American flag on campus. A bunch of ex-GIs who were students surrounded the flagpole and said, 'Come on, let's go.' I was standing there on one of the hills watching this all take place. It was close to getting really bad, like what happened in Carbondale."

But there was no destruction at SIUE, and troops were never sent to campus. Things played out much differently in Edwardsville, thanks in large part to the calm leadership of Chancellor John Rendleman.

"One evening, students decided to occupy the University Center," Ward recalls. "I learned that was going to happen, and we got John involved. Building hours ended at eleven at night, but we kept the doors open and set up microphones in the lounge for the students to speak. We facilitated the right and ability for students to vocalize what they were feeling and what they wanted. They were lucky they had someone who came that night and stayed there with them—John Rendleman. Later, I made a comment to him that it was great that he didn't close the building and allowed them to stay. He said, 'Lyle, we will let them stay in this building as long as they want to talk about their feelings on this.' That was just another example of how much he valued the students, and they knew it and appreciated it. We had no damage, no fights. We had some really different opinions there, but it all worked out fine."

"Chancellor Rendleman was an amazing man," Greg Drexelius remembers. "He was very much in tune with the students."

The Kent State aftermath was just the latest in a difficult series of challenges for Morris, as the unrest in Carbondale closely followed what was known as the University House scandal. Morris had led a project to build a multi-purpose structure in Carbondale, similar to a hotel, that would house university guests, host events, and serve as replacement living space for the university president and family. Plans were drawn up and money was spent. But Illinois media began to take a critical view of the project for its cost (in the hundreds of thousands of dollars) and method of financing (the use of "restricted funds" generated from grant income). The situation culminated in the fall of 1969 with a sharp rebuke from the Illinois Board of Higher Education and a major hit to Morris' reputation.

Now, in the wake of violence on the Carbondale campus, Morris' standing with Illinois legislators was waning. Students and faculty called him aloof and out of touch—interesting; considering how integral he had been in creating the festival that brought Baez and other anti-war artists to SIUE. Petitions calling for the 63-year-old president's ouster grew in number. On June 19, after 22 years at the helm, Delyte Morris announced he would step down in September. No doubt, Morris had played a crucial role in the creation, growth, and funding of the Mississippi River Festival. Without him, economics would become a major challenge moving forward.

The specter of Vietnam—and the larger social strife permeating the nation—would linger over the MRF, particularly in that summer of 1970. "It was the rebellion that had to do with the war and later the reaction against [the shootings] at Kent State," Ward says. "What I saw during the summer was an outcome of that and expressed by the musicians."

During a show that July featuring Delaney & Bonnie and Albert King, a female fan stormed the stage, grabbed the microphone, and made a statement both encouraging fans without tickets to crash the festival gates and soliciting contributions for imprisoned members of the Black Panther Party. Before her statement was complete, but not before the girl called concert police "pigs," the sound was switched off, and she disappeared back into the crowd.[37]

Reflecting the divided nature of the nation during that turbulent time, the MRF could also offer the occasional brief respite from the turmoil. During a 1970 St. Louis Symphony show conducted by Broadway veteran Franz Allers, nearly three thousand fans enjoyed music from *My Fair Lady* and *Camelot* in a program called "The American Musical Theatre." *Alton Telegraph* Music Critic John J. Ades—who moonlighted as Chair of the SIUE English Department—described a scene from a much simpler time than Vietnam War-torn America. "Most of the audience . . . looking back to their salad days when there were (or so it seems) no jitters, loosened a button or two, took their lady's hand, and sighed for melodic days past."[38]

"Welcome to the Dead"
The Grateful Dead (and Their Fans) Hit Edwardsville

The Mississippi River Festival was nothing if not eclectic, and a prime example came on July 8, 1970. After a relatively serene weekend of the SLSO and the New Christy Minstrels, the bill of fare took a sharp left turn with the arrival of the Grateful Dead, as well as nearly nine thousand local "Deadheads."

Uniting a variety of musical styles—including rock, jazz, country, and folk—the Dead created its own inimitable sound, complete with extended jams and psychedelic imagery. Formed in San Francisco in 1965, the Grateful Dead's original lineup, still intact for the band's first MRF show, consisted of lead guitarist/vocalist Jerry Garcia, rhythm guitarist/vocalist Bob Weir, keyboardist Ron "Pigpen" McKernan, bassist Phil Lesh, and drummer Bill Kreutzmann. Drummer Mickey Hart joined the band in 1967.

Just weeks before the concert, the Grateful Dead released its experimental third album, *Aoxomoxoa*, which was one of the first rock albums recorded with sixteen-track equipment and was described in *Rolling Stone* as the work of a "magical band."

The atmosphere was tie-dyed and cosmic even outside the SIUE campus, as fans driving in from the south via Illinois 157 were greeted by a large sign stating, "Welcome to the Dead." Despite arriving thirty minutes late and weathering a few technical challenges, the Grateful Dead's magic was on full display for three hours at the MRF, beginning with the hit "Casey Jones." Fans got as close to their heroes as possible. Much to the consternation of fire marshals, lawn ticket holders massed under the tent when the band appeared, claiming empty seats and filling the aisles and the apron at the front of the stage. This was fine with the band members, who encouraged the energetic response, dancing, singing, and clapping.[39]

Musically, Garcia's bluesy vocals and emotional guitar were highlights, with Weir and McKernan also taking turns at the microphone. "Pigpen" kicked things up a notch after an opening folk and country set, leading a 23-minute version of the Rascals' "Good Lovin.'" The Dead rarely stopped for applause or breaks between songs, giving the impression of a three-hour musical collage rather than a set of individual songs. The twenty-first and final song of the night was "Cosmic Charlie," the last song on the new album, and one rarely played in concert after 1970.

The band's partner in audio, Bob Heil, was proud to show off his newest toys at the MRF venue. This would not be the last time one of Heil's bands would plug into his MRF sound system—it would be done to historic effect just a year later.

Backstage, rambunctious fans, university officials, and band personnel mingled. The *Alton Telegraph's* Doug Thompson described the vibe: "Young girls and long-haired men crowded around the group's equipment and moved spasmodically to the music. A very young, brown-haired girl in white bell bottoms danced alone while patterns from the light show played across her and the screen behind her."[40]

All that exuberance led to a few minor injuries. "Nothing serious," an onsite nurse said. "Mostly bruises from falling down or falling over things. Just things like that."[41]

The Grateful Dead would continue touring relentlessly, but they would not return to the MRF for 10 years.

The Five-Timers Club (Part I)
Henry Mancini

Of all the performers who graced the Mississippi River Festival stage—and there were hundreds—only three could claim that they headlined five MRF shows. We'll discuss the other two soon enough, but the first of the three to arrive on campus was arranger/composer Henry Mancini.

Mancini's resume already boasted a No. 1 hit (1969's "Love Theme from Romeo and Juliet"), three Academy Awards (for *Breakfast at Tiffany's*, *Moon River*, and *Days of Wine and Roses*), and seventeen Grammy Awards when the 46-year-old made his initial MRF appearance in 1970. The Ohio native would conduct the St. Louis Symphony during all five of his visits and occasionally accompany on piano. Time and again, familiar tunes such as "Peter Gunn" and "The Pink Panther" proved to be crowd-pleasers.

In 1971, Mancini dodged a brief downpour and played the theme from the movie *Love Story* on the piano before announcing, "I sent that number up to the rain gods. I didn't write it, so I thought I could give it away."[42] Fans gave the celebrated conductor three standing ovations by the end of the show, which included Mancini originals such as "Baby Elephant Walk" and "Moon River." He also suggested audience members buy the new *Jesus Christ Superstar* album. "(Tim) Rice and (Andrew) Webber don't need the money, but you need the album."[43]

Similar shows followed in 1973 and 1975, and for his final MRF show in 1977, Mancini was in fine spirits, telling the audience, "You guys are all right" after the first of his two encores.[44]

During the festival's first three seasons, John Jarvis worked as a waiter at Rusty's Restaurant in Edwardsville, where he had the opportunity to serve MRF entertainers such as Bo Diddley, Gary "U.S." Bonds, and Judy Collins. Mancini was another, and years later, Jarvis again crossed paths with the star at the Ritz Carlton in St. Louis. "This was in the nineties," Jarvis recalls. "I asked him specifically if he remembered the MRF, and he said, 'Oh yeah!'"

Attracting crowds representing all age groups, Mancini played for about twenty-four thousand total fans at the MRF. "His music just made you happy," Greg Drexelius says. "He put on a great show. He was quite a showman."

"They were dead on"
Chicago Proves to Be Festival Favorites

Over the 12 summers of the Mississippi River Festival, attendance figures ebbed and flowed depending on the artist, weather, and numerous other factors. But there seemed to be one constant—Chicago would always pull a big crowd. Playing four MRF shows, the Rock & Roll Hall of Famers attracted nearly seventy thousand festival fans, the highest total number for any popular music artist.

One of the '70s most successful acts, Chicago fused rock, pop, and jazz, blending the talents of bassist/vocalist Peter Cetera, keyboardist/

vocalist Robert Lamm, guitarist/vocalist Terry Kath, drummer Danny Seraphine, and the horn section of Walter Parazaider, James Pankow, and Lee Loughnane. An early band press release described Chicago as "seven artists who work together in a creative community." Cetera added, "All of the labels mean something to everyone but us."[45]

The group first came to Edwardsville in 1970 as one of the hottest new bands in the business, riding high on the success of its debut double album released the year before. The *Chicago Transit Authority* album (the band assumed the name "Chicago" later in 1969 after the mass-transit operator of the same name threatened a lawsuit) led to a Best New Artist Grammy nomination and included hallmark songs like "Beginnings" and "Does Anybody Really Know What Time It Is?" By July 1970, Chicago's second album—soon to be known as *Chicago II*—was dominating FM radio coast to coast. The double LP would spawn three Top 10 hits—"25 or 6 to 4," "Make Me Smile," and "Colour My World"—and be nominated for three Grammy Awards, including Album of the Year.

Chicago's debut MRF appearance attracted 15,915 fans, making it the best-attended festival event to date. As was becoming customary, large crowds meant epic traffic jams pre- and post-concert. All entrances to the venue were jammed, and 15 minutes before show time, traffic on I-270 stretched four miles. Covering the concert for the *Edwardsville Intelligencer*, Judy Ronzio was fascinated by the sea of humanity on the lawn. "Thousands and thousands of youths streamed onto the site dragging their blankets—some of them still straggling in after intermission. Few of the youths looked as if they were twenty-four-hour-a-day hippies; more looked as if they just broke out their grubbies for the occasion."[46]

A few possibly overserved fans decided to set off Roman candles and firecrackers during the show, but the overall vibe was more laid back than raucous. "Chicago didn't seem to draw the thunderous ovations the symphony and some pop groups have been getting, but the group's appeal for Wednesday night's house couldn't be denied," Ronzio wrote.[47]

Jim Muffo was on the lawn that night. "I can tell you this," he recalls. "Of all the groups I had seen at that point, they sounded more like their album than any other group. I mean, they were dead on."

Three years later, Chicago returned. And this time, they nearly doubled their initial attendance figure by bringing in 28,377 devotees—the third-largest audience in MRF history behind only shows by The Who and the Eagles.

In the period since their first festival appearance, Chicago had only grown in popularity, enjoying a No. 1 album in 1972 with *Chicago V*, and the No. 3 hit single, "Saturday in the Park." The summer of 1973 saw the band touring behind *Chicago VI*, which also topped the album chart. The hits "Just You 'N' Me" and "Feelin' Stronger Every Day" would both crack the Top 10.

While Chicago had become a local fan favorite, the feeling was mutual for the musicians. "We love it," woodwind player Walter Parazaider said weeks before the show. "It's neat playing where the symphony performs."[48]

As seen with the band's previous visit, traffic jams were the norm before and after the show. Also, the larger crowd meant less space and more heated interactions between attendees. Scattered fights were reported, and one staff member was attacked and beaten by several men when they were told they could not enter the site through a back entrance. Numerous cuts, bruises, and scrapes were seen by SIUE Health Services.

One particular lawn dweller went above and beyond in his attempts to show off for fellow fans. "A man climbed a speaker tower," recalled concert attendee John Oeltjen. "The guy didn't have complete control of his faculties. I don't know if he was high or drunk or what. But he climbed up the speaker stand, did a vertical armstand, and then he lost it (falling groin-first onto a metal bar). Everybody in the crowd went, 'Ohhh!' They shared his pain."[49]

Chicago's third appearance came the following year, supporting the *Chicago VII* album. Again, radio airplay and record sales quickly followed. The double album featured two Top 10 singles, "(I've Been) Searchin' So Long" and "Call On Me," and the No. 11 hit "Wishing You Were Here," which included backing vocals by members of The Beach Boys.

The band's crew created a striking look for the '74 MRF show, installing white carpet on the stage and a plexiglass riser for the horn section, and topping it off with a powerful light display. The set list covered songs from all seven albums, with plenty of emphasis on the hits. The receptive crowd was pleased to hear Pankow announce, "Thank you. See you next year," before the band headed for the black limousines that swept them on to the next gig.[50]

The night was a quiet one for festival officials and staff, despite the largest crowd of the 1974 season. Bob Prosise, assistant chief of University Police, said traffic moved smoothly, although getting cars off campus "was like running a quart through a pint."[51]

In 1978, Chicago bid the MRF farewell. The band looked and sounded different from previous appearances, as founding member Kath had died from an accidental gunshot wound the previous January. New guitarist Donnie Dacus was now in the band, fresh off stints with Stephen Stills, Boz Scaggs, and other acts. The band's tenth studio album and first without Kath, *Hot Streets*, would be released a few months later. Chicago still played its hits for the fans in the house, but without the virtuosity and distinct voice of Kath, the sound was irrevocably different.

The Five-Timers Club (Part II)
Judy Collins

A performer who would go on to become a festival and university favorite made her debut on August 5, 1970. Folk singer Judy Collins was born in Seattle, overcame polio, and studied classical piano as a child. Inspired by the folk music of Woody Guthrie and Pete Seeger, Collins shifted in a new direction and headed for the coffee houses and clubs in Greenwich Village. Her 1968 hit "Both Sides Now" —written by fellow MRF alum Joni Mitchell—cracked the Top Ten and won a Grammy.

Collins accompanied herself on guitar and piano throughout her first show, her long hair flowing over a floor-length white gown. Rain throughout the day made for wet blankets on the lawn, but it didn't stop the large crowd from enjoying a refined performance. Perhaps the strangest moment of the evening came when a fan rolled a watermelon on stage. Collins laughed, thanked the fan, and allowed the watermelon to remain on stage to enjoy the show.[52]

"That first Judy Collins concert was just unbelievable," says Greg Drexelius, recalling one of the initial MRF shows he ever worked. "It was so beautiful and just so quiet under the tent—you could have heard a pin drop. There was no socialization. People were there for the music and loving it to the max. And that was so impressive. That changed over time. Things got more social as years went by. But that was such a wonderful way to begin."

One song Collins performed that night was her rendition of the hymn "Amazing Grace." But it took an act of God—in a way—for it to happen. "Some of the backstage student workers asked her before the concert if she was going to sing it that night," said Charlie Cox. "She said she'd forgotten the words but promised that she would sing it if somebody could find the words for her. Someone was dispatched to go find a copy of 'Amazing Grace.' I think they went to a local minister's house, and he went to his church and got a hymnal that had that song in it. The student brought the hymnal back to the festival site so Judy Collins could perform the song."

By this stage, Rich Dalton had made a habit of bringing a cassette recorder along to some MRF shows, including the first Collins concert. "I sat in the dressing room and interviewed her," he remembers. "The (Crosby, Stills & Nash) song, 'Suite: Judy Blue Eyes' was out then, and boy, she's got blue eyes, too! Holy cow. I told her, 'I heard 'Suite: Judy Blue Eyes' is about you,' since the story was that she and Stephen Stills were dating. She said, 'Stephen and I are friends.' That's all she said."

The next year, Collins returned to Edwardsville, receiving a rousing ovation when she announced that net proceeds from the show would go to the American Friends Service Committee and its Black Draft Resistance Program. "Basically, I'm a humanist," she told reporters backstage. "I think of myself as a citizen of the world . . . and I'm a pacifist."[53]

The conversation soon turned to the Vietnam War, and not surprisingly, Collins was candid. She called the U.S. "unresponsive" to what she called an "unprecedented" offer by the North Vietnamese to release prisoners of war in exchange for troop withdrawals. "I mean, this is something that is unheard of in war. This is an offer of peace, and we are not taking it."[54]

Collins also sang a subdued rendition of "Me and Bobbie McGee" as a tribute to her friend Janis Joplin, who had died nine months before.

After sitting out the '72 MRF season, Collins returned to SIUE in 1973 for her third festival performance. This time, she was backed by a six-piece band promoting her *True Stories and Other Dreams* album and accompanied by a nasty sunburn, which she covered with a "quarter-inch of Noxzema."[55]

Collins' fourth festival show came in 1975 and was the first to include a number that would become the artist's signature song, "Send in the Clowns." Written by Stephen Sondheim for the 1973 musical, *A Little Night Music*, Collins' version from her album, *Judith*, would earn Sondheim the Grammy for Song of the Year in 1976.

For this visit to Edwardsville, Collins brought along a special guest—symphony conductor Antonia Brico, her former classical piano teacher, and the subject of Collins' Oscar-nominated 1974 documentary *Antonia: A Portrait of the Woman*. Brico listened to Bach recordings in the SIUE music library and praised her former pupil for reigniting her career. "I say, 'God bless Judy Collins' every time another chance to conduct comes up because that came as a direct result of the movie," Brico said.[56]

"That was a really special event," Ward remembers. "Antonia was a wonderful woman and conductor, and it turned out to be a really magical couple of days. I think Judy appreciated it, too."

By the mid-1970s, the MRF was venturing more and more into the arena and southern rock realms, with fewer folk artists on the schedule than in earlier years. But there would always be an audience for the lighter fare. "Music like Judy Collins' is best suited for the summer festival," wrote Doug Thompson in the *Alton Telegraph*. "The Mississippi River Festival was conceived as a summertime music series where people could go and hear music at a reasonable price—not as a summertime rock festival where one becomes part of a mob who could care less what the group on the stage is doing. Unfortunately, good music and small crowds don't pay the bills."[57]

In 1976, Collins switched things up for her last festival show. The stripped-down acoustic guitar and piano sound was replaced by a six-piece backing group that added texture to her newer songs. The final show's attendance figure boosted Collins close to 40,000 fans over five festival shows. Decades later, Collins would return to SIUE to perform—indoors this time—in the University Center's Meridian Ballroom. "We had a lot of good times together, and I have very good feelings about Judy Collins on a personal note," Ward says.

Through her MRF visits, Collins also built a rapport with student hostess Linda Ruth Brubaker. "The first time I saw her, a great performer in the flesh, was amazing," Brubaker said. "After Judy's performance, she said, 'Where's a good place to go and eat?' And I said, 'Well, how about Rusty's? It's a really nice local restaurant, great food, and great ambiance.' So, we went over to Rusty's, and some of the guys that traveled with her went, too. I pulled out my harp and sang her some songs, bless her heart. She listened to some of my songs, and we had an interesting time talking. I saw her perform again several years later, and I went out to see her at the Holiday Inn the next morning, and we had a little short chat."

Festival Assistant Manager Gene Haffner says Collins forged a genuine connection with the student workers. "Judy Collins was just such a classy lady," he says. "I remember one of her concerts, she did a sound check in the afternoon, and then she just sat on the hillside back by the dressing rooms, playing her guitar and singing songs for some of the students who came out early to get ready and set up. They were just sitting out there on the hillside with Judy Collins, talking and singing songs and having a good time."

"Hell, yeah! Skip was quite a character"
The Legend of Skip Manley

Opening night in 1971. Pianist Van Cliburn and the St. Louis Symphony Orchestra were gathered on the MRF site, as were nearly four thousand fans in anticipation of an evening of music. Out near the tent, the *Edwardsville Intelligencer's* Dick Norrish overheard someone pointing out a large black thunderhead to tent master Skip Manley. "Aw, that's blowing the other way," Manley said confidently, and he soon would be proven correct. [58]

This level of meteorological acumen was nothing new for Manley, who seemed to have an uncanny knack for predicting festival climate conditions. "This guy could predict the weather two weeks in advance," recalls student worker John Klobnak. "I don't care who you would turn to from a meteorological standpoint, they were never as accurate. He was a circus tent guy. That's what he did. And he had to know if there was going to be a storm. He told us that TV meteorologists start watching when weather gets to California. Skip was tracking weather back in Asia and he would follow it across the Pacific. And he was always right about the weather. He just knew."

Rich Dalton says Manley eventually made his way onto WSIE to share his weather forecasts. "He would say it was going to rain," Dalton says. "Now, the weather bureau would say it wasn't going to rain, but if Skip said it was going to rain, it would rain."

Gene Haffner worked many nights at the festival site alongside Manley. "We would marvel at this guy. There were times when it would be mid-morning, mid-afternoon, and he would come busting out of that trailer gathering people to head for the tent, and they would start adjusting the cables and the ropes. We're sitting there going, 'What are you doing?' And he's going, 'We're going to have 60-mile-an-hour winds here in about two hours.' And we're going, 'Well, nobody's saying that.' And then, two hours later, it would either happen, or the weather forecasters would be saying to batten down the hatches. He was amazing."

One could make a persuasive case that Skip Manley is the most unforgettable character in the annals of the Mississippi River Festival. Enigmatic, peculiar, and one of only a handful of individuals in the world capable of performing the necessary job, Skip was irreplaceable. "How could you do it without Skip?" asks Bob Heil.

Roy Manley was born in 1903 in Peoria, Illinois. After finishing high school, he hopped aboard a train headed to the west coast with dreams of becoming a cartoonist dancing in his head. But before he could reach his destination, somewhere around Wyoming, he took a detour into another life with the circus.

"I was riding along on the Union Pacific in a coal car with several other fellows when one bum said that he knew we would all have jobs by the morning," Manley told SIUE News Service in 1976. "It seems he had noticed posters advertising a circus playing in the town where the train would stop the next morning, and sure enough, we all had jobs with the circus the next day."[59]

Manley quickly fell in love with the circus lifestyle and abandoned his cartooning pursuits. Years of work with some of the nation's top circuses (including Ringling Brothers) followed, leading Manley on the highly-specialized path toward becoming a tent master. Whether it was a circus, summer theater, or concert, or any other event that required a large tent, Skip Manley was in demand. Described in the *Edwardsville Intelligencer* as having a "personality that has been tinted by decades on the road with the top shows and circuses of a generation ago and accented in more recent years by working with some of the respected drama festivals presented under the stars," Manley had plied his wares in 48 states and several foreign countries.[60]

So, when the MRF came into existence in 1969, officials were fortunate to land (and retain) his unique set of skills. "I don't think any of us knew much about Skip," Ward says. "He was ageless. He looked like a little Mitch Miller, very thin and small but with muscular arms, and he always wore a goatee. He had no sense of humor. He was a tyrant when it came to that tent—that was his child."

Before the festival's inaugural season, Manley worked with U.S. Tent and Awning on tent design and supervised SIU crews in erecting the tent completely by hand. "They had refused to build the tent according to the architect's plans," Manley reflected in 1976. "They sent me the plans, and I could see there was no way the tent was going to work with the original plans. I told them to tell me what they wanted to put in it, and I would design one to my specifications."[61]

Ward says that the effort was much more detailed and complex than Manley made it sound. "Having a tent was only possible because the university located a true tent master," he says. "Skip was very much involved in the design of it because it was important acoustically, aesthetically, and from a safety standpoint to have the right tent. It was truly remarkable to see Skip orchestrate—that's truly what it was, the orchestration of raising the tent. It involved dozens and dozens of people from the university, electricians, carpenters, and all kinds of craftsmen who would be pulling on the ropes.

The period of time between the initial concept of the festival and the first concert was less than a year, and it was less than five months between the beginning of construction and the first date. Skip Manley was a remarkable man who was no stranger to barking orders to all of us in terms of how his baby was to be taken care of. He was a centerpiece of the festival during the years the university managed it."

Haffner agrees. "Skip was dedicated to what he did, and he was dedicated to making sure that it went right. In terms of his responsibilities, he pulled absolutely no punches. You always knew where you stood with Skip, and what he thought about you, what you were doing, and what you ought to be doing. But there is no question that he was a key, key person in the whole operation. The tent was vital to the magic of the venue, and man, that tent was his baby."

Manley and the festival faced their first big challenge just a week into the MRF's existence when a severe storm hit the site on June 28, 1969. The St. Louis Symphony and cellist Leonard Rose were playing for a crowd of 854 fans when violent winds smashed the tent during intermission. "We were right on the edge of a tornado," Manley recalled in 1976. "I hollered at the people to clear the tent, but they just wouldn't move until I jumped down into the audience and started yelling. We were lucky that no one was hurt."[62]

Ward adds, "The poles on the sides of the tent splintered like toothpicks. We had enough time to evacuate the tent—the musicians actually went underneath the stage. The outcome is that we had not a single injury and the student workers took over and ushered everyone out of the site and back to their cars. But it was a night none of us will forget."

John S. Rendleman remembers the phone ringing at his home that evening. "My dad was called away because the tent had 'blown down'—that was the word we got on the phone at home," he says. "It hadn't actually blown down, but wind had torn part of it and damaged it. So, dad had to go out there. The next day, he talked about meeting with Skip, who knew exactly what needed to be done. I think Skip's presence was important because everybody believed that he knew what he was doing. Even though he was a little bit eccentric, we were all happy to have someone like that holding up the tent."

The second half of the performance was canceled, and several tent poles were replaced before the next event. "I have to be in full control of the tent 24 hours a day," Manley said. "The weather does not punch a time clock, and when the weather gets bad, the tent has to be prepared to stand up to it."[63]

Bob Heil laughs as he recalled the sight of Manley's near-dictatorial control over all things related to the tent. "Don't you ever think you're going to go over there and pull that rope—you're in big trouble!" Heil says. "I'd seen kids do that before, and it was really weird. (Skip) would see some guy that was all buzzed out and he was gonna go over and pull a rope or something. I don't know where Skip came from. He would just fall out of wherever, and he solidified his rope. Trust me, you did not touch the tent. It was his deal—and bless him for that."

Manley's intensity and passion flashed during a 1971 concert by the rock group Mountain. Groupies congregated backstage with designs on catching the eyes of band members Leslie West and Felix Pappalardi—eventually, a handful of them wandered into the press room. "I want them out!" Manley demanded. A member of the band's crew countered that the girls were friends of theirs. "Friends, hell!" Manley exclaimed. "These girls have been here before. I want them out!" The girls were quickly evicted from the press room. [64]

Over the course of the MRF's run, there were actually four tents erected over the stage. Midwestern heat and storms could do a number on canvas, after all, and the proposed permanent site never came to fruition. Before the start of the 1974 season, the third tent was slowly making its way to Edwardsville—usually in place a month before the season, the new tent was still in Chicago just days before the July 7 opener. Receiving and installing the tent would be a last-minute job. "We're planning on working very long days," said Charles Moorleghen, SIUE's Assistant Vice President for Business Affairs. "If it rains, it may really put a damper on things."[65]

As it turned out, the tent arrived at 3 a.m. on July 3. Manley and his twenty-man team had it erected before Independence Day, fueled by some fifty gallons of soft drinks. "When I came here six years ago, they told me they would have a tent for that first season and then build a permanent building for the site," Manley said. "I just laughed."[66]

In addition to doing the job for the money (he reportedly earned a $13,400 salary for the 1971 season, which translates to almost $100,000 today), Manley viewed his MRF service as a duty to be performed for the good of his home state. "I was born here, and I felt this was my chance to do something for Illinois," he said. "I could see big possibilities for the MRF as a good event for this area, and, by God, it is."[67]

No doubt, when it came to his tent, Skip Manley wasn't about to suffer any fools. But for those who worked alongside him, the unconventional tent master became a figure they would remember fondly for the rest of their lives.

"He would come into Vanzo's every night after the show to drink and tell stories," John Klobnak says. "He was just the nicest guy. We'd stay up there sometimes until two or three in the morning listening to him. He'd tell stories about the places he'd been, tearing tents down and putting them back up. I'll never forget him."

"Skip was a unique gentleman with his green glasses, and he always wore his hat," adds Greg Drexelius. "He enjoyed the students very much, and he shared little bits of wisdom with us. He taught me that if you were going to smoke a cigarette in a dirty environment, you'd better open the other end of the pack so you could take it out by the tobacco end instead of the filter end. That way, when you put the filter in your mouth, it was clean. I had never thought of that before."

Festival worker Bob Gill also occasionally hit the town with Manley. "Hell yeah, Skip was quite a character," he said. "He had a little dog that he would take around to the bars. But he knew his tents. We'd get him talking about circus tents; man, he could talk all night."

"He managed to have a bottle of whiskey out there every now and then; I know that may or may not have been within the university guidelines," added Larry Medlin, an architect who worked on the initial creation of the concert site. "Students would find a way to come out, share stories with him, and so forth. Skip really became sort of a cultural institution. He was a wonderful guy."

Bryan Erdmann was MRF's Stage Manager and another social comrade of Manley's. "We became pretty close," he says. "I guess Skip liked my style because I was comfortable with people, and he liked that I had been on the road with a tent show before I got to the MRF. We would sometimes drink a shot of whiskey together and meet at Ronnie B's, or I would give him a ride down there. He thought the bigger place down the street was too phony, but he liked Ronnie B's because it was a little joint. So, I would take him there after we got the show buttoned up and the stage locked down."

Skip was also easily identifiable on the roads of the Edwardsville-Glen Carbon area for his mode of transportation. "Skip had a Cushman—it was like a golf cart—and he would drive it up to Rusty's and have drinks and dinner there," Jim Grandone says. "I guess the police eventually figured out that this guy was not supposed to be driving a car, so they just let him go. So, there he was, driving a Cushman on the road at night. He had a little triangular reflector on the back—that's how you knew it was Skip. Your car would come up on it and you'd go, 'Oh, there's Skip!' If you've ever driven a golf cart, you know how tenuous it is to keep going in a straight line. And for him to drive it out to have dinner—well, it's a risk that I would never take."

Drexelius was a frequent dinner companion of Manley's—specifically for trips to the Candlelite Lounge in Glen Carbon. "They had these delicious pork chops that you couldn't beat, and we would get in the car and go. It was a good time. I did a lot of traveling with him; there were a lot of trips to town and a lot of pork chops."

Some student workers were "lucky" enough to peek behind the curtain and survey the landscape of Skip Manley's trailer on the MRF site. "One night after a concert, he invited me into his trailer to have some Scotch with him," Grandone says. "I went in and looked in his room and there was a bathtub filled with artifacts and equipment from the stage and the tent. I said, 'Skip don't you ever bathe?' He says, 'Oh no, I don't bathe. Hell, the mosquitoes would eat me alive if I bathed. I don't bathe all summer.'"

Umm, he was exaggerating, right? "No, that was absolutely true,"

Grandone recalls with a laugh. "If you were downwind, you could tell."

"The trailer was an interesting place," Drexelius adds. "It was really cluttered, and it had its own aroma. If you ever were in there, you'd probably agree with that. It wasn't dirty per se, but it had a 'lived in' aroma."

Erdmann also spent time in the trailer. "It was an office and a workshop with a bed in the back. I mean, it was not cocktail party material. He lived in a workshop, pretty much. He had every corner filled with something."

Skip Manley turned out to be the living embodiment of the old adage, "You can't judge a book by its cover." "When Skip first came to campus, people sort of looked at him and thought, 'Well, this old bum won't be able to do anything,'" said Charlie Cox. "But Skip knew how to work with people. He took people who had never worked with tents before and taught them how to tighten the tent, how to loosen it."

Grandone adds, "The man was probably in his late seventies when I knew him, and his vision was not that good. He had pretty thick glasses. But he knew everything there was to know about that tent and safety regarding the tent, and when to put flaps down on the side of the tent when it was raining. He was just an amazing source of information, and he had stories that you could listen to for hours about the circus and life in Chicago and things that happened before I got to the festival. He was like a grandfather to us."

At the conclusion of the 1969 season, Tom Webb was given a special souvenir to remember his brief MRF experience. "On the last night, I was talking to Skip, and he said, 'Well, I'll see you next summer.' I told him I wouldn't be back – that in a month, I would be heading down to Texas for active duty in the Air Force. I was looking at the chairs they used under the tent. They were director's chairs, and they color-coded them based on section. I said, 'Are those extra director's chairs?' And he said, 'Yeah, you want one?' He grabbed it and said, 'Where's your car?' And boom, he threw it in the trunk."

Webb laughs. "I carried that chair around with me for 10, 15 years, until the seat ripped out of it and I had to replace it. Finally, one day, the hinges broke. I said, 'Okay, you've served wonderfully.' Into the trash!"

Drexelius still has a couple of MRF chairs in his home. But he also has something even more precious. "I have a large piece of the original tent. Skip gave it to me in 1972 after they replaced the first tent. I gave pieces out to folks that worked with me for years. That's where Lyle Ward got his piece of it."

"With the students in particular, Skip developed really good relationships," Haffner adds. "There were times he would demonstrate real caring and tenderness for them."

Manley faded into history when SIUE relinquished management of the festival following the 1977 season. In a 1991 interview, Ward said the tent master had passed away, but no details were provided—he seems to have simply disappeared from the public eye.

"In the mid-eighties, I went to Chicago to design a sound system for the Chicago Theater, and while I was there, I visited Skip just to say hi," Erdmann recalls. "He said, 'Well, come back when you can to have a drink.' So, I went back up a couple of months later. That might have been the last time I saw him."

Still, the memories Skip Manley created over nine summers at the MRF live on. "They realized he was an important guy, and they didn't want him running off to join the circus somewhere," Gill said. "So, they tried to give him a nice setup here. They gave him a place to live, his own little scooter, and the run of the place. I think he realized he was a special person here. Everybody treated him with a lot of respect. So, he never, as far as I know, got any inclination to run off and join the circus again. We were pretty lucky to have him."

Haffner sums up the tent master this way. "In my entire life, I have never met anyone, nor will I probably ever again meet anyone, like Skip."

"If nothing ever happens in my life again after this, musically, I'll be happy"
Old Time Rock & Roll Under the Tent

St. Louis holds a special place in music history as the birthplace of the legendary Chuck Berry. The man dubbed the "Father of Rock & Roll" showed off his talents for hometown fans at the Mississippi River Festival on two occasions. But he wasn't the only pioneer of the art form to perform under the tent.

In fact, Smokey Robinson and The Miracles were the first "oldies" act to play the MRF. Their 1970 show attracted more than six thousand fans and quickly turned into one of the most frenzied nights the young festival had seen.

Born in Detroit, Robinson's unparalleled career as a singer, songwriter, producer, and businessman made him one of America's most beloved artists. He founded The Miracles in 1955 and led the act to massive success with a long string of popular records and five Top Ten hits, including "Shop Around," "You've Really Got a Hold on Me," and "I Second That Emotion." But it wasn't until 1970—just weeks after their MRF performance—that Smokey Robinson and The Miracles released their biggest hit—and lone No. 1—"The Tears of a Clown."

The *Alton Telegraph's* Doug Thompson chronicled the evening's chaotic events, which began before the Miracles even appeared. "Backstage, a small but loud group of autograph seekers had hounded the dressing room for more than an hour, keeping the group of stage marshals more than busy," he wrote.[68]

Robinson hit the stage, accompanied by just two of his Miracles (Ronnie White and Bobby Rogers), to a roaring response. All three were dressed in purple vests, bright gold shirts, and boots that glittered in the lights. Thompson wrote that girls trying to get a piece of the star forced a campus police officer to relocate to the front of the stage to control the crowd. A festival official backstage barked, "Get down there and talk to them. Tell them if they don't get back and off the stage, we'll close the show down. If they want the show to continue, they'll have to move back."[69]

Robinson joined the effort, pleading for the crowd to remain calm. By the show's midpoint, the black Cadillac that would rush the performers to safety post-concert had already pulled up to the steps leading to the dressing rooms—all in the hopes of a quick, safe getaway from the adoring fans. Meanwhile, back on stage, a girl made her way through security and grabbed Robinson in a fevered embrace. The singer just smiled and kept singing until an SIUE police officer—cigarette dangling from his mouth—

arrived to haul her away.[70]

As the final song began, a member of the MRF team told others backstage, "Get ready, he'll be coming through." Following waves and bows, Robinson and The Miracles bounded offstage and headed straight for the Cadillac—a trip clocked at just 14 seconds. A group of fans took off running around the tent, hoping to intercept Robinson before he could get in the car. Alas, they were too late. The Cadillac was already speeding its way off campus.[71]

"Where's he at? Where's Smokey?" a girl asked. A stage marshal responded, "That man is long gone."[72]

The next year, Berry crossed the river—accompanied by Jerry Lee Lewis, Bo Diddley, and Gary "U.S." Bonds—for what was dubbed as the Rock & Roll Revival show. A crowd topping 4,600 dodged raindrops to enjoy a trip down memory lane. Local act Billy Peek and the Sound Company kicked off the night's revelry with a hard-charging set and then remained onstage to provide support for several of the legends. Peek had occasionally played with Berry for several years by that point, but this, by far, was the biggest crowd the guitarist had ever entertained. It would be a career-altering night.

"I was playing this little place called the Rainbow and Chuck showed up," Peek remembers. "He says, 'Billy, I'm gonna play a concert in Edwardsville called the Mississippi River Festival, and I want you to back me up.' I said, 'Well, man, I'd be happy to.' So, then he says, 'Also, you're gonna have to back up Bo Diddley and Gary U.S. Bonds and Jerry Lee Lewis; they're gonna be on the show.' And I got a little nervous about that because Jerry Lee had a reputation back then, you know? I thought, 'Well, if I don't do something right, this guy's gonna dress me down on stage.' As it turns out, lucky for me, Jerry Lee brought his own band that night, but I did back up the others."

Peek arrived on campus the afternoon of the show for rehearsal, where he quickly got a feel for the different ways each legend liked to prepare for a big show. "Gary U.S. Bonds had a proper rehearsal," Peek says. "He knew his keys and told me where the chord changes were. But Bo Diddley was the funny one. We were waiting all day to rehearse with Bo. Finally, he comes up and says, 'Okay, now here's what's gonna happen. If I shake my head yes, like this, that means you play. If I shake my head no, like this, that means don't play. Now, if I'm not in the key of A, I'll be in the key of G. And if I'm not in the key of G, I'll be in the key of A.' And with that, he just tilted his head back, tipped his little hat, and took off.'"

Showtime approached, and the fans started pouring in. Peek surveyed the activity, and what he saw left him breathless. "I peeped out there at the people and I thought, 'My God, I've never seen anything like this.' You know, I actually got chills about going on stage for this many people. For someone coming out of nightclubs, where you're talking maybe a hundred or two hundred people depending on the room, and here's thousands of people and they're all rowdy and ready for the show—it was an amazing thing for me."

Peek faced his fears, soldiered on stage, and backed Berry, Bonds, and Diddley during a crowd-pleasing evening. "These were heroes of mine when I was a little kid hanging out in a slimy pool hall," Peek says. "We'd always hit the jukebox and it would be Chuck, or it'd be Bo Diddley or Little Richard, or somebody like that. So it was such a big thrill for me to be on stage with these guys, and it was surreal to play to that big of an audience. I stepped back and thought, 'Man, what am I doing here? I'm a little kid from Tower Grove. And now, here I am playing with all these guys that were my heroes.' And to do it at the MRF was the biggest thrill because a lot of people from St. Louis that knew me came to the show. I thought this would be the biggest thing to ever happen to Billy Peek."

Ironically, his most vivid memories of the evening are of the performer he didn't perform with. "Because I didn't have to back Jerry Lee Lewis, I got to stand in the wings and watch him. I can still see it—he was wearing brown cowboy boots, and it was really funny because it was a lesson in how to control a crowd. He started playing his country tunes, and some of the people started booing. So, he stops midstream, looks out, and says, 'Look, I know what you want to hear.' And he sings, 'You shake my nerves and you rattle my brain!' And then he just stops, and the crowd was going crazy, yelling and hollering. And then he did a little 'Whole Lotta Shakin' Goin' On,' and he says, 'I know that's what you want to hear. And I'm gonna let you hear that. But this is what I wanna play. And you're gonna sit there and listen to it and then I'll give you what you want to hear.'"

Peek laughs. "He dressed that crowd down because they were starting to get on his nerves a little bit. And they listened to him, too. He had command of them. And when he went into those songs that everybody came to hear, he just tore the place up. It was an interesting experience."

Rich Dalton experienced a very different Jerry Lee Lewis when he interviewed him after the show. "All that aggression was gone," he says. "He was very docile and very nice. I guess he got it out of his system."

In hindsight, Peek believes the MRF gig was a challenge issued by his mentor. "Chuck never said it to me, but I've always thought he was testing me to see how I would react to a crowd that size," he says. "I mean, it was the biggest crowd I had ever played to in my life, so it was a big thrill. I thought, 'Well, if nothing ever happens in my life again after this, musically, I'll be happy.' As it turned out, after that gig was over, Chuck started taking me out on all kinds of one-nighters."

European tours and residencies in Las Vegas with Berry followed over the next few years. Then, in 1975, Peek got his biggest professional break. It all traced back to that evening at the MRF.

"In '75, I did a *Midnight Special* TV show with Chuck," Peek says. "Rod Stewart and Ron Wood were watching that night. Ron was leaving the Faces and the band was going to break up. When they saw me, Ron put this bug in Rod's ear, saying, 'You should hire that guy.' I guess I made an impression. It ended up being a six-and-a-half-year gig. I did three world tours and four platinum albums with Rod. It was one of the rides of my life, and it all stemmed from that first test of being at the Mississippi River Festival. I think all those things fell into place from that gig on. Without Chuck, it would never have happened. Things go that way in this business. People say, 'Well, you got a good break here and you got a good break there. You were in the right place at the right time.' And this may be true, but you have to be good at the craft or you won't remain there. I did get a lot of breaks. I did get lucky here and there. But you have to be ready when it happens."

In 1972, a second Rock & Roll Revival was held at the MRF, with twelve thousand fans turning out to see Chubby Checker, Freddy "Boom Boom"

Cannon, Bobby Comstock, The Coasters, and Bill Haley & the Comets. The timeless sounds of "The Twist," "Rock Around the Clock," "Yakety Yak," and "Palisades Park" reverberated around the natural amphitheater. Berry crossed the Mississippi River to greet his old friends, but when he asked to perform, festival officials declined the offer.

Four years later, one of the top hitmakers of the '60s was experiencing a renaissance, making it the perfect time to bring Frankie Valli & The Four Seasons to the MRF. The Jersey Boys' resume is matched by few, with nine Top Ten singles, including chart-toppers "Sherry," "Big Girls Don't Cry," "Walk Like a Man," and "Rag Doll." During a career downturn due to the changing tastes of music lovers, the Four Seasons survived as a popular live act. Valli scored a solo No. 1 hit in 1975 with "My Eyes Adored You," which seemed to kickstart the group's fortunes as they scored a No. 3 hit with "Who Loves You" later in the year. But in March 1976, after a 12-year dry spell, Valli and the Four Seasons hit No. 1 again with "December, 1963 (Oh, What a Night)." Sung by drummer Gerry Polci, the song would be an international hit and the last for the group.

In 1977, Berry returned to the festival along with Bonds, Bobby Vee, and Bobby Lewis for "Dick Clark's Good Ol' Rock & Roll Show." The *American Bandstand* host known as America's oldest teenager hosted the event, telling the aging crowd he would take them "so far back your face will break out again.

Each headliner performed with Bonds' four-piece band, and not surprisingly, Berry was welcomed with the biggest ovation. He delivered a blistering set of his classics, beginning with "Roll Over Beethoven" and concluding with encores of "No Particular Place to Go," "Nadine," and "Reelin' and Rockin.'" In between the artists' sets, Clark showed old *American Bandstand* clips and told stories. One sour note? Vee told the audience it was nice to be back in "Mississippi."[73]

Unlike the harder rock acts, one constant of "oldies" shows was the makeup of the audience. Truly, these artists attracted fans of all ages. Before his '76 performance, Bill Haley noted the generational mix coming out to hear the '50s hits. "It's surprising, but the younger kids are the ones who dig the old rock," Haley said. "We're finding this more and more as we play across the country. We've been playing the same stuff for twenty-one years and people still want to hear it."[74]

Clearly, when it came to old-time rock & roll, the MRF offered the real deal. But in addition, festivalgoers could experience nostalgia through an eccentric act out of New York City called Sha Na Na. How to best describe this group? A collection of '50s tribute doo-wop singers? Sure. A parody of New York greasers? Absolutely. A divisive lineup of singers, dancers, and actors that elicited both positive and negative opinions? Undoubtedly. "People come to listen to us because they don't like modern rock music," said band guitarist Vinnie Taylor. "Hell, rock's been dead ever since Buddy Holly died."[75]

Formed in 1969, Sha Na Na evolved from a Columbia University a cappella group called the Columbia Kingsmen. Just months into their career, the group caught the eye of Jimi Hendrix while performing in a New York City club, which led to a coveted slot on the Woodstock schedule preceding the festival-closing legendary guitarist. Their final encore, "At the Hop," was performed as the sun came up on Monday morning and included in the documentary film of the music festival.

Sha Na Na would play the Mississippi River Festival four times, drawing a healthy crowd for its first appearance in 1973. Some loved the harmonies, outfits, and overall '50s vibe. Others viewed the group as a hacky rip-off, capitalizing on old memories. Count Dick Richmond of the *St. Louis Post-Dispatch* in the latter camp. Calling the songs of the late 1950s and early 1960s the "Dark Ages" of pop music and "an embarrassment," Richmond added, "To keep that embarrassment alive is a 10-piece group called Sha Na Na, which thrilled an audience of 12,000 nostalgia freaks . . . with some of the worst music since Annette Funicello graduated from the Mickey Mouse Club to make her first beach blanket movie."[76]

But this being Sha Na Na, reviews were mixed. The *Alton Telegraph's* Doug Thompson was more complimentary. "Although their basic theme is a satire of the '50s sounds, Sha Na Na proved to be excellent musicians and performers with expertly choreographed routines and a varied program to please any nostalgia buff."[77]

Backstage after the show, band members were impressed by the MRF site, comparing it favorably to a recent show at St. Louis' Kiel Auditorium. "Kiel is a wipeout," Taylor said. "This place is much better for music. Kiel should never be used for musical shows."[78]

Sha Na Na would return in 1974 (the *Alton Telegraph's* review the next day would carry the headline, "Sha Na Na at MRF: Who cares?"), 1976 and 1978. The shows didn't vary much, remaining true to the content and style that had earned the group an appearance in the film *Grease*, as well as their own TV variety show.

For the 1976 show, Sha Na Na brought along legendary disc jockey Wolfman Jack to host the evening's festivities, which began withholding court for the staff backstage.

"We couldn't get away from Wolfman Jack," says Rick Stankoven, who through positions as a campus photographer working for Charlie Cox and at local newspapers such as the *Alton Telegraph* and the *St. Louis Globe-Democrat* would shoot MRF concerts for eight summers. "We kept saying we had to go, but he kept talking. I think he just liked talking to college kids. He had a cooler full of *Popsicles* and he offered us all *Popsicles*. I didn't take one because I was shooting photos and the last thing I needed to do was be all sticky from a *Popsicle* while I'm trying to take pictures. But a few years later, I saw the movie *American Graffiti*, and there's a scene where he reaches into a cooler and offers Richard Dreyfuss a *Popsicle*. I couldn't believe it. I said, 'That happened to me!' I just wish I had taken a picture of the *Popsicles* in the cooler."

Perhaps the final word on the polarizing Sha Na Na should come from Frank Absher, a veteran on-air talent and manager for several St. Louis radio stations, including KSHE, KADI and KMOX. Absher attended the '78 show with his young son. "I saw Chicago there, and all of the other popular groups at that time, but the family atmosphere and fun around Sha Na Na stands out," he says. "I know it was their schtick, but I had a little guy with me—around five or six years old—and he loved that show. It was a wonderful way for him to see a live concert."

"I'm telling that story fifty-something years later, so it couldn't have been that dangerous"
The Dedication, Passion (and Occasional Valor) of SIUE's Student Workers

The MRF was unique for many reasons—the diverse entertainment mix, natural amphitheater, and giant tent, to name just a few. But the fact that more than one hundred SIUE students each summer were gainfully employed to staff events featuring some of the world's top performers has to be near the top of the list.

Lyle Ward was tasked with organizing the student workforce, which made sense, considering he was still an SIUE student himself only weeks before the MRF's first summer began. "I was involved in student programming all four years as a student, creating the campus programming as president of the University Center board," he says. "I guess they must have been desperate, because they called upon me to work with another person to find students who could be employed. We ended up using those students for everything from parking, ticket collection and sales, security, ushering, artist hosting—everything that needed to be done was done by university students."

When it came to hiring, training, and managing that collection of students, Gene Haffner was Ward's right-hand man. Program Director in the University Center during the day, Haffner was granted the additional title of Assistant Concert Manager from 1970 through 1975. "Each year, we would have hundreds of students apply for job positions," Haffner says. "We would narrow them down to a number of people that we would interview, and we would have days of interviews. I honestly don't recall anybody turning down an offer because these were jobs that the students were so honored to be selected for."

"Gene created those teams, both within the groups and then between them," Ward says. "He trusted people and developed relationships with the employees. I don't know that anyone ever called him the boss because it wasn't that kind of a relationship. They knew to listen and do what they were expected to do, and all that had to do with Gene's personality. It really was simple. We enjoyed doing what we were doing. There were a lot of laughs backstage, no matter what was happening on stage."

Ward did set one criterion for all who were interested in working at the site—they had to be enrolled in at least one class during that summer. "Well, that went over well with both the faculty and the students," Ward says with a laugh. "But it introduced scores of young people to SIUE, and the impact was enormous. John Rendleman had faith in young people to always do the right thing and show the university at its best. The festival was driven by students. The rest of us on staff at the university had our full-time jobs during the day and did this at night.

No matter the role, each student worker had the same primary responsibility—making festival guests feel welcome and safe. "It didn't matter if they were receiving them in the tent, collecting their tickets upfront, or working in the beverage stands," Ward says. "They were there to make people feel comfortable and ensure they had a good time."

"All the workers out there were great people," adds Greg Drexelius. "They would bend over backwards to help you in any way possible. That was a great thing, especially for a new person coming in."

Those who attended concerts during the festival's early years recall Dodie Ladd, a.k.a. the MRF's "Bell-Tree Ringer." Ladd would roam the site during concert intermissions playing a bell tree to alert fans that the show was about to restart. The memorable role began when Ladd was working the MRF's opening concert as a festival usher and SLSO official Peter Pastreich approached, asking if she knew how to play a bell tree. Answering no, Ladd was connected with Walter Susskind, who gave her a 30-second lesson. That was all she needed. "When I saw the bell tree, I realized that it could be mastered in that amount of time," Ladd said in a 1969 university press release. "I really love the job."

Bryan Erdmann came to SIUE in 1972 and quickly landed a role working at the festival. "The season was already underway, so I worked on the grounds crew cleaning up and fixing the fence where people had cut through to get in to see the shows," he says. "It got around that I was also in the Theater department, so I ended up working as a stagehand. When the Stage Manager, Larry Gallagher, retired, the campus people waited around until two weeks before the first show of the next season before they realized, 'Oh my God, we don't have a stage manager!' So Lyle Ward called me and asked, "Can you do this?" I said, "Yeah, I can do that." And I was there until the MRF shut down in 1980."

Bob Heil notes that students interested in learning about the more technical aspects of the MRF were given a golden opportunity to roll up their sleeves and get their hands dirty, rather than observe from afar. "There were so many students that would help unload trucks, carry gear, hook up cables, climb towers to hang lights, whatever was needed for each of the groups that would come in," Heil says. "That was really a neat thing. These kids were great because they were passionate about being around the artists, but they also truly wanted to learn. They were a great help. Some touring companies would come in with a little bit of an attitude, and then they'd find out that these volunteers were pretty good. 'Oh, wait a minute. These kids do better jobs than the people we're hiring!' I always got a kick out of that."

Audio company Showco was one of the many vendors that toured with artists of the era and made several festival stops. Engineer Rance Caldwell, who accompanied James Taylor, Stephen Stills, and Jackson Browne on trips to Edwardsville, said Showco was impressed with the MRF's pool of student workers. "It was a bunch of kids that really didn't have a grasp of what we did as a traveling circus, but they were always eager to learn," Caldwell said. "They were affiliated directly with the college in order to save money and promote the festival because it was a low-budget kind of situation. If the festival had to pay maximum wages for union representatives or stagehands, they would never have gotten off the ground. So, that was a good thing."

Erdmann says the festival gave students a chance to "work in a professional situation because the road crews that came in wanted to work with people who had experience. It wasn't their first rodeo, you know? They wanted to work with people who knew how to unload a truck without breaking the glass."

No matter the role, the opportunities provided by the festival impacted the lives of scores of students. Rick Stankoven remembers a lunch he had with fellow MRF photographers several years ago. "We talked about how we went to a country club of a college," he says. "We got to do things that students don't get to do at a lot of places. I was a student photographer shooting big names. The security guards were students. The production crew was students. Those opportunities that students had were a big part of the MRF. I enjoyed working there."

Mark Rogers also spent many nights at the festival site as editor of the campus newspaper, *The Alestle*. "I had years of free seats and backstage access to rock & roll history," he says. "The Mississippi River Festival was as one of a kind as you could get."

Being an MRF student worker sounds pretty great, right? And it was! Seeing some of the era's top entertainers—and getting paid to do it—was certainly an attractive gig. But that doesn't mean the duties were always painless. On some nights, the glitz and gleam were overshadowed by sweat—and maybe even a few bumps and bruises.

In the summer of 1970, John Klobnak was weeks away from beginning his sophomore year when he accepted a position working the fence line surrounding the lawn. "The first night I was there, I asked, 'What do I do?' They go, 'Oh, well, see that fence? Make sure nobody jumps over that fence.' I had the fence on the right side if you're looking at the stage.

"So, I'm out there, and these two guys come up. One of them said, 'Come here.' So, I said, 'What do you need?' And he goes, 'We need you to stand over there. We're gonna jump the fence.' So, I'm dumb, and I point and say, 'Well, no, see that kiosk way down there? You have to go there and buy a ticket.' And the guy pulls out a gun and says, 'Yeah, we could do that. Or I could just shoot you—your choice.' I said, 'You want me to stand over there or *over there*?' They jumped that fence like it wasn't even there. First night. That was my introduction to it."

Not that Klobnak stared down firearms every night he worked the fence line. "No, definitely not," he says with a laugh. "I'm telling that story fifty-something years later, so it couldn't have been that dangerous. What else would I have been doing that night? Nothing. I also worked at Vanzo's, so I was not unfamiliar with the occasional altercation."

Ward says the fence workers deserve special recognition for dealing with the less attractive aspects of the festival experience. "I really think the hardest job was trying to monitor the people jumping over the fence," he says. "That was the one part of my involvement I was uncomfortable with—putting young people in a position of being more than monitors. There was some physical interaction. I never got any complaints from any of them, but that doesn't mean they were always happy doing what they did. They had the lowest level job, I think, in terms of being able to enjoy being part of the festival. They didn't see anything. But they did a great job."

Drexelius began working as a tent usher in 1970 after completing his freshman year. While he says most nights were relatively uneventful, a few crowds kept the staff on their toes. "It all depended upon the artist," he says. "Anything that was folk, there was absolutely no issue. Most of the time, there wasn't really any issue with rock shows. The War concert was a challenge. Some of the patrons cut the rope that we had at the end of the aisle because that would make it easier for people just to go in and harder for us to stop them. So, they cut the rope and I kept it. I still have it—I don't know who I'll pass it down to someday, but we'll see.

"Ike and Tina was a little touchy, too. We ended up on stage that night. They basically told us to leave our posts in the aisles and go up onto the edge of the stage. If somebody wanted up, we were going to try to stop them, or just try to be a force that they didn't want to deal with. But there weren't many of those nights, and that's a really good thing."

Klobnak eventually moved on from guarding the lawn fence and found himself working under the tent. "People would get stuck working in the concession stands and taking tickets and picking up cans, so working the fence wasn't that bad," he says. "But everybody's ambition was to get in the tent because that was where everything was going on."

Despite the move, trouble continued to follow Klobnak. "Sometime during the summer of '71—I don't remember the show, but it was packed—I was standing in the tent and this guy was like 50 or 60 feet from the stage just throwing . . . well, I'm not talking about firecrackers," he adds. "This was back in the day when you could go over to Alton or West Alton and get, you know, quarter sticks of dynamite. These things would literally blow your hand off. And he was just throwing them in the air. Well, there were people everywhere, so one of the big supervisors comes up to me and tells me to go over and throw that kid out."

Klobnak laughs. "So, I tell the guy, 'Excuse me, you're gonna have to leave.' He goes, 'Oh, yeah? What if I don't?' I said, 'Well then, I'm gonna have to take you.' So, I grabbed the guy's arm. He had like nine or ten friends with him, and they jumped me. So, I've got this guy down on the ground and they're kicking me. Fortunately, about forty feet over, my fraternity was sitting there together. They looked over, saw what was going on, and jumped in to help. We had about 30 guys and they had nine. Finally, I remember taking the guy and dragging him to the back gate where the VIP parking area was, and literally picking him up by the back of his pants and throwing him out. This all happened during the concert."

Whether it was a rowdy rock concert or a serene symphony show, the work was hard. "We were sweating from the moment we got there, until the moment we left," Jim Grandone says. "I had very good people surrounding me. They all did their jobs and did them well. It sounds glamorous to work in the production area and interact with all these stars. But it wasn't an easy job. Most of the time, during a concert, we sat in the office. Sometimes, we would go out to the crowd, especially if it was a major event, to see how things were working out. I can hardly hear out of my left ear now, probably because this is the ear that faced the stage when I was in the wings. Poco was probably one of our favorite bands from a production standpoint. We were all excited when Poco came, and God, the music was just fantastic. I went out into the crowd and listened that night. I abandoned my post, as it were. I can't remember a concert I didn't enjoy. Each one was a unique experience."

The efforts of the MRF's student workers did not go unnoticed, even earning a shoutout from Doug Thompson in the *Alton Telegraph* after a 1975 show by Roberta Flack and Ramsey Lewis. It was another rainy night, and the side screens designed to keep rain out of the tent were set up. A few lawn fans tried to make their way under the tent to grab open seats, causing interruptions to Lewis' set as security chased down the crashers. Some even set up lawn chairs in the aisles. "The MRF tent ushers handled the seating problems with patience and tact, keeping their heads in a situation that could easily have gotten out of hand," Thompson wrote. "The calmness of the tent crew in handling these troublemakers was the only thing that kept a nasty situation from getting a lot nastier."[79]

The aggravations occasionally extended backstage, as Erdmann and the stagehands dealt with what he calls "I'm With the Band" Syndrome. "It was a fairly open area, and there were always people representing themselves as somebody from the record company, or somebody from the booking agency, or saying, 'I'm here because Jerry Garcia hired me to bring him his whatever . . . ,'" he recalls. "Often, it was my job to tell them that I didn't believe them. If you were with the band, we'd have your name already. It was pretty easy to spot the fakes. We also had to kick more than one drunk off the back loading dock as time went by. They would come up after the show as we would be starting the load out, and there would be a truck backed up to the dock, and here comes some guy crawling up there trying to help us push stuff. You know, 'I can help.' 'No, you can't. Get outta here.' 'No, no, I'm with the band.' Sometimes they would give us a name none of us had ever heard of. So we would have to kick them off. I had a couple of pretty big stagehands on the crew."

Okay, so sometimes student workers had to handle sticky situations. And they certainly weren't out there for the salary—in the neighborhood of $1.10 an hour (about $6.50 today). Jim Grandone served as Artist Host Coordinator and later Production Supervisor, from 1973 to 1977. "We didn't get paid much. I guess it was beer money. And we were capped on how many hours we could work, so we were on the clock for a certain amount of time and the rest was volunteering. You worked as long as you were allowed to work and then whatever more you put in was up to you. We had many meetings that lasted all morning, and then class, and then the concert that night. There were 16-hour days. But we wanted to be there."

Of course, they did. What other job allowed you to enjoy personal interactions with the stars?

Klobnak was working backstage before a 1973 Seals & Crofts concert when Jim Seals approached with news. "He goes, 'Hey, we're having a party after the concert in that room backstage. Tell everybody.' I said, 'No kidding? Okay!' They didn't announce it to the crowd, just to the people who worked there. After the show, I go back and there's 50, 60 guys who worked there all sitting around in a circle, and they're talking about the Baha'i religion. So, I raise my hand, and I go, 'Is there gonna be beer at this party?' They said no, and everybody got up and left," Klobnak says with a laugh.

That same summer, Klobnak was present for a humorous exchange between folk singer Jose Feliciano and a fan. "Jose was just the nicest guy. On stage he said, 'I'm gonna be in the back of this tent after the show, and I'll be happy to meet you all and shake hands with anybody who wants to shake hands.' There must have been 500 people who stayed. I was standing right next to him, and I'll never forget this. This older lady—maybe 50 at the time, so I thought she was old—she goes, 'Oh, you are just the cutest little guy. I'd love to take you home with me.' And he says, 'Well, why don't you? I'm blind. You think I got someplace to go?'"

Gary Kochan worked MRF security for three seasons, putting him in prime position to join a spirited pre-concert game of Frisbee with Linda Ronstadt and her crew in 1976. "She was a free spirit," he said. "She was definitely her own person."[80]

Mark Rogers recalls a 1971 visit from the power trio Mountain. "I watched as drummer Corky Laing called into the darkness of the hill behind the dressing room trailers, trying to locate guitarist Leslie West, who had fallen and rolled down the hill. It was like rock & roll Marco Polo. 'Corky!' 'Leslie!'"

A 1975 show by Jefferson Starship illustrates another of the popular perks available to student workers—the leftovers. "I recall Grace Slick had to be escorted to the limousine after the show," Grandone says. "We had iced down a trash can full of Heinekens and ice for Grace. Now these artists, almost without exception, drank a lot, but they couldn't drink it all. So, the production area was a very popular place to be after concerts because of all the extra liquor that was left. And Grace Slick's half trash can of Heinekens was consumed readily by the production staff."

While some may have relished the opportunity to rub shoulders with the stars, Grandone was never comfortable in the role. "It was intimidating as hell," he recalls. "I was terrified of these guys. I was 19, 20 years old, and these people were stars. I didn't want to talk to them because I figured everybody wants their autograph; everybody wants to talk to them because they're cool. One time, Andre Kostelanetz came in to conduct the St. Louis Symphony and I was charged with picking him up. I got him in the car, and he says, 'Where can I go to have lunch?' I took him to a restaurant in the Hyten Building, pulled up to the door, and let him out. He goes, 'Aren't you going to join me?' And I froze and said, 'Oh no, sir. No, sir. I have to do something else.' So, I let him eat lunch all by himself. And he was very disappointed that I didn't join him. I found that out later."

One MRF worker who wasn't faced with that internal roadblock—he went so far as to ask to introduce a band he loved on stage—was Bob Gill. "The Nitty Gritty Dirt Band was one of my favorite bands at the time, so I actually requested if I could be the one to introduce them, and they let me do it," Gill said. "I got up there in front of this big audience and said, "Ladies and gentlemen, let's give a warm Mississippi River Festival welcome to the Nitty Gritty Dirt Band!' It was a high point in my life to be in front of all those people and get to introduce them. I got to hang out with John (McEuen) after the show on the back deck. He played banjo and I added a little harmonica to it. It was a great, great time."

For those working front of house, mingling with the stars was rarely in the cards. "Under the tent, you really didn't get that many opportunities to deal directly with the artists unless they came out there for some reason—and most times they didn't," Drexelius says. "They stayed backstage for the most part, and you had Jim Grandone back there and he wasn't going to let any trouble go down."

However, there were benefits to being a tent worker. "By being out front, I did pick up some interesting memorabilia," Drexelius adds. "I got Rod Stewart's empty wine bottle. I got pearls that flew off of Tina Turner's dress and landed on the stage. And I had one of Keith Moon's drumsticks that I just picked up off the stage. Just little bits and pieces of stuff."

Does he still have these fragments of rock & roll history? "No, I recycled them about 20 years ago. I mean, how could anybody ever really know that was Keith Moon's drumstick? I knew it was, just like I knew it was Rod Stewart's wine bottle. But sometimes you have to draw the line on what you're going to keep. At least I still have the memories of them."

Of all the keepsakes Drexelius still holds dear from his MRF days—including a box full of original festival pins and stickers—the greatest of all is his wife, Gloria. "We met when she was a volunteer under the tent in 1974," he says. "Honestly, my college degree initially was in the MRF. I wouldn't say the MRF was a distraction, but it was definitely a driving force because there was nothing else like it. You would have visions of, 'Maybe I could really do something with this. Maybe I could parlay this into something else.' But no, that wasn't going to happen. You kind of knew that after a certain point, it was time to go on with education and get it done. By 1975, Gloria was telling me I needed to start thinking about getting out of SIUE someday. So, I really became a much more serious student. I realized this was not my life, and, while it was great while it lasted, I couldn't do it forever. It really gave me wonderful memories that I'll always have. But getting out of college and being with her was the best. We've had a great life together and I wouldn't change a thing."

In 1977, Drexelius graduated from SIUE and married Gloria. They celebrated their forty-fifth anniversary in 2022.

While we will never know how many marriages were born at the Mississippi River Festival, it's clear that the camaraderie forged among the student workers led to countless lifelong friendships. "They developed relationships," Haffner says. "One of the things that always amazed me was, by a couple weeks into the season, they would have designated a gathering place where many, if not most, would go after concerts to have a drink and socialize with each other. Whether it was the Granary, Vanzo's, or somewhere else—it seemed to change each year. But that was a meaningful thing to see."

Grandone speaks lovingly of the many festival workers he served alongside, but two stand out. Bob Gill is one. "Bob was the essence of a hippie. He looked the part, and his spirit was the part. He brought calm to situations that other people would panic in. I would put him out on Poag Road because he could handle people being hostile. Not very many people could handle road rage the way Bob did. These guys would want to park in the back because it was close. Well, Bob explained to them that no, you can't park here, but you might want to park over there where they've got extra spaces. He diffused the situation completely. He covered me many times when conflicts arose. He brought a loving spirit to work with him." A well-known Edwardsville resident and MRF advocate, Bob Gill passed away in 2022.

In many ways, Grandone's guide in all things Mississippi River Festival—and SIUE—was Neil "Buzzy" Butler. "I enrolled at SIUE in 1973," Grandone says. "I walked into Student Government to tell them I wanted to get involved, and I ran into a fellow by the name of Buzzy Butler. We talked, and I told him I was interested in the Mississippi River Festival. He said, 'Well, I happen to be the production supervisor for the festival. Maybe you could work for me.' Ultimately, I ended up replacing Buzzy in that role.

"Buzzy was my mentor. He was there to modify my radical positions on things. Buzzy was the guru. He was the go-between. Sometimes there were conflicts between Skip and Lyle and other officials, and Buzzy acted very much as a mediator, preventing a lot of confrontations. He could have been a diplomat in the U.S. State Department. He was very good at calming people down, getting them to reach an agreement and compromise."

Drexelius also has fond memories of Butler. "Buzzy was a unique force out there. He was a very special person. If you had an issue or a problem and you needed to vent, he would listen to you and make you feel better. He was very, very good at that. He was a good friend. His heart was always in the right place."

Erdmann actually lived with Butler for a year. "Buzz was a professional student and man about town. He was the very image of a 60's hippie. I mean, he had long, long hair with gray streaks and wire-rim glasses. He was a pretty cool guy, and people knew him. It really wasn't much of a surprise to me that artists and crews would come here and say, 'Oh, it's good to be back here in this place. Is Buzz Butler still around?'"

Neil "Buzzy" Butler died at 48. "Everybody loved him," Grandone says. "Before his funeral, I went up to his mother and I said, 'Buzzy Butler was my best friend.' And she said, 'Everybody says that.'"

As special as the opportunity to work at the festival was for the students, it was equally appreciated by the artists. "The people took good care of you there," said Richie Furay, who played the festival as a solo artist and with the Souther-Hillman-Furay Band. "I remember that you were taken care of when you came to do that event."

Jeff Hanna of the Nitty Gritty Dirt Band added, "I think that when you get a venue that gets used through several months of the year, everybody gets into a groove. The technical people do, the people working backstage, the people making sure that everybody parks their car in the right place— people get into a rhythm, and it makes it a lot more comfortable when you show up for something like that."

"Every performer I talked with or eavesdropped on had nothing but praise for the stage, sound, accommodations, and audience," Rogers says.

Perhaps Concert Manager Vicky Holt put it best. "Having students working at the festival, I think, is one of the things that makes the MRF the success that it is."[81]

And on one hot August night in 1971, it was "all-hands-on-deck" for the student workers, festival officials, law enforcement, and practically anyone else within a 20-mile radius. This was the biggest night in Mississippi River Festival history.

"The craziest night of them all — just a sea of people"
The Who Invade SIUE

The Who. Angry, loud, aggressive, melodic, trailblazing, iconic . . . you could spend all day listing adjectives to describe Pete Townshend, Roger Daltrey, John Entwistle, and Keith Moon. Those descriptions would run the gamut of all possible shades, tones, and emotions and likely, they would all be true.

Bursting onto the scene in 1965, the band quickly became one of the biggest acts in the world through a string of hits like "I Can't Explain," "My Generation," "Substitute," and "I Can See for Miles." Their instrument-smashing set at the 1967's Monterey Pop Festival was immortalized in the subsequent documentary film. In 1969, The Who released the rock opera *Tommy*, which led to a slot at Woodstock. Shows from the *Tommy* tour were captured on the Live at Leeds album, regarded as one of rock's greatest live recordings.

Which brings us to 1971 and the question of how one of the most influential and popular bands in rock history found themselves in lil' old Edwardsville, Illinois, on Monday night, August 16, 1971.

This was no concert. This was an *Event*, with a capital "E." And the buzz across the entire St. Louis area was far beyond anything seen for a prior MRF event—or even a rock concert of any kind. Prior to this, the largest attendance for a pop-rock concert in St. Louis history had been 25,000 for the Beatles' 1966 concert at Busch Stadium. MRF officials expected a large crowd, even one surpassing Chicago's season one attendance of 15,915. Maybe around 18,000 sounded about right . . .

It's not as if university and MRF officials didn't anticipate what might happen. Frank Peters of the *St. Louis Post-Dispatch* wrote a detailed assessment of the work that surrounded staging a concert of this magnitude. In it, he described Lyle Ward (and Gene Haffner) attending a concert by the band in Saratoga, New York, to study audience behavior. After witnessing the spectacle that was The Who—and the passion elicited by their fans—SIUE's expected crowd number began to soar.

"We had a rule in the ticket office," Haffner says. "There was a point in time before a concert that we could look at the number of tickets sold and triple it, and that would be about what the total attendance would be. I don't know why it worked, but it was something that we tended to do. Well, when we had booked The Who, I remember Lyle coming into the office one day and saying, 'Uh, we have some planning to do because we've sold 10,000 tickets.' That meant, by tripling it, we had like 30,000 people coming. We were like, 'My God!' We knew that we were going to have people arriving days in advance to camp out in line to get the best lawn seats. That meant we had to do something to keep them entertained. They were going to need food, and we had to bring in porta-potties. We knew we didn't have enough parking and that we would have to use the campus parking lots, so we had to arrange a system to shuttle people out to the festival site. There was just a string of events and planning that needed to occur."

Ward adds, "We learned a lot in Saratoga. The first thing I decided to do was make changes at the front entrance to try to keep the young people waiting to get in from running through the gates all at once. I hired some local bands so we would have entertainment out there."

Barbed wire was added to the peripheral chain-link fence. The team of student workers was bolstered in number. Loudspeakers were added to better reach the furthest points of the lawn and beyond. And as the St. Louis Symphony played a pops concert 24 hours before The Who would take the stage, fans were already waiting on blankets outside the gates to be among the first to get tickets when the box office opened the next day. "The night before The Who concert, four of us spent the night out there to help keep people from coming in before the proper time," Drexelius says. "A lot of people were showing up really early and camping out. It was a big thing."

What Ward witnessed at 8 a.m. Monday morning was alarming—parking lots were full, and thousands of fans were swarming the MRF grounds. Now, anyone affiliated with the festival, the university, or the symphony was on high alert.

The box office opened at noon, and the 12,000 yellow tickets printed for the concert were gone in the blink of an eye. Sellers grabbed unused tickets from previous concerts—more yellow tickets, then green, orange, pink... anything they could find.

"We told fans at the box office, after the first 15,0000 or so, that they had little chance of seeing the show," one symphony official later said. "They didn't care. It's the crowd itself, the experience apparently, that they are after. They might snuggle up against the fence, a couple of those young people, with their bottle or whatever it is, and be set for the evening. Or wander around and talk. They want to hear the music though, and they could: Oh, how they could hear it! My ears ached and I had to leave."[82]

Rick Haydon was playing in a band called Globe Theater that got the call to, in effect, open for The Who. "They asked us if we would play in front of the turnstiles because there were people camping out two days before the concert," he recalls. "So, they had us come up and play for those folks before they opened the gates. We started around 10 o'clock in the morning and played until about two or three in the afternoon."

At 5 p.m., the MRF team gathered to assess the situation. With more than twenty thousand rowdy fans holding tickets and waiting for the gates to open—and thousands more in line to purchase tickets—officials knew they already had more people coming in than could fit into the venue. The decision was made to open the gates immediately—90 minutes earlier than scheduled—to start letting people in. Appeals were also made to local radio stations to ask those who had not yet made their way to SIUE to stay home. That accomplished little, as most folks wanting to see The Who were already on site, or stuck in nasty traffic jams on the roads leading to Edwardsville. Interstate 270 was backed up from Rte. 157 to Rte. 3—about five miles.

Haydon and the rest of Globe Theater rushed onto the site to witness the invasion. "When we were done playing and they opened the gates, we went down and sat right in front of the tent to watch the people come in over the top," he says. "It looked like ants taking over the whole hill, man. That was probably the largest group of people I had seen in one place at that age."

Now 12 years old, John S. Rendleman accompanied his father to the MRF site for the show. He had been doing so since the festival's earliest days, but this night was much different. "In the early years, my father was interested in seeing the performances, so he would ask any of the family if they wanted to go," he says. "None of us wanted to go see the symphony, although he would make us go on occasion. But once in a while, we'd go to some of the rock & roll acts. And in those years, dad would just drive out and we would pull in the back right behind the band shell and get out. He'd say, 'Meet me back here at 10' or something like that. So, we got to go run around and listen to the bands.

"But The Who—everybody knew who that band was. I had not planned to go, but I know that my father recognized that that was an important night. So, he took me out there. It was almost like an Abbott and Costello routine—my father is like, 'Who's The Who, son?' I'm like, 'He's on first.' We played that game a little bit as we walked around. I remember we saw some people climbing over the fence and some of that. I know my father eventually had to leave and take care of business. I think it was important to him to be available if they needed to talk to him, and he didn't need me helping him with that aspect of the evening."

Jack Twesten was 13 years old on this night—one year older than

Rendleman. But he wasn't as fortunate, as his father deemed him to be too young to face the onslaught at SIUE. Instead, he mowed the lawn while his older sister, Terry, set out for the show.

"I had just turned 16, and I was a music lover, although I had only attended one concert so far—Three Dog Night," Terry Twesten says. "I was so excited to go with my Aunt Jeanne, who was only five years older than me, to see The Who! People were parking wherever they could find a spot, and the closest we could get was near the west end of St. Louis Street. There were massive numbers of people walking toward the entrance. People were everywhere! I recall wondering how we were going to get through the crowd. The music had already started, and it seemed there was no clear line to get in. Trying to stay together, we saw many people go under an opening in the fence, so we did, too!"

Throughout the site, fans were amped as showtime approached. One of them was Steve Porter, a Journalism student about to begin his junior year, who was sitting in one of the best seats in the house. "I was Sports Editor at *The Alestle*, and there was an MRF ticket booth by the Meridian Ballroom," he remembers. "The tickets went on sale at 8 a.m., and since I had to work that morning, I got there about 7:30 or 7:45. I was like the tenth person in line. They got to me and asked how many tickets I needed. I said, 'Four. Can you give me the best tickets you've got?' They said, 'Well, sure, how about fifth row right in the middle?' It was closer than being on TV. I could hear the band members talking. If there was a break, I'd yell a song for them to play and they could hear me. I went with a buddy of mine and two girls—they were pretty impressed!"

Sitting with Porter that night was his childhood friend John Jarvis, a student at Belleville Area College. "I still can't believe he got those tickets," Jarvis says with a laugh. "That was just amazing. I was looking at all these people behind me and thinking, 'I hope to God they don't rush the stage or we're dead!'"

While the party raged on the lawn, band members were tucked away backstage, having a pre-show dinner and some fine wine. And as Charlie Cox learned, they were not in the mood to share. "I recall that Frank Peters of the *Post-Dispatch* was backstage, and you could look through the door into the area where the band was and see that they were drinking wine and enjoying some fine food that had been provided for them," Cox said. "Frank said, 'I wish I could have some of that wine.' I remember saying, 'Well, that's no problem. I'll just take a cup in there and ask them to pour some wine in it.' I didn't know who The Who were—they were just a group of entertainers to me. So, I went in and asked, and they looked at me like I was some sort of a freak. I backed out of there pretty quickly. Frank Peters didn't get his wine that night."

J'Deanna Twesten was in her customary spot on the side of the stage for the MRF's biggest show. "I had a new copy of *Who's Next* with that now infamous album cover picture and remember being on the ramp with some of the security guys. I thought it was funny when two of the band members came out of the restroom and walked past us down the ramp to the stage."

Somehow, someway, the festival team pulled it off. When The Who stormed the stage, an official tally of 31,756 fans was packed in every crevice of the site. That attendance record would never be broken. Fans perched in trees and light poles to get a better look. The aisles under the tent were filled with bodies. There was no room to move on the lawn, where Frisbees, beach balls, and the occasional football flew through the air. How accurate was that 31,756 number? We'll never know, as the number of gate crashers in the house is impossible to quantify.

"We ended up putting our blankets down somewhere just inside the entry gates," Terry Twesten says. "We couldn't see the band onstage, but we sure could hear and feel it! The sound system, with lawn seating being in a bowl-shaped area, carried quite nicely. Jack was mad that he had to stay home to cut grass. But we lived close to the campus, and when he shut down the mower, he could hear Pete Townsend's guitar."

"It was so jam-packed under the tent that people had to stand on their chairs," Porter adds. "I was standing on a chair to see because you were elbow to elbow. And these weren't chairs made for people to stand on. They weren't real sturdy. People came down the aisles and stood there. The four rows in front of us were standing up. At the end, you were sort of worried that people were going rush the stage."

Mike Reinhardt was in the seventh row that night. "Everybody was standing," he says. "I know we were standing on top of our chairs, and those cloth chairs weren't too stable. People were taking the cloth off the backs of the chairs and throwing it on the stage. Everybody was just packed in there because people rushed into the tent."

"Eventually, they made it down every aisle and filled up every seat that wasn't already filled in," adds Drexelius. "There wasn't a lot we could do to stop them because they wanted it that bad. I found some friends that were there, and they helped us bolster the line under the tent. That was all we could do. They were going to come. Basically, all we did was slow them down without anybody getting hurt, either on our side or their side."

John Moorman remembers this being one of the nights when an unofficial band of MRF peacekeepers known as the Goon Squad sprang into action. "Early arriving audience members finding time on their hands and nothing much to distract themselves with would wander the property. 'Goon' is probably a bit of a misnomer, but sometimes a heavy hand became necessary to quell some action not related to the show. The squad was mostly made up of friends and associates of Buzzy Butler. This was long before 'Security' as it now exists was really developed. No cross-armed bullies lining the front of the stage wearing 'SECURITY' on their head or shoulders. Just a few 'take no crap' brothers helping keep order."

"Sure, I remember the Goon Squad," adds Haffner with a laugh. "The layout of the site gave opportunity for lots of different things to happen out there. There were a lot of places for people to roam and do whatever they felt like they should be doing. So, should something get unruly, Buzz and the others could be called upon to come help. It didn't occur very often, but they were ready."

In describing The Who's performance, Thomas B. Newsom of the *St. Louis Post-Dispatch* referred to the "pulsating wall of sound" delivered by the foursome that once held the Guinness World Record for loudest concert at 76,000 watts (120 decibels). Their equipment alone at the MRF weighed more than 10 tons.[83] Bob Heil was like a proud papa, as the band he was now providing sound for was performing in one of his favorite venues. The audio wizard had been hired by The Who for their 1971 tour, and the partnership would prove long-lasting and fruitful.

"The Who is something I will never forget," Heil says. "That was one of the most magnificent nights I've ever had with any artist. It was incredible because you had thirty thousand-plus, and these kids really enjoyed it. The Who is the best rock & roll band, no question about it. You get all these things about, 'Oh, this band and that band.' No. If you ever saw The Who live, they had more energy than all of them. They were incredible. And at the MRF, they were really cranked up, and we had a lot of sound for them. That got their adrenaline going, as well as their musicianship."

"I had already thought ahead on what to do if one of the artists we toured with played the festival. When we put our stuff together for the tent, all the plugs coincided with our road gear. So we could bring the road gear in and augment it as much as we wanted. Ed (Drone) and I figured out a way that everything would couple up, so we could augment it very easily. And that's what happened with The Who. The sound that night was incredible because we had the magnificent system that was already there, but then we had this monster that the band had on tour. We hooked it all up and let it go. It was just incredible. We were happy that we could do that at the Mississippi River Festival."

The band's set list was heavy on songs from *Tommy* and *Live at Leeds*, including the show opener "Summertime Blues." The Who classics like "I Can't Explain" and "Substitute" also made the cut. But it was the album released just two days before the MRF show that would arguably be The Who's best, and one of the greatest rock albums ever recorded.

Who's Next contained such classics as "Won't Get Fooled Again," "Bargain," and "Behind Blue Eyes"—all of which were played at SIUE—as well as "Baba O'Riley." The album would go on to sell more than three million copies in the U.S. and be labeled "the best hard rock album in years" by *The Village Voice*. In 2003, *Rolling Stone* ranked it No. 28 on its list of the 500 greatest albums of all time.

The evening's final song was "Magic Bus," and, of course, Townshend smashed his guitar to pieces before leaving the stage. "One fan went flying across the stage, diving for pieces of the guitar," Reinhardt recalls. "Security dragged him off. It was a wild concert. Best concert I ever saw."

"I wasn't working, but I was in the crowd," John Klobnak adds. "They were great. I mean, just fabulous guitars and the drums were insane. Then, at the end, they banged the guitars into the drums and destroyed things."

Porter concurs. "I've been to a lot of concerts, and this was the best one I've ever been to in my life. And I've seen the Rolling Stones and Stevie Wonder at Kiel Auditorium. That was my second favorite. The Who was so loud and so good. This was The Who at its peak. They played a lot of the songs that were on *Live at Leeds*. If you listen to that album, they sounded quite a bit like that."

Rich Dalton, who went on to enjoy a long career on the radio at KSHE-95 in St. Louis and attend countless concerts, calls this performance, "My single best concert experience, and I've seen The Who many times. Keith Moon threw a drumstick out into the audience, which I caught. I was in the sixth row. But I gave it to a friend of mine, the drummer in my high school band. I bought us all tickets because we were all very much into The Who. To this day, Ray remembers it as him having caught the drumstick. I've never bothered to correct him. It's better that way."

J'Deanna Twesten also brought home a keepsake that night. "Pete Townshend gave my dad his guitar pick, which my mom framed, and I still have to this day."

The band even impressed one non-rock fan in the house. "I thought The Who were remarkable performers and entertainers," Ward says. "It doesn't matter that it's not my taste in music. It's easy to see skill and talent, and they had it."

After the show ended, Dalton lugged his tape recorder backstage and obtained the interview of a lifetime with the legendary Moon. "Things were different then—they were looser—so I just walked right up to him," Dalton says. "His shirt was off, and he had a towel around him. He had been thumping the drums all night, but he was very nice, very gentle, and we just talked. They had just finished a tour where they were doing nothing but *Tommy*, and he mentioned that he was tired of it. He said, 'If I'm at a party and somebody puts *Tommy* on, I want to take it off and smash it.' I started working at KADI a few months later, and I'm sure I played that interview on the radio."

Then, in a flash, The Who disappeared into the night. "I happened to be backstage, along with a couple others from the Goon Squad, as the boys in the band wrapped the gig up with Pete Townshend smashing a guitar and shucking the remnants off the stage," Moorman says. "We were there to get the band off stage and out to the limos and off the property. The crowd exploded with applause and cheers for one more song—it didn't happen."

For exhausted festival staff, the long day wasn't quite over. There was still the matter of getting more than thirty-two thousand people off campus safely, a task that took until 3 a.m. Some clever fans strategized earlier in the day to save themselves considerable time and hassle after the show.

"Because of where the MRF was, parking was not very good," Porter says. "So, we got there real early, parked in one of the outer lots, and walked about a mile or so to the tent. After the concert, I remember everybody trying to get out of there, but it was easier for us because we kept walking and walking back to the parking lot. And once you got there and you left, it was easy getting out. But a lot of people had parked on the hills down there on the side of the road, and they were just stuck. We got out of there earlier because we knew what was going on."

It was exactly this sort of chaotic scenario that kept some MRF regulars home for the night of the festival's biggest show. "I was a student janitor in the Library and the Peck building," Jim Muffo remembers. "I took one class every summer so I could keep working. When I drove to campus that morning, traffic was already heavy, and it continued all day long. You could see cars just going through campus constantly. You'd hear people saying, 'Man, you ought to see all the people out there!' I don't like crowds now, and I didn't like crowds then. So, I went the other way and got out of town."

He laughs. "I was a great Who fan. *Who's Next* had just come out, and that is my favorite rock album of all time. I don't think there's a better rock album start to finish than *Who's Next*. But the crowd was just too big."

John S. Rendleman enjoyed the show, but he decided to head for home before the post-concert crush. "I didn't stay for the whole performance as a true fan would," he says. "I remember coming home and we could still hear them three-quarters of a mile away at our house. They were superstars. You could just tell. You could feel it when you listened to them and you saw the audience react."

In total, The Who received a guaranteed $15,000 and 60 percent of the box office receipts. With $68,000 in the till at the end of the night, that meant the band earned $55,800 for a 90-minute show. Not bad, by 1971 standards. St. Louis Symphony Ticketing Manager Anna Rice headed to the Holiday Inn with a load of cash for the boys. As she sat on a hotel room bed counting money, the band members were too intoxicated to accept it. Accompanied by armed security and police, Rice headed back over the river to Powell Hall, where the money was locked away for later distribution.[84]

From a safety and behavioral standpoint, relatively speaking, the show was uneventful. "Given the fact that there were thirty thousand people there, the incidents were very, very small," Drexelius says. "There may have been some fireworks, there may have been some cuts or bruises from stepping on cans or whatever, but the instances were very few."

Future Edwardsville Alderman Jack Burns worked several MRF shows as a member of the SIUE Health Services ambulance crew. Having received training as a combat medic for a reserve unit out of St. Louis, Burns returned to school in 1969 and found himself working backstage at the The Who concert. "The audience was very enthusiastic and rowdy," he remembers. "There were several injuries from flying objects. I was working on an injured person when a man with a British accent tapped me on my shoulder requesting assistance. I said, 'Just a second, let me finish here.' A few minutes later, I went over to him and asked how I could be of help. He introduced himself and asked for *Band-Aids* for his blistered fingers. I applied them, and he politely thanked me and moved on. I asked someone who that person was, and they said he was the band's drummer. I wasn't really into music. A few days later, I was talking with someone and telling the story. She asked if his name was Keith Moon, and I told her I believed that was how he introduced himself. She went crazy!'"

More than fifty years later, Haffner still regards the night as one of the greatest of his life. "We planned in great detail, and to have that many people come and have everything go so smoothly with no major glitches was probably one of the proudest moments, certainly of my MRF experience, if not my career," he says. "During a concert, I would sometimes walk around the site and disconnect enough to just appreciate the artist and listen. But even more than the music, my favorite moment was standing at the edge of the lawn watching the audience or standing at the edge of the stage in the wings looking out at the audience in the tent, and just looking at their faces. Seeing the smiles, the look in their eyes, the applause, their response to the venue, the artist, the experience. To be able to stand there and feel in your heart that you had something to do with that evening for those people was just the best moment every night. And I thought The Who was just amazing; one of the best rock concerts that we had done."

Before closing the book on The Who's historic MRF concert, let's take a moment to recognize the bands who warmed up the crowd—if they even needed warming—before Pete Townshend hit his first chord. In addition to Globe Theater, a pair of St. Louis groups—Titus Mother and Magna Crunch—kicked things off before England's Wishbone Ash hit the tent. The harmonizing guitars of Andy Powell and Ted Turner were the catalyst of a band that influenced many and emerged at the forefront of progressive rock.

"Wishbone Ash was great," Porter reflects. "They still come back to the Wildey Theater, and I had Andy Powell sign my *Argus* album there. I told him, 'Man, you guys were so good that night. The Who was one of the greatest rock bands in the world, and I thought you guys matched them.' He said, 'Yeah, I remember that night. That's why we come back here to this little town—because people remember us at the MRF.'

"He said that after the concert, Pete Townshend came up to him and said, 'You guys outplayed us tonight.' Wow, what a thrill! I don't think Pete Townshend is a guy to throw around compliments, so for him to say that . . ."

Powell recalls what it felt like to open for The Who, and how the opportunity came about in an unexpected way. "We found ourselves on our first U.S. tour, and I remember we were stuck in Wildwood, New Jersey, of all places for about a week," Powell says. "We knew we had maybe a Steppenwolf gig and then we had nothing, so we were just hanging out and fishing. This promoter—I think his name was Ron Sunshine—made us the offer to open for The Who, and I believe the Mississippi River Festival was our first date. So we flew to St. Louis and were suddenly catapulted into this situation that gave us a real sense of what was possible. To open for The Who was really a dream come true because I had been a follower of that band since they were a small club act in the U.K."

The magical MRF site and immense size of the crowd is a memory Powell will never forget. "To walk out and see this beautiful amphitheater—it was a natural bowl. We had man-made bowls like the Hollywood Bowl, but this was a beautiful setting. People were sitting on blankets in the sunshine, and it was a spontaneous outpouring of good feeling. No violence, no aggression. It was a very warm feeling of all that was good about America."

"And then, wow . . . I was confronted with the biggest crowd that I'd ever performed in front of. We were all just blown away. I went up to the mic and the sound was just massive. That first note of the guitar was wondrous. It was so much power, and we did a blinding gig. I think that's what really broke us in the St. Louis area, and people still talk about it to this day."

One final note from Powell on The Who's visit to the MRF. Keith Moon chose that evening to express contrition for an act of destruction sometime before and a continent away. "Back in the day, we used to play at the Speakeasy Club in London, which was a notorious musicians club," Powell recalls. "Any given day of the week you could see, George Harrison, John Lennon . . . and we were like the house band at the time. One night, Keith Moon decided to come up on stage and jam. I think we played 'Johnny B. Good.' At the end of the performance, Keith simply took a bow and walked through the drum set. It was a brand-new set our drummer (Steve Upton) had saved up to buy, so he was distraught.

"So, the fortuitous thing was that at the River Festival show, Keith was waiting backstage as we came off with an old bottle of nice Cognac in hand to commiserate to Steve, and to make amends for the drum set that he'd completely annihilated. But that was Moon's style. He didn't give any thought about those kinds of things, you know?"

Mississippi River Festival

TRIUMPHS
1972-75

"If you're ever in Canada, give me a call"
The Stars Fall to Earth at Local Establishments

Unlike a concert in St. Louis—where the headliner emerged from a dark, shadowy backstage area, played for 90 minutes, and disappeared into the ether—the Mississippi River Festival allowed for possible interaction between stars and their fans. It really wasn't that difficult, as there were plenty of entertainers who fell in love with the MRF's small-town collegiate vibe and embraced it with gusto. Imagine popping into Stagger Inn for a post-show beer and finding Arlo Guthrie performing on stage and signing autographs for fans . . . those kinds of things happened!"

"As the artists learned more about the facility, we would find them getting more involved with students and staff during their time here," Ward says. "Some of them actually would come in a day early and attend a performance incognito. I remember Emerson, Lake, and Palmer were sitting on the grass watching the concert the night before their own. It scared me to death; they could have been mobbed any minute, but I don't think they were noticed. We had entertainers who would go out with the student workers following the concerts and others who would go out and play golf with some of the university staff. I know that might have been the most enjoyable part of (SIUE VP) Bill Hudgens' involvement, that he got to take them out for a round of golf before the evening performance.

One star who wanted the full experience during his 1972 visit was John Denver. Arriving a day early, the singer toured the SIUE campus, hit the golf course with university administrators, and visited the nearby Cahokia Mounds archaeological site. In addition, he drank beer, ate hamburgers, and played foosball late into the night with students at the local hangout The Granary following his show, which attracted more than eight thousand fans. That's a full 48 hours!

"John Denver came over to dinner at our house after he played golf with my dad," John S. Rendleman says. "Most of us were a little suspicious of him because he didn't play hard-driving electric rock & roll. But he was a really nice guy, in contrast to David Cassidy, who my dad met and did not bring home for dinner because he was an ass. My dad enjoyed the company of some of the celebrities. I was playing football in high school at the time, so if I came home, I was exhausted and probably taking a nap about the time of day my father would bring some of these people home. Many of them may have stopped by when I was asleep in my room upstairs."

Ward remembers, "John Denver was a really wonderful human being. He gave a great performance, and afterward, he was feeling so good he asked if we could get a group to go out with him. So, we got together a whole group of student workers, and I went with them, and we went up to the local establishments. He's there playing pinball and just having a great time until late in the night with people. Just a great night."

One interesting note on John Denver uncovered by John Moorman— the singer was also a juggler. "I asked him why he juggled, and he said, 'It pays to have a backup. This whole song thing may not last.'"

Another amateur golfer was Mac Davis, who preceded his 1975 show with a round at Sunset Hills Country Club that included Hudgens and Larry Hepler, husband of MRF Board member Sue Hepler. "After they played golf, he came over to our house on St. Louis Street for a visit," Sue Hepler recalls. "We laughed because the kids in the neighborhood were looking in our windows. He was pretty well-known at the time because of his TV variety show. I remember we just sat in the living room and had a nice conversation about what he was doing. He was interested in what we were doing, too. He was just really nice; it was a lot of fun."

Davis also paid a visit to the Hudgens family. "I was home from school and the doorbell rang," J'Deanna Twesten remembers. "My mom called from another room and asked me to answer the door, and there stood Mac Davis. He walked right in and gave me a surprise kiss on the cheek! I thought I'd never wash my face again. Mom had prepared dinner, as she often did for the many entertainers who visited our house."

The popular Edwardsville watering hole, Vanzo's, was the scene of a night fueled by hockey talk and alcohol, when Canadian rockers The Guess Who came to town in 1970. The band members were ready to mingle even before their show began, as described by Doug Thompson in the *Alton Telegraph*. "Backstage, a long-haired girl tries to enter the stage area when she is stopped by a stage marshal. 'But I'm with the group,' she protests. The stage marshal asks one group member if the girl is part of the group. 'Yeah, she's with us,' he replies. 'For tonight anyway.'"[85]

Another female attendee explained the "groupie" perspective to Thompson. "The groups are it. This is where it's at for us and where we should be. Some groupies think status is how many musicians they've sacked with. I say it's not how many, but who you've sacked that counts."[86]

After the show, the merriment continued. Festival student worker John Klobnak had not attended the show, instead spending the evening at his other employer's, Vanzo's. "I'm standing by the jukebox, and I noticed there were some guys I knew who worked at the festival hanging out with some guys, and I see them point to me," he recalls. "So, this guy comes over and starts talking to me. I could tell he was from Canada because I was interning with the St. Louis Blues that year and everybody had Canadian accents. The guy says, 'They said you know all about hockey,' so we started talking about hockey and the Blues. We're talking for about an hour, and I didn't know who the guy was. So, I said, 'I can tell you're from Canada; what are you doing now?' He goes, "Oh, I'm in a band and we were playing somewhere tonight, someplace that had a big tent.' I go, 'What's the name of your band?' He said, 'The Guess Who, ever heard of us?' This is (lead singer) Burton Cummings I'm talking to."

"So, Vanzo's is closing, and he goes, 'What are we gonna do now?'" Klobnak laughs. "I said, 'Well, what do you wanna do?' I still lived with my parents, so that's not gonna work. I knew a couple of girls who lived in a little house by the library, so like half the tavern goes. Burton Cummings bought armloads of fifths—you know, *Crown Royal*, all that stuff. I left at four a.m., and they were all still there. He gave me his phone number and said, 'If you're ever up in Canada, give me a call.' Of course, I have no idea where that number went, but he was just the nicest guy. You couldn't tell him from some other guy who just happened to come into the tavern that night. He was that unassuming."

And these chance meetings were not limited to the Edwardsville city limits. In 1977, the Ozark Mountain Daredevils played under the tent, with an up-and-coming singer from Pascagoula, Mississippi, named Jimmy Buffett opening the show. It was a dream lineup for local fan Mary Kay Leach.

"I knew of the Daredevils, but I was a Parrot Head from the early days," she said. "The manager of the Daredevils offered coveted tent seats to me and my cousin, and while we were thrilled, what I *really* wanted was to meet Jimmy Buffett. Well, there was no security, so we just meandered to the back of the tent after the show and there they were—the Coral Reefer Band. We were invited to the Holiday Inn in Collinsville where the band was staying. Of course, we went as fast as our car could get us there, and the Reefer band sat at tables in the lounge area and sang and strummed for us." Leach walked away with autographs from Buffet and his band on an Ozark Mountain Daredevils flyer.[87]

A frequent MRF lawn dweller during the late '70s was Buddy Fendler, a student at St. Louis Parkway West High School. His first concert was a 1976 appearance by the Marshall Tucker Band, and, while memories of the songs played that night have faded, a brief moment on the side of Route 157 remains vivid.

"A friend and I took Interstate 270 and got off at 157 to go up to the university," Fendler remembers. "At the time, there were two lanes going in each direction with a center grass median and rock on the shoulders on either side of the road. We had creeped along trying to get to the concert, and we started seeing cars driving up the rock shoulder. We said, 'Screw it, let's follow 'em.' So, we hopped onto the rocks, and naturally, we got maybe a quarter mile up and then we were stopped.

"A big old white limousine pulled up behind us as we were just sitting there. We figured it had to be somebody, so we decided to go be nosy. You know, we're 16-year-old punk kids—we've got all the guts in the world back then, right? So, we walked back there, and they rolled down the window. We were like, 'Hey, who are you guys?' I had heard of the band, but I didn't know what they looked like. And they're like, 'Well, we're Tommy and Toy

Caldwell of the Marshall Tucker Band.' I go, 'Really? Hey, cool! We came out here to hear your great music. Can we have your autograph?' Nobody had a pen, but they were back there smoking a joint."

Fendler laughs at the next part of the story. "Toy handed it out the window to my buddy, who was older than me, and he said, 'Here, take a hit off this joint and you can tell people you smoked pot with Tommy and Toy Caldwell of the Marshall Tucker Band.' "We were like, 'Awesome! Wow!' That's a story I've been telling for 40 years now."

A lifelong fan, Fendler stills see the band in concert (lead singer Doug Gray is the last remaining original member). "I can't say I'm great buddies with him, but I've seen him so many times I can walk up to him and say, 'Hey, Doug,' and he'll say, 'Hey Buddy, how you doing?' I told him the story once, and he laughed and said, 'Oh, that sounds like the boys, I'm surprised I wasn't with them.'"

Fendler agreed with Ward's assessment that eagle-eyed fans were liable to spot the occasional celebrity just strolling the concert site. "These guys would just walk around out there," Fendler says. "I'd be asked, 'Oh, did you see so and so?' And I'm like, 'What are you talking about?' They'd go, 'Oh yeah, they're just walking around out here in the crowd.' A lot of the headliners would walk out and see how it was for the guys that were playing before them. People would always come back and say, 'Oh, look, I got a guitar pick from this guy I saw over here by the Johnny on the Spots.'"

Fendler's southern rock fanhood led him to another brush with celebrity in 1979 when the Charlie Daniels Band played the MRF. Fully embracing the country and western trend that swept the nation in the late '70s (culminating with the John Travolta film *Urban Cowboy*), Fendler was dressed for the occasion, from his feather-adorned cowboy hat right down to his cowboy boots. "I was kind of like Burt Reynolds: I only took my hat off for one thing," he says with a laugh. "Actually two, the other one was to sleep."

While awaiting the band's set, Fendler encountered a friend who, via a connection through her father, said she could get him backstage. "She was like, 'Do you guys want to come backstage and meet Charlie?' And we're like, 'Yeah, sure! Why not? What else are we gonna do?' So, I get back there, and good old Charlie Daniels is grilling barbecued pork steaks and drinking a *Heineken*. He says, 'Son, have a beer and talk to me.' They had a barrel of *Heinekens* sitting in ice, and we just sat there and talked a little bit. Finally, he said, 'Well guys, I gotta go get ready,' and off he went."

Drinking a beer with Charlie Daniels while he grilled pork steaks? Truly amazing. Eating your mother's lasagna with the band Orleans in your own dining room? Priceless! That was the experience of 12-year-old Katy (Krchniak) Katzenberger one night in June 1979, when the band rolled into town to open for Stephen Stills.

As a child growing up in Long Island, New York, Orleans' lead singer Larry Hoppen had lived down the street and received trumpet lessons from a teacher named Stefan Krchniak. In the late '60s, Krchniak and his family (including daughter Katy) relocated to Edwardsville when he accepted a position at SIUE. Hoppen and two friends formed Orleans in 1972, and the band enjoyed Top Ten hits in 1975 ("Dance With Me") and 1976 ("Still the One"). Orleans' 1979 album, *Forever*, brought their third and final hit, "Love Takes Time," which peaked at No. 11.

When Orleans was booked to open for Stills at the MRF, Hoppen gave his old teacher a call. "They had kept in touch," Katzenberger recalls. "He contacted my dad and said he was coming to town. He invited us to the show, but he also came to my dad's classroom the day of the show. He introduced himself to the students, and they knew who he was and were happy to meet him. He said they were having a sound check right then, so he thought he'd come over and say hi."

But that wasn't all. Hoppen and the entire band came to the Krchniak home on Weber Street for a pre-show dinner of homemade lasagna. "I was embarrassed, you know?" Katy recalls. "I think 12-year-olds are embarrassed by just about anything, right? Two of my good friends came over, too, and we were like, 'Oh, these are rock stars!'"

After dinner, Katy and her family ventured the short distance to the festival site, where they toured Orleans' tour bus, handed down by Linda Ronstadt. "I remember sitting there, and they offered me *Pringles*," Katy says. "I thought that was cool."

Backstage, Katy had a brief encounter with the evening's headliner. "I remember (Stills) was just tall, skinny, and very aloof. He shook my hand and kept walking. He was eating something. I'm sure he didn't want to meet a 12-year-old that night." Katy laughs. "The funniest thing is that I ended up living up in the mountains here in California, and I lived right by Neil Young. At one point, Stephen Stills was walking down the street and my husband was out in the yard. He was like, "Oh, Stephen Stills just went by." I thought maybe I should go reintroduce myself, you know, but I didn't go there. It was funny to be in the same area as him again."

Festival worker Bob Gill discovered one evening in 1976 that country singer Emmylou Harris was an admirer of small kids . . . and jewelry. "I was a big fan, and I didn't have to work the night of her concert, so I brought my daughter, who was probably less than a year old at that point," Gill said. "They let me come backstage to meet Emmylou. So, I'm standing on that walkway between the stage and the dressing rooms with my daughter. Emmylou comes out, sees my daughter, and just goes crazy. 'Oh, she's so pretty. She's beautiful. She's so cute.' Emmylou was wearing this very expensive turquoise bracelet. It was gaudy almost. And my daughter was just fascinated with it. She hands it to my daughter to play with, and my daughter looks at it, and pitches it into the shrubbery off the deck. It's getting to be dark at that point, and I'm going, 'Oh my gosh!' So, I'm crawling underneath the platform, digging through all these weeds, trying to find this beautiful, turquoise bracelet. Fortunately, I found it eventually, but I was a little embarrassed about it. Emmylou was a good sport. She said, 'Oh, that's what kids do.'"

"That was bloody amazing!"
Progressive Rock Hits the MRF

Progressive Rock Hits the MR The bombastic assault of progressive (or prog) rock captivated millions in the 1970s, as bands like Jethro Tull, King Crimson, and Genesis fused elements of rock & roll with classical music, lofty concepts, virtuosity, and a large dose of wild imagination. Two of the leading prog-rock acts of the era brought their distinct styles and sounds to the MRF in 1972.

One of the MRF's largest crowds came out on August 8 to see Emerson, Lake & Palmer, and opening act Jo Jo Gunne. The British "Supergroup" had formed just two years earlier—the combination of keyboardist Keith Emerson (The Nice), vocalist/bassist Greg Lake (King Crimson), and drummer Carl Palmer (The Crazy World of Arthur Brown). ELP was unlike any other band of the time, blending rock, jazz, and classical into a synthesizer-driven wall of sound. The group's third album, *Trilogy*, was released the month before the MRF show, peaking at No. 5 on the album chart and containing the Top 40 hit and rock radio staple "From the Beginning."

Fans filled every nook and cranny of the festival grounds, throwing Frisbees and blasting fireworks on the lawn. The band emerged just past 10 p.m. after a large banner displaying their name dropped from the ceiling above the stage. Visually, they were prog rock all the way—Emerson wore a grey jacket with three large round collars overlapping down the front, Lake was dressed in a pure white suit, and Palmer wore a Japanese kimono.

Beginning with the opening song—a cover of composer Aaron Copland's "Hoedown"—Emerson was the focal point of the performance. Coaxing incredible volume from his $25,000 Moog synthesizer (the first such instrument to grace the MRF stage), Emerson eventually jumped off the stage and walked up the aisle with a remote control to create "cosmic contortions of sound." During the set's finale, Emerson threw his equipment à la Pete Townshend and created even more sonic noise.[88] The music, which included the classic ELP song "Lucky Man" and the 21-minute encore of "Karn Evil 9," was accompanied by a light show courtesy of The Electric Rainbow Company.

ELP played their final note just minutes before midnight. And following the bombastic nature of what occurred on stage, attendees were probably worn out. But sadly, they soon realized the enormous crowd of 25,747—second highest in MRF history to that point—had created a traffic nightmare on the roads surrounding the campus. It took until 2 a.m. for the festival grounds to clear, with police handling several accidents and a few car break-ins.

Meanwhile, the night was just beginning for the band, and John Klobnak was about to impress the musicians with his own ability to break into cars. "I was working in the back of the tent, and they come back to leave and see like three hundred to four hundred girls around their limo," he remembers. "So, we got like six or eight guys, and we formed a diamond around them. We pushed our way through these girls, and they're grabbing at the band and trying to pull their clothes off. We get to the limo, and the keys are locked inside. Now we're stuck with a mob around us.

"I yell back, 'Get me a coat hanger!' Keith Emerson says, 'Uh, what do you want a coat hanger for?' I say, "Watch this, man." And I put it into a loop, reach it down there, and pop it open. He looks at me and says, 'That was bloody amazing!' That's how they escaped. I've still got the scars to prove that one, too. Those girls were vicious."

Once safely inside the car, Emerson, Lake, and Palmer asked their artist host coordinator to drive around the area, which he did until almost 1 a.m. One band member still wasn't finished exploring—he wanted to see a movie. This triggered a high-speed drive to St. Louis County. Twenty minutes into the film, the artist was bored, and it was back across the Mississippi River to the Holiday Inn.[89]

Also, in '72, Rock & Roll Hall of Famers Yes made their first festival appearance (with Jackson Browne opening). The band had recently welcomed former Plastic Ono Band drummer Alan White to its lineup, after the departure of Bill Bruford to join King Crimson. Personnel changes would be no stranger to Yes over the next 50 years, but the fourteen thousand fans on hand at SIUE that night enjoyed the band's classic lineup: singer Jon Anderson, guitarist Steve Howe, bassist Chris Squire, keyboardist Rick Wakeman, and White. Yes was touring behind its fourth album, *Fragile*, which would go double platinum, peak at No. 4, and contain Yes classics "Roundabout," "Long Distance Runaround," and "Heart of the Sunrise."

The pomp and circumstance that was prog rock was on full display. Wakeman was surrounded by eight instruments, including a grand piano, an organ, two mini-Moog synthesizers, and two Mellotrons—one containing pre-recorded snippets of violins, cellos, and flutes, and the other housing male and female vocals and bird sounds. Squire wore a purple satin butterfly costume, complete with flowing scarf wings and a sequin butterfly on his back.[90] Mary Jost of the *Belleville News-Democrat* was impressed. "It is a break from the past, perhaps a basis for the future, something which new artists will pick up and expand upon. But it's doubtful if any will equal the fresh, sheer beauty and originality of 'Yes.'"[91]

The band's departure from nearby Bethalto after the show was described as "like something out of a James Bond movie" by Buzzy Butler. "We drove to (Bethalto's Civic Memorial Airport) after the concert, and everything was completely dark," he said. "Then, as soon as the car lights hit on the plane, the jet engines started, the airplane lights went on, and, in a few minutes, they were gone."[92]

Gone, but not forgotten. Three years later, Yes was back, and one of the MRF's largest crowds—25,574 people— packed the natural amphitheater.

While the latter half of the decade was a bit of a dead zone for the band in terms of classic albums and radio hits, it didn't stop Yes from selling concert tickets in large numbers. Keyboard whiz Wakeman had left the band in 1974 and was replaced by Swiss musician Patrick Moraz. The rest of the previous MRF lineup—Anderson, Howe, Squire, and White— was back, and the band rewarded the large crowd with a long, intricate show full of lights, smoke, 200 pounds of dry ice, a backdrop depicting clouds and trees, and any other accompaniment necessary for a 1975 prog rock show. "A Yes concert is like a race car going flat out all the way," wrote John S. Cullinane in the *St. Louis Post-Dispatch*.[93]

It was a challenging evening for the MRF's student workers, as stagehands representing Local 6 of the International Association of Theatrical Stage Employees had established a picket line at the performers' entrance. The group was demanding the SIUE civil service stagehands and student workers be replaced by St. Louis local members at established union rates. The picket line would come down the next day.

"It was up to our production crew to put the show together and make sure it started on time," Jim Grandone says. "We provided the muscle to get the amps and everything on stage. I had to cross a picket line to get into the back of the site. That was a major challenge because I'm a Democrat and I had to decide whether I would go with my politics or my job. I went with the job, much to the stagehands' consternation."

A third Yes concert was scheduled for 1976, but the show was moved to Kiel Auditorium because the band's elaborate staging demands could not be met at the MRF site.

"If you see Mike Love, tell him he still owes me a quarter"
The Legendary Beach Boys

It's become a popular conversation piece—"What is your Mount Rushmore of . . . *fill in the blank*." Well, if the topic were American pop music artists, it would be very hard to make the case that The Beach Boys would not hold one of the four available spots.

A continuous presence on the cultural scene for more than 60 years, The Beach Boys' resume is unmatched: More than one hundred million records sold worldwide, 36 Top 40 hits (the most by an American band), the landmark 1966 album *Pet Sounds*, and a 1988 induction in the Rock & Roll Hall of Fame. No doubt, the creative vision of Brian Wilson changed the world.

Making the first of four MRF appearances in 1972, the Beach Boys were without the eldest Wilson brother, who was playing intermittently with the band while dealing with mental health challenges. His brothers Carl and Dennis were on hand, along with fellow original members Mike Love and Al Jardine, and newcomer Blondie Champlin. The short hair and matching shirts of the early '60s were replaced by the current styles of shaggy hair, baggy clothes, and scraggly beards. But to the more than twenty-two thousand fans at the MRF, the music was still the thing.

The newer songs in the setlist didn't always land, with a *Belleville News-Democrat* review describing them as "unimaginative and often just noisy."[94] In addition, issues with the sound system created balance and feedback problems that affected the band's classic harmonies.[95] But when they pulled out the classics, it was 1963 all over again. "Good Vibrations" closed the set, followed by encores of "I Get Around" and "Fun, Fun, Fun" that had fans dancing and singing along.

Student worker John Klobnak would be closer to the action on this night than anyone aside from the musicians themselves. "My job was to sit under the piano and when girls jumped on stage, I was supposed to grab them and get them off the stage," he recalls. "I think I caught three girls. But that was a real experience being on stage with The Beach Boys."

In addition, Klobnak had a pre-show interaction with Mike Love that seems a bit backward—college student loans rock star money. "So, we were just kind of standing around backstage, and he asks me for a quarter. He says, 'I'll pay you when I get off.' I go, 'Sure,' and give him a quarter." Klobnak laughs. "Still waiting for that quarter! Fifty years!"

And what did Mike Love spend the 25 cents on? "He bought a Diet 7-Up from a vending machine," Klobnak says. "If you see him, tell him he stills owes me a quarter."

It would be five years before the Beach Boys returned to Edwardsville, and, unlike their initial show, the lineup that closed the '77 season included all three Wilson brothers—Brian joined Carl and Dennis, as well as Love, Jardine, and Billy Hinsche. Arriving late and without the benefit of a sound check, The Beach Boys dealt with some technical issues. "I know this may seem like bungling to you," Love told the crowd, "but all this stumbling around is really a finely orchestrated ballet."[96]

The fans didn't seem to mind, as they heard a set packed with The Beach Boys' classics, beginning with "California Girls" and rolling through to encores of "You Are So Beautiful," "Barbara Ann," "Rock and Roll Music" and "Fun, Fun, Fun."

It was a magical night for a couple of fans in particular. Shari Faltus and her future husband, Tim, were on the lawn. "I think we fell in love at a Beach Boys concert," she said. "It seems like that night was extra special. Everyone was hugging each other. It was a very romantic night for everyone, but I think it really cemented our relationship."[97]

In 1979, the band visited for a third time, again closing out the season. The Beach Boys' final appearance was one of the final MRF concerts ever, and the band's leader chose to sit this one out.

"We didn't let 'em down, did we?"
Younger Fans Get the Blues

Some musical styles come and go (disco, anyone?). But the blues are timeless. And, while the decade of the '70s may not have been the prime era for the great blues artists, several of them passed through Edwardsville, thrilling longtime fans and even cultivating some new ones.

Rather than just delivering the symphony and crowd-pleasing rock shows, Ward adhered to the university's original commitment to education and culture when creating summer schedules. The blues was one category where this came into play. "I was not a great fan of rock & roll," he says. "I was more interested in folk, blues, and jazz. So, when I was in a position to decide what to bring in, I decided to commit every Tuesday to those three forms of music. Look at any calendar of events and you'll see the pattern. Of course, there were some exceptions. But I tried to get as many top Black artists as possible to fill in the dates, particularly with blues, because it was appropriate to do so."

The man known as "The King of the Blues"—B.B. King—first came to town in 1972. It must have been challenging to carry such a lofty title, but King was always up to the task, electrifying the crowd with his raspy voice and his favorite Gibson ES-355 guitar, Lucille.

Born on a cotton plantation in Mississippi, young Riley B. King learned his first guitar chords from a local Pentecostal minister. In 1948, the 23-year-old relocated to Memphis to work as a disc jockey and sing in local clubs. By the early '50s, King was releasing hit records and playing shows throughout the East, South, and Midwest.

Accompanied by a nine-man band, including horns and piano, King's first MRF set brought fans to their feet from the opening chords, with some of the more excitable ones standing on their seats under the tent. King opened with "Every Day I Have the Blues" and never let up, closing his set with his biggest hit, "The Thrill is Gone," which won a Grammy in 1970 and a Grammy Hall of Fame award in 1998.

In 1974, King returned with another blues pioneer. Born McKinley Morganfield in Mississippi, Muddy Waters began making a name for himself in 1950s Chicago while recording on the famed label created by Leonard and Phil Chess. Waters' Chess albums and singles—including "Mannish Boy" and "Hoochie Coochie Man"—are renowned.

In an interview before the MRF show, King was pessimistic. "I think the blues is a deteriorating art," he said. "It is dying because we haven't taught our children to love the great men who made the blues, like Muddy Waters, T-Bone Walker, and Lightnin' Hopkins. The gain of young Blacks is few."

King added that the new keepers of the flame were predominantly white and British. "The blues is being imported. People like Eric Clapton, John Lennon, Mike Bloomfield, and the Rolling Stones; they listened to the blues, and when they started playing in front of big crowds, they mentioned our names and people began listening to us again."

Waters passed through the room and asked King, "We didn't let 'em down, did we?" King responded that the legendary blues men had not, adding "If I had it my way, your name would be in the schoolbook."[98]

The fans attending festival blues shows—largely representing all age groups—did not give the impression that the genre was on life support. Waters returned in 1975, capping off his set with a lively encore of "Got My Mojo Working." Opening act Luther Allison, a purveyor of the more contemporary Chicago blues style, catered to the locals with a set paying tribute to Chuck Berry. The *Alton Telegraph's* Doug Thompson said the small crowd "heard the best of the blues performed by some of the best in the business. Nothing fancy, mind you, just good, driving blues performed by competent musicians in a straightforward manner . . . That's because this is blues, basic honest music, performed by musicians who have paid their dues."[99]

Another Mississippi product, guitarist Albert King, played on two MRF bills, opening for Delaney & Bonnie and Friends in 1970 and Roberta Flack in 1971. Known as "The Velvet Bulldozer," King was an imposing figure on stage, well over six feet tall and around 250 pounds. Playing his distinctive Flying V guitar and tearing through such classics as "Stormy Monday" and "Born Under a Bad Sign" during his first visit, King was visibly spent on a muggy evening, according to the *St. Louis Post-Dispatch*. "His white vest was crumpled on the floor, his suspenders hung around his legs, and his purple shirt was soaking wet."[100]

As B.B. King mentioned, the blues had crossed the Atlantic and become an integral part of the British rock sound. One of the musicians leading this new wave was John Mayall, who headlined at the MRF in 1973. Best known for fronting the Bluesbreakers, Mayall surrounded himself with some of the greatest musicians of the era: Eric Clapton and Jack Bruce (who later formed Cream); Mick Fleetwood, John McVie, and Peter Green (who would go on to create Fleetwood Mac); and Mick Taylor (who joined the Rolling Stones in 1969).

One blues artist who came to SIUE in 1976 didn't need a guitar. In fact, Bobby "Blue" Bland didn't play an instrument of any kind. But like B.B. King, Albert King, and Muddy Waters, Bland's vocal talents would earn him enshrinement in the Rock & Roll Hall of Fame.

"The Maestros"
The World's Greatest Conductors Visit SIU

The St. Louis Symphony is one of the world's most revered and decorated orchestras. So it only seems appropriate that the era's top conductors wanted to come to Edwardsville and lead the SLSO at the Mississippi River Festival.

Anyone flipping the channel to their local public television station in the 1970s was likely familiar with the snow-white hair and mustache of conductor Arthur Fiedler, who led the Boston Pops Orchestra from 1930 until his death in 1979. The PBS series *Evening at Pops* ran from 1970 to 2004 and featured Fiedler and the Boston Pops for its first decade. The conductor's first MRF show came in 1971, and while in town, Fiedler, a lifelong fire truck aficionado, hopped aboard an old Ahrens-Fox pumper fire engine and enjoyed a ride with the St. Louis Fire Department. Fiedler returned in 1973, guiding the symphony through a wide range of pieces, including selections from *Show Boat* and *Carmen*.

"When Arthur Fiedler was going to be there in 1971, I noticed Skip Manley's helpers were doing something up on the stage," Greg Drexelius says. "I found out they were putting a back on the conductor's podium so he wouldn't get too excited and fall off the podium. Before that, there had never been a back on the podium. And if you go to almost any concert now in almost any place, you'll find that there is a back on the podium. But that was the first time they ever put one on at the festival. Fiedler got very exuberant. He was quite the director, you know?"

Aaron Copland was known as the Dean of American Composers, creating music that captured the spirit and heritage of the American story. In 1945, he received the Pulitzer Prize for music for his composition *Appalachian Spring* and added an Academy Award in 1950 for composing music to the film *The Heiress*. At his first MRF concert in 1972, Copland led the symphony through original works, including "Our Town" and the Suite from "Billy the Kid." Copland made a return engagement the next year.

Also in 1972, Mitch Miller made the first of two festival appearances. Best known for his *Sing Along with Mitch* television show that aired on NBC from 1961 to 1964, Miller presented a variety of styles at the MRF, ranging from light classical, standards, and the popular "Sing Along with Mitch" section. Miller returned in 1973, leading the SLSO through favorites such as "Four Leaf Clover," "Shine On, Harvest Moon," "Hava Nagila," and "Good Night Ladies" during the singalong section of the show.

At some point each December, it's a certainty that you will hear the familiar, jingly sound of the holiday classic "Sleigh Ride." The song's most popular rendition was arranged and conducted by Leroy Anderson, one of the most successful American composers of the twentieth century. The Boston native studied music at Harvard before catching the eye of Fiedler, who asked for original pieces he could perform with the Boston Pops. After serving in World War II, Anderson's career took off. "Sleigh Ride" was released in 1950, and the next year, "Blue Tango" climbed to No. 1 on the Billboard chart and became the first instrumental recording to sell one million copies. His pieces "The Typewriter" and "The Syncopated Clock" used everyday objects as percussion instruments. Anderson made his only MRF appearance in 1974, with Illinois Governor Dan Walker in attendance.

That same summer, Frenchman Michel Legrand directed the St. Louis Symphony through works from some of his more than two hundred film and television scores, including Oscar winners from *The Thomas Crown Affair* and *Summer of '42*. Over his career, Legrand was nominated for thirteen Oscars and won five Grammys.

A pair of trailblazing conductors stepped into the MRF spotlight, as well. On August 8, 1970, Dean Dixon became the first Black conductor to lead the St. Louis Symphony. Born in New York City, Dixon left the U.S. in 1949 and was serving as Music Director of the Frankfurt Symphony in Germany by 1970. His MRF appearance marked his first return to American soil in 21 years. Four years later, Henry Lewis stepped on stage to lead the SLSO. In 1948, at 16 years old, Lewis was invited to join the Los Angeles Philharmonic, becoming the first Black instrumentalist in a major symphony orchestra. He became the first Black U.S. symphony orchestra conductor when he was named musical director of the New Jersey Symphony Orchestra in 1968.

Working multiple symphonic concerts each summer spawned a love of classical music in Drexelius that never before existed. "The MRF is the reason I appreciate the symphony orchestra the way I do now," he says. "When you were out there, on a beautiful night with this wonderful music that they were creating with their guest artists, it was just magical. I was into Creedence (Clearwater Revival) and Peter, Paul and Mary. I had no exposure to classical music before the MRF, so this was such a nice way to break into it. Now, my wife and I are season ticket holders for the symphony."

The Five-Timers Club (Part III)
Harry Chapin

The third and final member of the Mississippi River Festival's Five-Timers Club made his debut on July 17, 1973. Not only was Harry Chapin one of the most gifted artists to play under the tent, but he is universally viewed as the most beloved entertainer to play the festival. "Harry Chapin was a very special performer who was sincerely honest with people and shared joy with them," Ward says. "I didn't find a single negative about him. I loved working with him."

Born in 1942 in New York City, music was in Harry Chapin's DNA, with his father being a jazz drummer and brothers Tom and Steve also growing up to be singers. The subject of a bidding war, Chapin signed a multi-million dollar recording contract with Elektra Records in 1972 and promptly released his first album, *Heads & Tales*. The LP went platinum, containing the Top 25 hit "Taxi," and Chapin was nominated for the Best New Artist Grammy. By the summer of 1973, Chapin was finishing work on his third album, *Short Stories*, which would be released in December and contain the hit, "W-O-L-D."

In his first MRF show, Chapin vividly shared stories through 12 original songs. "It is likely that the Chapin style will remain free from imitation because there is no one on the present rock or folk scene with as much ability to tell a story through song," wrote Jim Landers in the *Alton Telegraph*.[101]

Greg Drexelius was one of Chapin's many fans at SIUE. "Harry Chapin was always so interesting. What can you say about Harry's music? It wasn't always very uplifting—it was very serious and spoke to tragedy a lot. But it was very interesting, and he always told a great story."

But beyond the music, it was Chapin's warm personality that made him a favorite of MRF fans, as well as officials, student workers, and anyone else affiliated with the festival. "From the moment he strode on stage, the MRF crowd was aware that this was not the typical rock performer—sullen, disinterested, ego-tripping," Landers wrote. "Chapin looked like he was glad to be at the MRF and maintained this enthusiasm throughout the concert."[102]

Chapin returned in 1975, hot from the success of his biggest album, *Verities and Balderdash*, which sold more than two million copies behind the No. 1 hit, "Cat's in the Cradle." Dressed in a navy-blue turtleneck, with jeans and sneakers, and supported by a band including brothers Tom and Steve, Chapin was his usual approachable, generous self. Following a full set and three encores, the musicians went backstage to unwind. With fans still standing and cheering for more, Chapin and the band grabbed their instruments and headed back on stage to play several more encores.

As if that weren't enough, Chapin then gave interviews with local reporters on his signature issue, world hunger. Hearing fans gathered outside his dressing room door, he went back out to sign autographs well into the night.[103]

"He was going to have this press conference about world hunger, but unfortunately, that press conference didn't take place until 1:30 or 2 in the morning or some ridiculous hour because he decided to have like twenty-seven encores," Rick Stankoven says with a smile. "That was a long night."

Stankoven had the chance to speak with the artist hours earlier, before the show began, but specifics of the conversation have been lost to time. "God, that was so many years ago. It's hard to remember the details. We just chatted. He was nice. He always talked with people a lot."

"One of the shows I still remember is when Harry Chapin came and he brought his brother Tom," John S. Rendleman says of the '75 show. "He wasn't as big an act as some of the others, but I remember enjoying that concert quite a bit."

On June 30, 1976, Chapin made the most memorable entrance in MRF history. Delayed at New York's LaGuardia Airport by a tornado warning, the singer was clearly in danger of missing his third festival show. "Shortly before the gates were to open at 6:30, I got a phone call from Harry," Ward says. "He said, 'Lyle, I don't know what to do. We had a problem here and we've missed our plane. Do we need to cancel the concert?' I said, 'No, Harry, the people are on their way in. We need to have the concert no matter what.' He said, 'I'll get there.'"

As they say, the show must go on. Officials located a student who was friends with local musician Terry Beck, who grabbed his guitar and rushed to Edwardsville. Warmly greeted by a crowd of more than six thousand, Beck performed for an hour and was rewarded with a standing ovation. "He is a good singer and a very capable guitarist and deserved the reception he received," wrote Dick Richmond in the *Post-Dispatch*.[104]

Meanwhile, in New York, Chapin had leased a jet, and as soon as the weather cleared, he flew directly into St. Louis. The singer then arrived at the MRF site via a helicopter piloted by a Vietnam veteran hired for a mere $500. Again, the connection was made by a student who knew the pilot. "We've had a lot of strange arrangements to get people to the festival, but this has to be the strangest," Concert Manager Vicky Holt said.[105]

Bryan Erdmann describes the chaotic scene. "It was ten minutes to eight, and Harry still wasn't on site. As soon as he landed in St. Louis, he called to tell officials that he had landed and was on his way. The helicopter landed on the hillside to the side of the stage. And in front of thousands of people, he jumped out of the helicopter, ran down the hill, ran up onto the stage platform in the back, and came on stage. Everybody was watching him and cheering, and Harry went right on stage and said, 'Well, I made it,' or some casual greeting."

The Herculean effort to make the show align with the reputation Chapin was building among the university and festival communities as an artist who would always go above and beyond for his fans! "I wanted to play here," he said after the show. "I've played here before, and I love this place."[106]

MRF fan John Jarvis was there that night. "Harry Chapin was my favorite," he reflects. "The guy was phenomenal. I loved his music, but he was just an everyday person. They brought him in by helicopter, so he played really late because he felt bad. I never saw a better concert than Harry Chapin."

In 1978, Chapin played the festival for the fourth time, again earning the positive feedback from fans and local critics that had by then become customary. Chapin was as close to a sure thing as the tent would ever see. "He is undoubtedly one of the most dynamic talents to ever set foot on the MRF—or any—stage," wrote Walt Sharp in the *Alton Telegraph*.[107]

A Harry Chapin concert was more than just music. It was storytelling and fan interaction, basically, an evening-long conversation. Early arrivers to the '78 show were waiting at the gates when they opened at 5 p.m., three hours before Chapin took the stage. Many staked their favorite spots on the lawn and huddled under plastic sheets to avoid light rain. "You can always count on the people in the cheap seats," Chapin later said in acknowledging the lawn sitters.[108]

After a few acoustic numbers, Chapin's backing band (including his brother Steve on piano) came out to electrify the sound. "I like to open that way," Chapin said of the fuller sound. "Kinda makes me feel like Neil Diamond."[109] Chapin would continue performing well into the night and then nearly apologize as if it wasn't enough. "It's frustrating to perform for three hours as we did tonight and still have so many more songs we want to play for you," he told fans before inviting them to continue the show at his upcoming Kiel Opera House appearance.[110]

Always promoting his world hunger message, Chapin mentioned a recent meeting with President Jimmy Carter about the imminent passage of new bills that would create a commission focused on the issue, of which Chapin himself would be a member. To drive home the topic's importance to the singer, Chapin announced that he would meet and greet fans at a T-shirt stand after the show. All proceeds from sales of the $5 shirts would go to the World Hunger Year program. Not surprisingly, a large crowd gathered at the stand, and Chapin spent an hour talking to fans and signing autographs. "I still have my autographed T-shirt," Stankoven says.

Well past midnight, the long evening behind him, Harry Chapin left campus and headed back to the Holiday Inn, where he said he planned to call his wife.[111]

The last time Harry Chapin would play SIUE came on June 28, 1979. Just over two years later, Chapin died in an automobile crash on the Long Island Expressway. He was thirty-eight years old. "I was very depressed the day I heard he was killed," Jarvis says. "I mean, such a waste to lose somebody like that. There was nobody better."

"The Harry Chapin crowd loved him more than any other fans loved their artist," Stankoven says. "He had such a way of connecting with the audience, and you could see that in all of his concerts here. He really liked coming to SIUE. Once, I gave a friend a large, mounted photo I took of him at the MRF. She took it with her to a concert someplace and showed it to him. He was like, 'Oh, where did you get that?' She said her friend was a photographer at SIUE, and he said, 'Oh, that's one of my favorite places.'"

Though his music lives on, the true legacy of Harry Chapin is one of humanitarianism. His manager, Ken Kragen, was so inspired by Chapin's example that he spearheaded the USA for Africa and Hands Across America campaigns in the 1980s. Multiple organizations created humanitarian awards in Chapin's name. And in 1987, on what would have been his forty-fifth birthday, Harry Chapin was posthumously awarded the

Congressional Gold Medal.

"One night, Harry Chapin conducted an interesting experiment," Erdmann remembers. "He said to the audience, 'I'd like you all to do me a favor. If anybody has keys in their pocket or their purse or anything jangly that makes a sound when you shake it, could you get it out and hold it up for me, please?' People dutifully reached into their pockets and their purses, and they brought out their key rings. He said, 'Now, please hold them up in the air and shake them.' And all of a sudden, there was this sound. It was really pretty and kind of spooky at the same time. Who would have thought of that? That was one of my favorite things that happened out there."

"You get that one shot. It's like somebody flips a coin"
Local Acts Enjoy 15 Minutes of Fame Under the Tent

The story of Billy Peek illustrates the opportunities local artists could receive through the Mississippi River Festival. But for others, an evening under the tent was nothing more than a brief glimpse of what might have been. Take, for example, The Guild, a Collinsville, Illinois, band that opened for Sha Na Na in 1973.

The seeds of The Guild were planted in a mid-'60s cover band from Mascoutah, Illinois, called the Del-Rays, which had the distinct honor of playing on the bill when the Beatles made their lone St. Louis appearance at Busch Stadium on August 21, 1966. After the Del-Rays disbanded, band members and brothers Rich and Tom Lang formed the Guild.

Through a rotating cast of members (including St. Louis native and future Steely Dan contributor and Doobie Brother Michael McDonald), the band became mainstays on the 1970s Illinois rock scene, sharing bills with REO Speedwagon and building a loyal following through shows at the Collinsville Park Ballroom, The Granary in Edwardsville, Stonehenge in Lebanon, and Ricco's in Belleville. The Guild even opened for The Who at a show in Lake Geneva, Wisconsin.

But the music business is a fickle one, and while REO went on to achieve worldwide success, the Guild's story ended much differently. The band never got a record deal. "They were supposed to be a giant act," John Klobnak remembers. "I mean, they were so good. They would pack Collinsville Park every Thursday night—you couldn't get near the place. They toured all over. You get that one shot. It's like somebody flips a coin, you know? What are you gonna do? Michael McDonald goes and joins Steely Dan. Two other guys go off with Dan Fogelberg. It's just never the same. I always feel sorry for them because they were just so good."

As Klobnak mentions, The Guild members Denny Henson and Tom Kelly left the band and formed Fool's Gold in 1974, opening for and backing Peoria, Illinois, native Dan Fogelberg at his 1977 MRF show. "Playing in front of people you know is often a strain on the performers because they know the audience is pulling for them and they want to be as good as their fans think they are," wrote Dick Richmond in his *St. Louis Post-Dispatch* review of the Fogelberg concert. "If there was any nervousness by Henson and Kelly, they sure didn't show it."[112]

Kelly would eventually become one of LA's top session vocalists, lending his talents to the Grammy-winning *Toto IV* album and touring with the band. But it was as a songwriter that Kelly left his most lasting mark. With partner Billy Steinberg, Kelly would pen five No. 1 singles and scores of hits. The list is impressive: "Like a Virgin" by Madonna; "So Emotional" by Whitney Houston; "True Colors" by Cyndi Lauper; "Eternal Flame" by The Bangles; "Alone" by Heart; "I'll Stand by You" by The Pretenders; "I Touch Myself" by Divinyls . . . No wonder Steinberg and Kelly would be inducted into the Songwriters Hall of Fame in 2011.

In the mid-'70s, there seemed to be a pipeline from Champaign, Illinois, down to the St. Louis area—Fogelberg and The Guild were two artists who spent time honing their chops in the shadow of the University of Illinois. Another was REO Speedwagon, a band that played the MRF in 1975. The group dated back to 1966 when Belleville's Neal Doughty met fellow University of Illinois student Alan Gratzer. With Doughty on keyboards and Gratzer on drums, a band was soon formed to play at fraternity parties, university events, and local bars. With Peoria native Gary Richrath joining on guitar, REO Speedwagon landed a record deal in 1971 and soon gained a Midwestern foothold, thanks in part to radio support from KSHE.

The role of vocalist changed three times on the band's first three albums, with Terry Luttrell giving way to Kevin Cronin and then Michael Bryan Murphy for the 1973 album, *Ridin' the Storm Out*. For the band's lone MRF show, Murphy, Doughty, Gratzer, Richrath, and bassist Gregg Philbin were promoting the *This Time We Mean It* album, which would be their last before Cronin rejoined the band as lead vocalist.

Following a long intermission to address feedback issues that plagued the opening set, REO took the stage and a large, younger crowd erupted. Playing early hits like "Keep Pushin'," "Like You Do," "Ridin' the Storm Out," "157 Riverside Avenue" and "Golden Country," the band felt right at home in downstate Illinois. In fact, the evening was a homecoming for Doughty, whose parents and four brothers were in attendance. "The crowd was fantastic," Murphy said. "This area, the St. Louis–Edwardsville area, contains one of our most loyal audiences."[113]

After leaving The Guild and contributing to Steely Dan, Michael McDonald played before the home folks three times with the Doobie Brothers. For the first show in 1976, the McCluer High School graduate with the thick beard and soulful voice was in the early stages of his career-changing stint with the band.

Hailing from Northern California, the Doobie Brothers were the creation of guitarist/vocalists Tom Johnston and Patrick Simmons. Their second album, 1972's *Toulouse Street*, garnered attention, but it was 1973's *The Captain and Me* that placed the Doobie Brothers into rock's stratosphere with the classics "China Grove" and "Long Train Runnin'." The band's first No. 1 single, Simmons' "Black Water," followed in 1975. But at the height of their success, the Doobies faced a major crisis. Johnston was suffering from health problems, including a bleeding ulcer, making it impossible to tour. The band's newest member, former Steely Dan guitarist Jeff "Skunk" Baxter, recommended McDonald, and the '75 tour was saved.

Come 1976, Johnston was still unavailable, and a new album was contractually required. The Doobie Brothers again turned to McDonald for the *Takin' it to the Streets* album, which landed at No. 8 on the album chart. The band rolled on, although the hard-rocking earlier sound established with Johnston was evolving into a more mainstream, soulful style with

McDonald.

In a premonition of things to come, rain fell on the Doobie Brothers at the MRF, but it didn't dampen the mood of 16,695 fans. Backed by the Memphis Horns, the Doobies gave fans the best of both worlds, as Johnston was feeling well enough to attend and play alongside McDonald. But not long after the MRF show, Johnston's health challenges returned, and he stepped away again. This time, he wouldn't return to the band until a 1987 reunion tour.

Two years later, with McDonald firmly established as the band's frontman, the Doobies returned to the MRF. Once again, stormy weather hit the festival site. An extensive smoke and light show accompanied the hits as the band thundered through a set few other '70s rock groups could rival. Since their previous appearance two years before, the Doobie Brothers had released the hit album *Livin' on the Fault Line* and memorably appeared in two episodes of the ABC sitcom *What's Happening!!*

The final Doobie Brothers appearance came in 1979, and, as lightning again filled the evening sky, McDonald belted his way through newer songs from the *Minute by Minute* album, including "What a Fool Believes." Released seven months before, both the album and the single would reach No. 1 and win the band three Grammys in early 1979.

Other performers also made the MRF a homecoming of sorts – a special occasion to show friends and family how far they had come. In 1970, a Granite City, Illinois, native named Bonnie Bramlett and her husband brought their act, Delaney & Bonnie and Friends, to Edwardsville. Born Bonnie O'Farrell, Bramlett sang in a local church and St. Louis area clubs before heading to California to seek fame and fortune. Seven days after meeting in 1967, Delaney Bramlett and Bonnie O'Farrell were married, and their professional act was formed as well.

The "Friends" aspect of the band was an ever-evolving list of some of the era's top musicians, including Eric Clapton, George Harrison, Leon Russell, Bobby Whitlock, Dave Mason, Rita Coolidge, and King Curtis. At the MRF, the most notable "Friend" joining Delaney and Bonnie in promoting the *To Bonnie from Delaney* album was guitarist Duane Allman of the Allman Brothers Band, regarded as one of the best slide guitar players ever.

"I remember my brother asked if I wanted to go see 'Bonnie and Delaney and friends.' That's how I remember him saying it," John S. Rendleman says. "I'd never heard of Bonnie and Delaney or their friends—I didn't know who they were. But I wanted to go to the concert with my brother. He told me that Eric Clapton would be playing with them, and of course, I knew who Eric Clapton was. So, I went to hang out with my brother and his friends and listen to Eric Clapton play. Well, apparently, he didn't show up. But Duane Allman did, and he was a pretty good substitute."

Bonnie Bramlett was welcomed home by a typical Southern Illinois summer night—one band member asked, "It's hot as hell here, isn't it?" upon emerging from a Cadillac and being smacked in the face with the 93-degree heat.[114] After gathering in front of a small TV backstage to watch their recorded performance on *The Smothers Brothers Summer Show*, the headliners took the stage to a large crowd of sweaty fans and encouraged them to sing along, dance, and get into the music. The *Edwardsville Intelligencer* compared Bonnie's vocal style to that of Janis Joplin, "with perhaps a little less volume, but a lot smoother."[115]

Connie Rosenbaum of the *St. Louis Post-Dispatch* also was impressed, depicting Bonnie in a clingy burgundy knit sweater and luminous brown slacks. "Clutching one microphone in each hand, she moaned, stamped, shouted, and shimmied through the rippling rock without ever sounding raw, and she usually managed to smooth the shrill out of her screams."[116]

After the energetic two-hour set, a "dragging and drained" Bonnie Bramlett returned backstage to greet old friends from the area and Granite City High School classmates. "I couldn't really tell how it sounded, but it sure felt good," she said with a smile.[117]

Delaney and Bonnie ended their personal and professional relationship in 1973. Bramlett would return to the MRF years later, both as a solo artist and a member of the Allman Brothers Band.

In 1971, the woman who had inspired Bramlett to follow her dreams also played at the MRF; also with her husband. While neither was born in the St. Louis area, Ike and Tina Turner cut their teeth across the river in 1950s East St. Louis. Ike's band, the Kings of Rhythm, came to the region from Mississippi at the urging of his sister, who lived in St. Louis. Shortly after, a high school singer from Tennessee named Anna Mae Bullock turned up in the Gateway City and caught Ike's band playing at the local Manhattan Club. Soon, she was singing with the Kings of Rhythm on weekends and recording her first song with Ike in 1958. Ike renamed his musical muse "Tina Turner," and the fledgling act performed and recorded under the name The Ike & Tina Revue before the pair married in 1962. For three short nights that year, a seventeen-year-old Bonnie Bramlett filled in for backup singer Jessie Smith and became the first white Ikette before her mother pulled the plug on the arrangement.

Ike and Tina moved to Los Angeles, and industry success soon followed. By 1971, the act was established, with their hit cover of Creedence Clearwater Revival's "Proud Mary" reaching No. 4 on the Billboard charts in January. The record would go on to win a Grammy Award.

At the MRF, Tina stole the show with Ike, the Rhythm Kings, and The Ikettes laying down the structure that freed the singer to soar. The *Alton Telegraph's* Doug Thompson summed up her sizzling mix of soul and sex: "She didn't just sing, she creamed the words. She didn't just hold the microphone, she caressed it and seduced it . . . Each thrust of the hip, each twine of the white costume only brought more cheers and screams." [118]

Thompson also painted the backstage picture, focusing on a 22-year-old fan named Bruce Carlton, who approached Tina for an autograph after the show without a piece of paper. Wearing a bathrobe, the star signed "Love, Tina" on Carlton's right hand. "Now, what do I do with it," he asked. "Maybe if I had the hand laminated. You know, she really bore down with that pen. It left furrows in my hand."[119]

It was a memorable evening, and it almost didn't happen. Before the show, Ike Turner approached Ward and demanded his $12,000 fee in cash. Right now. "He refused to let Tina go on stage until I paid the guarantee," Ward says. "I went to the box office, and there were bills all over the floor, mostly ones and fives. (Staffers) Clarice Moulton and Randy Hart were grabbing money and loading it into my briefcase, which I then walked backstage and delivered to Ike."

Ike and Tina Turner's musical impact was memorialized in 1991 when the duo was inducted into the Rock & Roll Hall of Fame. But their turbulent partnership had come to an end long before with their 1976 divorce. Tina enjoyed a renaissance in the 1980s as a solo artist, with her 1984 album *Private Dancer* going multi-platinum and spawning a series of hits, including "What's Love Got to Do With It," which topped the Billboard chart and won the Grammy for Record of the Year. She was inducted into the Rock & Roll Hall of Fame as a solo artist in 2021, making her the second female to be inducted twice.

Also in 1971, a local product with a deep love for the Mississippi River performed at the festival alongside his idol. John Hartford was born in New York City but grew up in St. Louis, where his passion for the Mississippi would greatly influence his musical destiny as well as his non-music pastimes (Hartford would earn his license in the 1970s to work as a steamboat and towboat pilot). By the time he reached John Burroughs High School in the early 1950s, Hartford was already accomplished with both the banjo and fiddle. He later added guitar and mandolin to his musical arsenal.

After studying at Washington University, Hartford set out for Nashville, signed a record deal, and released his first album in 1966. He was discovered there by Tommy Smothers, who brought Hartford to Los Angeles and made him a regular on *The Smothers Brothers Comedy Hour*. This opened the door for regular slots on *The Glen Campbell Goodtime Hour* and *The Johnny Cash Show*. Hartford wrote "Gentle on My Mind," a song that won four Grammy Awards in 1968 (two for Hartford's original and two for a version by Glen Campbell).

No doubt, Hartford was a musical force in 1971. But he remained in awe of Earl Scruggs, the man whose banjo skills had inspired him since childhood and with whom he would share the MRF stage. During the encore, Scruggs joined Hartford and his band on stage for classics, including "Let Me Be Your Salty Dog." Hartford called sharing the stage with his hero "an ego trip."[120]

One of the university's, and festival's, best allies was state senator Sam Vadalabene, who held office from 1971 until his death in 1994. Vadalabene was an ardent supporter of the MRF during some trying times when state funding—and the MRF's survival—was in doubt. He also fought for years to establish a civic center in Edwardsville that could serve as a permanent festival site—a project that would never come to fruition. Today, Vadalabene's name graces the athletic facility on the SIUE campus—the 4,000-seat Vadalabene Center opened in 1984.

But there was an even more direct connection between Sen. Vadalabene and the Mississippi River Festival. On July 24, 1976, fiddle player Doug Kershaw and his group, Slidin' Jake, served as a warmup for the Ozark Mountain Daredevils under the tent. Observant fans may have noticed that Slidin' Jake's drummer had a familiar last name—Vadalabene. Yes, Marty Vadalabene was the son of Senator Sam.

"When that boy quit school at SIU and said he wanted to go off to Denver and be a rock drummer, I just threw a fit," said Marty's mother, Mary Vadalabene, at a pre-concert reception. "I absolutely told him he couldn't do it. But Sam said, 'Oh, mother, let the boy go.'"[121]

The twenty-five-year-old drummer got his start playing with local bands in Edwardsville, following in the footsteps of his father, who was a drummer in the Pana, Illinois, High School band in the 1930s. "I'm very proud," the senator told the *Post-Dispatch*.[122]

Seated in the crowd, Sen. Vadalabene told those around him that Slidin' Jake's version of the "Orange Blossom Special" would "bring the roof down." Sure enough, the fast-paced bluegrass classic got the crowd up and dancing, and when Kershaw gestured toward his drummer after a nifty break, mom and dad beamed with pride.[123]

Marty Vadalabene would play with Kershaw for two decades, a gig that would take him to the Grand Ole Opry, Farm Aid, and many other destinations. Now based in Seattle, Vadalabene continues his music career.

The festival's symphonic concerts also presented their share of local headliners, but one, in particular, stands out for her additional role as a member of the SIUE family. Legendary American pianist Ruth Slenczynska accompanied the St. Louis Symphony on four MRF occasions. A child prodigy born in Sacramento, California, in 1925, Slenczynski was seemingly groomed from birth by her challenging violinist father. At age four, she gave her first recital, and by age seven, she had performed in both Berlin and Paris. But the stress at such an early age took a toll, and during her high school years, Slenczynski stopped performing for nearly fifteen years. In 1964, Slenczynska accepted a full-time position as Artist-in-Residence at SIUE, holding the title until 1987.

"Change Partners"
Crosby, Stills & Nash Play the MRF . . . But Not Together

Yes, David Crosby, Stephen Stills, and Graham Nash all played the Mississippi River Festival. But Crosby, Stills & Nash never did. Confused? It's simple, really, when you understand the complicated relationships that permeated the supergroup in the 1970s (and still exist today).

CSN's 1969 self-titled debut album and 1970 follow-up, *Déjà Vu*, had firmly placed the group at the forefront of American music. "Crosby, Stills & Nash just blew all of us away," Jim Muffo says. But by 1973, that success had faded. Over the last three years, the individual artists had spent their time working on solo projects and talking about getting back together, with little to show in the way of results.

Stills had created the country-rock side project Manassas in 1971 along with former Byrds' and Flying Burrito Brothers' bassist Chris Hillman. The band was more successful as a live act than through its recordings—two albums sold well but spawned no hits. Fans turned out in large numbers for Manassas' 1973 MRF show primarily to see Stills and Hillman, not so much to hear the band's new songs. The *Alton Telegraph's* Doug Thompson was less than impressed, describing the performance as "a mixed bag of music... their performance never seemed to jell and ventured constantly into the out-of-date and overdone era of rock music ... (Stills') performance was loud, but little else."[124]

To close the '73 season, Stills' most famous musical collaborators made their first trip to Edwardsville. Crosby and Nash had recorded a self-titled album as a duo in 1972, which reached No. 4 on the chart. They spent the following summer headlining shows and supporting Neil Young on his U.S. tour.

At SIUE, the pair was greeted by high winds, lightning, and thunder. The biggest victim of the conditions was the opening act, J.D. Souther.

Predominantly known as a songwriter for the Eagles and Linda Ronstadt, Souther lost power during his set due to a lightning strike. An emergency generator restored light and sound to allow Souther to proceed, but the lingering storm forced fans on the lawn to seek refuge under blankets and jackets and caused staff to lower the plastic weather shield around the tent. This obstructed the view of some fans, whose complaints led staff to continue raising and lowering the shield as the rain increased and lightened up.

Musically, Crosby and Nash delivered, performing CNS hits "Wooden Ships," "Our House," "Guinnevere," and "Almost Cut My Hair" and "giving a 'relaxed, professional performance of easy songs that made for a very mellow evening.'"[125]

By the end of the year, Manassas was history, and Stills rejoined Crosby and Nash for a successful reunion tour in 1974. But the following summer, Stills was back on his own, headlining an MRF show as a solo artist for 7,500 fans. The evening was reminiscent of the festival's early days, complete with a younger crowd tossing Frisbees on the lawn, passing wine bottles, and enjoying a set lasting more than two hours from rock royalty. Stills opened with "Love the One You're With" and played a mix of songs from throughout his storied career, complete with an acoustic set in the middle that included a cover of Harry Nilsson's "Everybody's Talkin.'"

In 1976, Crosby and Nash were back, outdrawing their previous MRF show by bringing in a crowd topping 10,000. A handful of those fans even had the chance to meet one of their heroes on the lawn that evening, but the opportunity was missed. "David Crosby was a little off," says Jim Grandone. "The band was doing their sound check and he was standing out on the lawn listening. It was time for the gates to open, so I said, 'Mr. Crosby, in about ten seconds, there's going to be thousands of people coming down that hill. I think you might want to get back to the dressing room.' And he said, 'Oh, I don't care.' Sure enough, people start to come in and lay their blankets down, and Crosby is still out on the lawn listening to the sound check. Nobody recognizes him. Nobody says hello to him. And he finishes the soundcheck and goes back to the stage. He blended in like any ordinary person, even though he had that mustache and that hair. He was the most distinctive person on the lawn that night, and no one noticed he was there."

Backed by members of The Section (top Los Angeles session musicians including guitarist Danny Kortchmar, drummer Russ Kunkel, and Jackson Browne's right-hand man David Lindley), Crosby and Nash were supporting their third album together, *Whistling Down the Wire*. Their set was diverse, mixing acoustic ballads and rockers, and always blending in the harmonies that had made them famous. Although songs recorded with Stills ("Wooden Ships," "Long Time Gone," and "Déjà Vu") were included, the pair also focused on songs they had recorded as a duo, including "Immigration Man." They closed with "Teach Your Children."

After the '76 tour, Crosby and Nash would reunite with Stills for 1977's *CSN* album, and the Crosby/Nash tandem would be shelved for 28 years.

In 1979, Stills was back on his own, arriving in Edwardsville with his California Blues Band. He gave the MRF crowd a sneak preview of a Crosby, Stills & Nash hit they wouldn't hear on radios for three more years, "Southern Cross," before closing with a couple of Buffalo Springfield chestnuts, "Bluebird" and "For What It's Worth."

CSN was welcomed into the Rock & Roll Hall of Fame in 1997, and they were the first act to have all members inducted twice (Crosby with the Byrds, Stills with Buffalo Springfield, and Nash with the Hollies). Continuing to perform sporadically, the act was put on ice in 2016 because of tension between the artists. Sadly, Crosby died in early 2023, forever ending hopes of yet another reunion.

"A forklift and a clean, made-up bed"
The Booking Process, Cost Structure and Contract Riders

By the mid-1970s, the Mississippi River Festival had become a destination of choice for performers in nearly every conceivable entertainment form. This put SIUE in the catbird seat when it came to booking the artists fans wanted to see. But it didn't begin that way.

"All of the big contemporary performers were there," Ward says. "I mean, anyone who was anyone in the 1970s came to the festival. But at first, it was very difficult to get them because they'd never heard of us. We had no reputation. It didn't take very long, only a couple years, and the word got out between musicians that this was a great place to play. All of the stars loved it, and I think they got an ego boost from being part of an academic endeavor. They loved the outdoor setting. There wasn't much opportunity to do that at that time. The artists would speak from the stage about what a remarkable facility it was and how happy they were to be there."

University Center Director Bob Handy was responsible for booking talent during the inaugural festival season. But when he left the university in 1970, Ward stepped into the role. His previously noted lack of knowledge about rock & roll might sound like a hindrance to the task of selecting artists for a popular music festival, but Ward knew his limitations. He also knew that a college campus was teeming with knowledgeable, passionate rock fans.

"The students were very involved in everything, and I mean that in a positive way," Ward says. "A committee was formed that was instrumental in helping to select performers. I used them the whole time I was there, and it was very rare that I overrode their recommendation. They all knew music better than I did."

Jim Grandone was a member of the committee. "We asked for ridiculous things like the Rolling Stones and Crosby, Stills, Nash and Young," he says. "Of course, the Beatles had broken up by then, but it would've been nice to have a couple of Beatles. And, you know, Lyle, God love him, did the best that he could with what he had to work with. These rock bands were hot, and they cost a lot of money to bring in. So, we got what was touring plus whatever Lyle could miraculously pull out of his hat. The question was, can we make up the money we're putting up front with the crowd that we expect to come to the concert?"

Ward also connected with the heads of other popular American music festivals to align efforts and maximize mutual benefit. "We would meet every winter to talk about the groups we were interested in," he says. "At the beginning, I often rode on what they were going to do. They had statistics that I didn't have, such as attendance figures of these artists, and, equally important, they often had experience with artists they had booked before. There were some people we didn't bring in because of the information I got there. Often, we ended up with a chain of events across the country when all of us decided to do the same groups. It was to the artists' advantage to be in these locations."

After a list of targeted acts was put together, it was time to reach out to their representatives and talk business. And while Ward says he was never given a budget for booking talent, he created a structure that specified how much artists would be offered based on their ability to draw a crowd.

"I arbitrarily made a decision that I would not pay more than $15,000 guaranteed for anyone," he says. "But I would reference some of our larger groups, whether it was the Eagles or The Beach Boys, and allow certain acts to take 60 percent of everything we brought in. Well, they liked that. That was the general way of determining the cost of these events. I only made one exception to that pay structure." More on that story to come.

Interestingly, Ward's price range was in the same ballpark as what top artists earned at Woodstock, where Jimi Hendrix collected the largest check ($18,000) and just three other artists—Blood, Sweat & Tears; Joan Baez, and Creedence Clearwater Revival—reached the $10,000 mark.

Three years later, Jim Landers of the *Alton Telegraph* obtained some of the MRF's numbers from the 1972 and 1973 seasons. Artists earning above $10,000 included David Cassidy; Chicago; Yes; Emerson, Lake & Palmer; the 5th Dimension; America; Loggins and Messina; and Manassas. This level of artist also received a percentage of gate receipts. Next, in the range of $5,000 to $9,999, were names like John Denver, Bobby Goldsboro, Judy Collins, Seals and Crofts, Curtis Mayfield, and Sha Na Na. Harry Chapin and Ferrante and Teicher received less than $5,000, while opening acts were earning between $1,000 and $1,500. Performers were expected to pay their own travel expenses and motel costs, with the MRF providing transportation from the airport to the concert, as well as a car to use while in town.[126]

"Groups at that time were not charging exorbitant fees compared to today," Ward says. "The most we ever paid in terms of a guarantee for an artist in the nine years that I did the contracting was $20,000. I mean, that's inconceivable today. Now, what they wanted to do was make their money based on the percentage of the gate. That's what drew them here, knowing that we had the potential to easily do 20,000 people."

So, who were some of the near misses? The big-name artists who wanted to play the Mississippi River Festival, but their demands exceeded what officials were willing to pay? "We were told that Lynyrd Skynyrd wanted to come, and we would've loved to have had them," Ward says. "They were at the top of their game at that time. But their agent would not come down to the fee level that we had established for ourselves. They asked for $30,000, and Bill Hudgens said, 'We didn't pay The Who that much!' Elton John was the same. He wanted to be here, and I wanted to bring him. But the agent would not come down on the guaranteed figure, and we kept that number firm."

Some who did sign a contract to perform under the tent attached certain demands to the deal, better known as contract riders. Landers also had access to a few of these, and, while some appear routine, a few might make you scratch your head. For instance, the members of America requested non-processed nuts, assorted cheeses, and sandwiches, while Seals and Crofts simply asked for grapes. Sha Na Na's contract called for a 24-bottle case of soda before the show and another after. David Cassidy didn't ask for much—just a "clean, made-up bed"—while, for some reason, Manassas demanded a forklift.

The task of fulfilling these artist requests—and many others—fell to the student workers, primarily the production team. "Being production supervisor was about making sure the artists were comfortable and that they had everything they wanted," Grandone says. "Sometimes, that included items that were not allowed under state law—for instance, you couldn't use a university vehicle to go get liquor. We also had to drive to this little shop in the Central West End to get *Perrier* for the artists because there was no place to buy it on the Illinois side of the river. This was before bottled water was available everywhere, and they wanted *Perrier* because they were going from town to town and drinking all that local water might cause them to spend most of their time in the bathroom."

One final interesting rider request: Bette Midler asked for an eight-foot artificial palm tree. An unusual request. But then, Bette Midler was rarely conventional.

"The Divine Miss M"
The One and Only Bette Midler

Any time Bette Midler came to your town to perform, you were guaranteed a spectacle. So, when the burgeoning, multi-talented star came to the MRF in 1973, scores of devoted fans turned out to pay homage to their hero. Many were spotted in the crowd wearing Midler's unique style of clothes, bright fingernail polish, and tall platform shoes.

But before the show, Midler gave no indication of the transformation to come. "Bette Midler is a premier entertainer," Ward recalls. "I learned at her performance that she is as much a performer as a singer. She was standing side stage with me just before the concert lights came on, talking in a normal voice like any other person that you'd know. And then it was time to go on and she became the Divine Miss M—a persona that was totally different than this quiet person. And she gave such a wonderful concert."

The *St. Louis Post-Dispatch* described Midler as "the last of the truly tacky women, a performer who has become the '70s most potent pop-cultural symbol."[127] Midler was joined on stage by The Harlettes, her trio of androgynous backup singers, and led the crowd on a bawdy journey of music and comedy. Songs ran the gamut from the World War II standard "Boogie Woogie Bugle Boy" to early rock & roll hits "Chapel of Love" and "Leader of the Pack."

Photographer Charlie Cox remembered the brutal warmth of the evening. "The tent gathered heat during the day and retained it at night," he said. "They had fans on poles, and there was air conditioning that came up through the floor of the stage to cool (performers) off. But it was so hot at the Bette Midler concert that she went offstage, took off her dress, and came back out and sang in her slip."

It turned out to be a very eventful evening for Ward, who attended the show with his wife, Shirley. "I was pretty much living at the university, doing my regular job during the day and concerts at night," he says. "My wife was nine months pregnant with our first child, but we thought she had another week. This was one of the few concerts she came to, and she was sitting in a very good spot in the front with three good friends. She enjoyed the show and came backstage for a little bit, and then we went home and got in bed. I think I may have just had time to fall asleep and she was up saying, 'My water's broken. Let's go to the hospital.' So, we're talking about just a few hours from when she was sitting there in the audience. I'm just so glad that we got home in time. That was our son, Andrew, and it changed my whole life."

One last word on Bette Midler. Remember the eight-foot palm tree in her rider? She got it, courtesy of Ward. "My father used to be in charge of holding dance parties for the glassworks union, and I had an artificial palm tree that had been a prop for one of his dances," he says. "I kept it in my basement. Following Bette Midler's show, the roadies and the trucks left, and my fake palm tree was gone. Later, I saw a palm tree in the background of one of her TV performances. I'm not sure if it was mine or not."

"This is so awesome! We've gotta come back!"
Don Henley Kisses Lyle Ward

As Lyle Ward likes to say, the MRF never hosted a performer who didn't want to return. But no artist ever expressed this sentiment more emphatically than Don Henley of the Eagles.

The seeds of the Eagles were planted in 1971 when Texas-born Henley and Detroit native Glenn Frey were hired as part of Linda Ronstadt's backing band. They soon were joined by Randy Meisner from Rick Nelson's Stone Canyon Band and former Flying Burrito Brother Bernie Leadon. It didn't take long for Henley and Frey to pull Meisner and Leadon into a band of their own. The Eagles' eponymous debut album was released in 1972 and contained three Top 25 singles, "Take It Easy," "Witchy Woman," and "Peaceful Easy Feeling."

Around this time, Ward and Gene Haffner caught a glimpse of the up-and-coming band and immediately took steps to get them to Edwardsville. "There was a national entertainment conference, and the agencies would put their rising acts on stage for all of us bookers from around the country to see," Haffner says. "Lyle and I were at this conference in 1973, and there was a group that just blew people away, and we decided that we would book them right then and there. That was the Eagles."

In those days, the university held a concert or two in the spring as a trial run for the upcoming MRF season, allowing the student workers and festival staff a rehearsal before the summer schedule commenced. In May 1973, the Eagles were that warm-up concert. "I want to say that we booked them for like 1,500, 2,500 bucks to play the university concert that spring. The students all came, and that concert was so incredible that we turned around and booked them for the festival either that same night or that same weekend."

By the time the Eagles made their MRF debut in July 1974, they had released the hit albums *Desperado* and *On the Border*, and added guitarist Don Felder to the lineup. It was another hot Midwestern evening and Jim Grandone was charged with driving to Lambert Airport and bringing Don Henley back to campus. "The university cars we used were all out on other jobs, so I had to borrow a friend's car, which was a Chevy something or other, and it didn't have air conditioning," he recalls. "It was hot and humid, and Don Henley gets into the right side of the car with his afro, and he is livid. He didn't say a word the entire way. We made up for it on the way back and got him a better car with air conditioning. He was more friendly then. He was exhausted, but friendly."

Ironically, the co-headliner of the show was Joe Walsh, who would join the band a year later. Nearly fifteen thousand fans were on hand as the Eagles opened with "Take It Easy" and progressed through a series of their country-rock hits, culminating in an encore of "Tequila Sunrise." The *Alton Telegraph's* Doug Thompson found their performance the perfect accompaniment to an evening on the lawn. "The Eagles blend country and rock better than most groups and their end product has style and melody. That's the kind of rock that goes best in the grassy environs of MRF."[128]

It was quite a scene backstage, too, as another popular act chose that evening to pay a visit and check out the festival site. "The Eagles were performing, and I looked backstage, and we have Joe Walsh and there's REO Speedwagon," Ward says. "They were all having a reunion backstage. (REO) had come out on their own and flown into the Bethalto airport. So, that was kind of a unique evening for any festival." REO would play the MRF the following summer.

The Eagles continued to rule the airwaves before returning to SIUE in 1975, and if not for The Who, the 29,941 fans who attended their show with J.D. Souther on July 29 would be the festival record. MRF officials were pleasantly surprised. "I expected about twelve thousand people," Ward said. "Looks like I was wrong."[129]

Ward remembers the band members being ecstatic as they left the stage following the concert. "The Eagles were a special group," he says. "They put on tremendous performances. That night, the fans would not stop demanding encores, and the band kept responding over and over again. Finally, the show ended, and they were so emotionally high about the experience—the crowd, the tent, the open air, all of it. They said it was the biggest crowd they'd ever played to. I'm waiting on the walkway right below the stage, and they're whooping and hollering and having a good time. Suddenly, Don Henley comes up and just grabs me and gives me a kiss on the head! He said, 'This is so awesome! We've gotta come back!' I was kind of in shock, I think."

The crowd size failed to top the legendary '71 concert by The Who, but in terms of headaches for MRF staff, this show may have reigned supreme. Health services dealt with an array of cuts, bruises, and other injuries from tossed bottles and fights, moving patients into an empty dressing room when their own treatment area filled up. "I've never seen anything like this," one staff member said.[130]

Ushers and security staff also took their lumps while dealing with the rowdy fans, and the Crisis Intervention Unit had their hands full with fans who had overindulged in drugs and alcohol. In addition, a light pole was torn down by fans hoping for a better view of the stage, and some fencing was damaged. As had become customary for highly attended shows, the traffic jams leading away from campus took hours to clear.

In an editorial, the *Alton Telegraph* took fans to task. "If rock fans want to hear their favorite attractions, they'd better shape up . . . The traffic through the first aid emergency center hit a new high, and missiles were thick in the area. Ushers were punched and shoved around. This is no way for an audience to act."[131]

The Eagles had one more MRF visit up their sleeve, and this time, they would be presenting songs from their biggest album, *Hotel California*. Released in 1976, the album vaulted the band to majestic heights, winning two Grammys and selling more than thirty-two million copies worldwide. In 2012, *Hotel California* was ranked No. 37 on *Rolling Stone's* list of "The 500 Greatest Albums of All Time."

The band's 1978 MRF show was professional and smooth, as might be expected from Southern California's premier music act. But Walsh, ever the character, stood out with abundant personality, energy, and guitar chops. The Ohio native had played the festival twice before joining the Eagles—the co-headlining 1974 gig and an opening slot along with his band, Barnstorm, at the Manassas show in 1973.

For the 1973 Barnstorm album, *The Smoker You Drink, the Player You Get*, Walsh used a talk box on the classic track "Rocky Mountain Way." On the band's ensuing tour, Walsh joined forces with MRF audio whiz Bob Heil to create the first talk box made for use in high-volume, rock concert settings. Walsh would play it on stage for "Rocky Mountain Way" throughout his career. It was just the latest milestone in the long friendship between Heil and Walsh.

"Joe and I started with the James Gang; we did a lot of dates for them in the late '60s," Heil says. "One of the things that held our friendship was that we were both ham radio operators. Joe was very serious about it. He does a lot of building and restoration. He loves all that stuff. You go to his home, and he just has radios everywhere. I remember, several times, the stage manager would come back and say, 'Hey, Joe, you're supposed to be on stage.' 'Wait just a minute, man. We're trying to make this contact to South Africa.' The fans were out there clapping and carrying on, waiting for Joe. They didn't know we were in the back of the bus trying to talk to a guy in South Africa!

"Joe was in Marissa one day and we're going, 'What do we do about this talk box thing?' And he said, 'Well, we're gonna have to do it live and it's gonna have to be a lot louder.' We went out and put something together, and that's what he used for the Barnstorm tour. Right after that, I thought,

'Wow, this could be a commercial effort.' So, we started creating the 100-watt version and built tens of thousands of those things. The rest is history. I gave one to Peter Frampton for Christmas in 1974 (made famous on the *Frampton Comes Alive* album) and helped Bon Jovi with it (Richie Sambora used it on "Living on a Prayer"), and so on. But Joe, when he appeared at the festival with Barnstorm, that was another magnificent night. We had augmented the sound system for him because he likes big sound, and he got it!"

The Festival's Longest Night
A Celebration of Jazz

In the annals of the Mississippi River Festival, there were some very long nights on campus. Any show that attracted more than twenty thousand fans meant hours of post-concert traffic issues for fans, festival staff, and local law enforcement.

But when it comes to the actual product on the stage, one evening reigns supreme. On Tuesday, July 30, 1974, a collection of the finest jazz musicians in the business played the longest concert in MRF history.

Dubbed "A Celebration of Jazz," the show proved to be more of a marathon for the 3,397 fans in the house. McCoy Tyner, former pianist for John Coltrane, opened the show with his band at the late hour of 9 p.m. His set focused on selections from his recent live album, *Enlightenment*, which was recorded at the Montreux Jazz Festival in Switzerland. Next up was a group led by trumpeter Freddie Hubbard, and, for some reason, this middle act on the bill played for two full hours.

It was now midnight, and headliner Chick Corea and his group, Return to Forever, had not yet set foot on the stage. One tired fan headed for the exits. "He took up all the time, man, he took up all the time," he said, referring to Hubbard.[132]

Thirty minutes passed as the stage crew set up the headliner's equipment. Finally, Corea emerged from the wings, and his talented group, which included bassist Stanley Clarke, kicked in. Having honed his craft in Miles Davis' band, Corea was an accomplished keyboardist and bandleader, and he and his band showed it as the night/morning wore on. When all was said and done, the clock approached 2 a.m., and the hearty fans who remained were calling for an encore. At least they could say they got their money's worth.

Like most other forms of music, the crème de la crème of jazz played the MRF. The biggest of all was the "First Lady of Song"—Ella Fitzgerald—who performed in 1973. Fitzgerald had been on the festival schedule the year before, but an eye injury forced cancellation. Rain kept the crowd below three thousand, but the hearty souls in the house certainly got their money's worth. The fourteen-time Grammy winner and recipient of the Presidential Medal of Freedom delivered songs from contemporaries like Billie Holliday, renowned composers such as Cole Porter, George Gershwin, and Duke Ellington, and even sprinkled in a few popular songs like "Mack the Knife" and "What's Going On?" Fitzgerald showcased her improvisational "scat" singing style throughout a performance Ward remembers as being "just remarkable."

The evening also had a remarkable impact on the trajectory of Rick Haydon's life. The SIUE student and member of local rock bands would nab front-row seats to MRF concerts by agreeing to write reviews for *The Alestle*, where his best friend served as editor. One of the shows he covered was Ella Fitzgerald.

"That night was an epiphany for me," Haydon remembers. "The band was Ray Brown, Joe Pass, Tommy Flanagan, and Connie Kay. At that time, the top of the heap. All legends. They were backstage playing poker after the show, and I went back and hung out with them. Joe Pass bummed a cigarette off me. Ray Brown was taking everybody's money, and I didn't want to get in the way and kill his streak, you know? So, I knocked on Ella's door and said, 'Ms. Fitzgerald, I'm here to interview you for the school paper.' And she said, 'Well, honey, come on in.' So, I went in and sat down, and she asked me what I needed. She was so sweet. I said, 'Well, what was that first song that you played?' And she just gave me this look, like I was one of her kids, and she said, 'Honey, that was 'Satin Doll.'' Years later, here I am, Professor of Jazz at SIUE, and I was telling some kids about that interview and the review in *The Alestle*. I went over to the library and dug it out just to make sure I hadn't written anything stupid.

"The MRF changed me. I don't think I'd be here playing and teaching jazz guitar, being a recording artist, if this didn't happen. The festival changed my whole outlook. I listened to all kinds of music because of the MRF, not just rock & roll. It opened the doors to how much music is out there, as opposed to, 'I'm just going to listen to Jimi Hendrix.' It took the blinders off for me."

The first jazz act to appear at the MRF back in 1969 was the Modern Jazz Quartet, a group that featured two veterans of Dizzy Gillespie's band—John Lewis (piano) and Milt Jackson (vibraphone). In 1970, legendary saxophonist Julian "Cannonball" Adderley performed under the tent following stints with Ray Charles and Miles Davis. New Orleans' Preservation Hall Jazz Band made three crowd-pleasing festival appearances, bringing the sounds and flavor of the Big Easy to Edwardsville. "The crowds are always great," saxophonist Emmanuel Paul said before the band's 1972 show. "There's not always a lot of them, but the ones who come love the music."[133]

The next year, English guitarist John McLaughlin and his Mahavishnu Orchestra provided a different take on the jazz experience. A pioneer in the genre of jazz fusion and contributor to four Miles Davis albums, McLaughlin's talents earned mention by *Rolling Stone* and *Guitar World* on their lists of 100 Greatest Guitarists of All Time. The Mahavishnu Orchestra included noted drummer Billy Cobham and keyboardist Jan Hammer, with the group creating a complex, unique sound mixing Indian music, jazz, and rock. Clayton Frohman in the *St. Louis Post-Dispatch* called the result "perhaps the loudest rock concert to hit this season's Mississippi River Festival. The flailing instruments united from nowhere, peaked in perfect order, and halted abruptly with such precision that it sounded as if someone had lifted the needle off the record."[134]

A handful of jazz artists found a way to break free of the "jazz" label and achieve mainstream success in the late '70s and early '80s. American flugelhorn player Chuck Mangione played at the MRF in 1976 and 1978, and in the year between tallied a Top Five hit with the instrumental "Feels So Good," which would be nominated for Record of the Year at the Grammys. Grover Washington Jr. and Al Jarreau shared a bill in 1978 just before scoring mainstream hits. Washington's saxophone stylings reached No. 2 in 1981 with the Grammy-winning "Just the Two of Us," sung by fellow MRF veteran Bill Withers. Jarreau reached No. 15 that same year with "We're in This Love Together," but he may be best known for singing the theme song to the Bruce Willis TV show, *Moonlighting*.

George Benson was one of the era's greatest guitarists, and when he made the first of three festival appearances in 1977, he was at a career apex. His fifteenth studio album, *Breezin'*, topped the pop, R&B, and jazz charts in 1976 and became one of the best-selling jazz albums of all time. The single "This Masquerade," written by Leon Russell, would win the Grammy for Record of the Year, one of three Grammys Benson won on the night, and one of ten he has taken home during his career.

As good as Benson was at the '77 concert, opening act Minnie Riperton stole the show. The 29-year-old singer from Chicago with a four-octave voice had reached No. 1 in 1975 with "Lovin' You." Co-written with her husband/producer Richard Rudolph, the song would be memorable for Riperton's high whistle register and her singing of "Maya Maya" on the fadeout, a reference to her daughter (and future *Saturday Night Live* star) Maya Rudolph.

At her lone MRF show, Riperton wore a purple-sequined dress and demonstrated her one-of-a-kind vocal range. It was the rare occasion when an opener received a standing ovation and responded with an encore. Benson and Riperton teamed up for the evening's final song, a cover of the standard "Misty."

Tragically, Riperton was living with a terminal cancer diagnosis. In 1978, she received the American Cancer Society's Courage Award from President Jimmy Carter. She died on July 12, 1979, at the age of thirty-one.

"It's still a long uphill climb"
MRF Finances Remain a Challenge

Though not as sexy as the music and the personal stories, one of the more fascinating chapters in the MRF story is the never-ending set of financial challenges faced by the university, symphony, and festival officials. To put it mildly, the Mississippi River Festival never had it easy.

For example, the initial season of 1969 exceeded expectations in terms of attendance (about ninety thousand fans) yet lost roughly $150,000. Immediately, the festival's future was in doubt. But John Rendleman believed in it. "This campus needs something like the festival to add to the total educational concept of the university," he said. "It's a good thing for the campus and the area. Sure, it's still a long uphill climb, but it has to continue. And I'll be in there fighting to make it continue."[135]

Through local fundraising efforts, grants from the Illinois Arts Council, and commitments from the SIU board of trustees and the Symphony Society, the MRF found ways to survive, even turning slight profits in 1970 ($6,401) and 1972 ($15,850). The 1973 season was the first to bring in more than two hundred thousand fans, thanks in part to a longer schedule. But even with the attendance record, the festival showed losses of close to $65,000. The cost of bringing in big-name artists combined with low ticket prices did not add up to financial success. Though the Mississippi River Festival was never designed to be a money-maker, the losses were piling up. But time after time, those in charge worked hard to keep the festival alive.

To aid the situation, ticket prices for rock and pop events were raised by $1 for the 1974 season, fifty cents of which would be used as a facilities utilization and parking charge. This surcharge would go straight into festival coffers, as it could not be claimed by artists who received a percentage of ticket sales. But MRF '74 was a disappointment, with attendance dropping by more than 25 percent and financial losses approaching $100,000. The reasons included competition from rock concerts in St. Louis, the fuel crisis leading to higher gas prices, inflation, and the SLSO performing free concerts in area parks.

For the first time, Rendleman's air of confidence deflated. "I can't even sound hopeful about it," he said of a 1975 season before asking his team to create a proposal to save the festival. All options were on the table.[136]

"The festival will never make money"
The St. Louis Symphony Bows Out

The disenchantment experienced in 1974 was the final straw for one of the festival's pillars. On November 7, a game-changing announcement was made—the St. Louis Symphony was stepping out of MRF management. What began as a joint venture with SIUE had become too much of a financial burden for the symphony to bear. On its way out the door, the SLSO would absorb $138,000 of the festival's debt.

Rendleman recommended that the university assume full management of the Mississippi River Festival, and this was unanimously approved. "We have to accept the fact that the festival will never make money, but its importance as a cultural institution goes far beyond any question of profits and losses," Rendleman said.[137]

In December, Rendleman told the trustees that the university could operate the festival with a balanced budget if $150,000 in grants could be obtained from the Illinois Arts Council, the National Endowment for the Arts, and donations from a Friends of the Festival group. Unfortunately, that's not how things would play out.

Over the next three MRF seasons (1975-77), the St. Louis Symphony's involvement would be limited to a handful of concerts each summer. After that, the symphony would have no role between 1978 and 1980.

Finally, SLSO official Peter Pastreich was replaced as festival managing director by a man who had played a fundamental role since the very beginning—Lyle Ward.

Have you talked to Lyle Ward?"
The Man in Charge Gets a Promotion

"Hi, I'm working on a book about the Mississippi River Festival . . ."
"Have you talked to Lyle Ward?"

It seems to be common knowledge in the Edwardsville area that all roads leading to the MRF pass through Lyle Ward. He is the festival's leading authority and advocate, possessing an astonishing array of photos,

T-shirts, signage, and other memorabilia. Ward's collection has been displayed numerous times over the years at SIUE, and, more recently, in a popular 2022 exhibit at the Wood River, Illinois, Museum.

Simply put: No one was more connected to the inner workings of the Mississippi River Festival from 1968 to 1977 than Lyle Ward. What makes his essential part in the saga even more astounding is that he was still a student when it began.

"I was born in Alton and lived there until I went to college at SIU," Ward says. "I don't know that I had a lot of options because of the expense of it, so my mom called some legislators, and I was fortunate enough to get a scholarship that allowed me to go to the university for $30 a quarter."

After spending his first collegiate quarter at SIU's Alton residence center, Ward moved over to the shiny new Edwardsville campus in early 1966. It didn't take him long to become a key player in the university's operations. "I got involved very quickly because I knew some of the upperclassmen from other volunteer work I had done," he says. "I joined a number of organizations and ended up serving as President of the University Center board, which was writing all the policies for the building that would open the next year."

University Center Director Bob Handy was so impressed with the undergrad that he hired him as an assistant for 30 hours a week. By fall of 1968, the beginning of Ward's senior year, he was a fly on the wall as plans ramped up for the school's new summer music festival. "My idea of the festival was very limited; I honestly didn't understand the concept," Ward admits. "My first real introduction was an invitation to a board meeting. There I sat as a twenty-one-year-old, watching Delyte Morris and John Rendleman and Bill Hudgens and Stanley Goodman talk about concepts I'm not sure I could even grasp. But I knew it was exciting, and I knew I wanted to be part of it. This really was a huge bi-state effort. Sitting in the meetings and listening as the biggest names in business, media, and industry in the St. Louis area gave up their Saturdays for two months to meet on this showed me they were very interested in making it work."

Soon, Ward was called in from the sidelines. "One of the first things they asked me to do was to get some help and go purchase the outfits that the student workers would be wearing during the first summer. We did that and brought it back to the board, and they approved it. The assignments just grew and increased from there."

By making himself indispensable, Ward earned a permanent job with the university upon graduation in 1969. "I had a great opportunity that first festival year," he says. "I don't know how I got there, except that I worked for the people who were making the decisions. We had built relationships through my work with the UC. I had been responsible for organizing and setting up events and those related things. I'd say Bob Handy was the reason that I was able to do it."

As noted, when Handy left SIUE after the festival's first season, the role of booking artists landed in Ward's lap. He was 22 years old. "I was honored to have the opportunity, but I did not know what it was going to grow into," he says. "If I have any talent, it is organizing people and planning events, and the MRF fit in very nicely with that. My role with the festival was very comfortable in terms of my status and my relationships on campus. It was particularly easy because the top administrators, such as Bill Hudgens and Bob Handy, had faith in me. There was nothing intimidating about making decisions around those people. I felt very comfortable with it. I was probably crazy and young, but I did it."

Hudgens and Handy hold special places in Ward's heart as the men who believed in a recent graduate and gave him the opportunity to spread his wings and fly. "Bill was always very nice to me, and I always admired his respect for those who reported to him. He trusted his group of directors and gave them room and support. As an assistant to Bob Handy, I was fortunate to observe Bill's style of management, which was a team philosophy that Bob emulated and taught me by example. Despite the many festival challenges, I did my best to manage my staff and our student area supervisors with courtesy, trust, and support."

Ward also credits a pair of SLSO officials—Symphony Manager Jim Cain and Concert Master Max Rabinovitsj—with helping him navigate through this new, foreign landscape. "I had to go through Max to get anything approved by the musicians," Ward says. "Jim was a mentor to me. He introduced me to all of the managers of the other American festivals of the era, and he handled the contracts of the guest conductors and symphony artists."

Though Ward was just a few years older than the students he managed, the age difference often felt more like a wide chasm. "Sometimes they thought of me as being 60 instead of 21," he remembers, "so they didn't tell me a lot."

Jim Grandone describes Ward as a "CEO working with hippies" at the MRF. "He was a very serious individual despite his age. He brought such professionalism to the position. I didn't realize how close we were in age until long after the festival ended. Essentially, we were children running the MRF, and Lyle brought the business head. He paid attention to the contracts, making sure the I's were dotted and the T's were crossed. Lyle kept the heart beating. He was wise beyond his years."

"Lyle may have been the MRF's true father," adds John S. Rendleman. "He was one of the people that my dad would have allowed a lot of freedom to put the festival together. My dad was an education administrator, not a performing arts administrator. I think he recognized some of the people who worked on the MRF knew what they were doing and enjoyed what they were doing, and he let them do what they needed to do."

Gene Haffner adds, "Working with Lyle was an experience that gave me a good base for my career and as a person. He had high standards for customer service and for performance in the job. But he was very understanding when there were challenges. He was always available."

In his new role as managing director, Ward hired SIUE graduate student Vicky Holt to fill his shoes as concert manager from 1975 to 1977. "Vicky was known for her phrase, 'I need,'" says Jim Grandone with a laugh. "She never said, 'Please.' She never said, 'Would you mind?' She said, 'I need.' And that was the order of the day—you did it!"

Ward's MRF service ended in 1978 (more on that later), but his SIUE career lasted until his retirement in 2000. Since then, he has continued to beat the drum for the Mississippi River Festival, keeping it alive for those who experienced it themselves and introducing it to subsequent generations.

"I was just a lucky person that was in the right place at the right time," he says.

"We're bridging the generation gap"
The Diverse Entertainment of the MRF

One point of pride for university and festival officials was the diversity of entertainment offered under the tent. Yes, the symphony and big-name contemporary stars triggered the headlines and brought out big crowds. But it was important to all involved that the Mississippi River Festival stands for more than that. If Lyle Ward could bring in an act that checked a cultural box—but might only draw a few hundred people—he was going to do it.

"What made the MRF unique at that time—and even today—is the scope of what it did, and the fact that it was focused on ensuring excellence in every part of the program," Ward says. "There was never an income-driven goal in the festival. It was artistic, it was innovation. It was trying to identify the up and coming and the very best of the day. And it was to ensure that the broadest diversity of people from our whole region would be served by it."

"People may remember Arlo Guthrie, Harry Chapin, Judy Collins, Joan Baez, the Eagles . . . but we also had a series of excellent chamber music performances with musicians from both the St. Louis Symphony and the SIU School of Music, as well as top musicians from around the country. We brought in true craftsmen of the area who were producing different crafts that were popular during that time. Everything from macrame and silver work to leather, all those people were there, creating their products. So, when you take all of those things—from craft fairs to chamber music to contemporary music to theater to dance—it may have been the most complete festival we've seen in this country."

Jim Grandone agrees. "When you take away the diverse culture of the university-run Mississippi River Festival, what you have is a concert venue. You don't get the dance, the symphony, the jazz, the soul, the R&B. You don't get the scope of American culture that the festival offered to the St. Louis area."

Even the popular music artists recognized and appreciated the university's diverse mission. "One of the things I love about a concert series is when the diversity of music is so broad, which is where I am as a music fan," said Jeff Hanna of the Nitty Gritty Dirt Band. "You know, I love all kinds of stuff. Everything relates back to food for me. You can get bored—like 'Let's have Italian tonight, you know? Let's have Chinese tomorrow.' I think being able to run the gamut from folk to blues to pop to jazz to symphony stuff is pretty amazing, and that's the way it ought to be. At the MRF, it all worked in just a wonderful way that made for this great kind of gumbo . . . very tasty!"

MRF fan-turned-performer Michael "Supe" Granda of the Ozark Mountain Daredevils agrees. "I went time after time after time. And not only did they have rock & roll people, but they had other people – they had jazz people. They had such a diverse palette that I just went there all the time."

"For several summers, I was there almost every night, and there were so many great nights," Rick Stankoven adds. "There was a bluegrass festival and I loved that. They'd have barbershop and so many other great events. There was a variety. They had a formula and it worked pretty well."

"The MRF gave you opportunities to experience things you weren't necessarily interested in," says SIUE alum and festival worker Jack Twesten. "I didn't think much of Gordon Lightfoot at that time, but I went because it was a two- or three-dollar lawn seat and I was a poor college student looking for something to do. But to this day, I'm so glad I went because now I really appreciate his music much more than I did before that night."

And it went beyond performances under the tent. Behind the vision of Dr. Lloyd Blakely, MRF Education Director, many classical musicians and conductors, theater performers, and dancers participated in educational programs at the university, ranging from speaking to a class to guest residencies.

A few of the more niche styles championed by the MRF include:

Dance
The MRF's initial dance event arrived in 1970, as the National Dance Troupe of Zambia made its first-ever trip to the American Midwest.

The group of seventy dancers, ranging in age from fifteen to fifty-seven, performed traditional dances while wearing tribal masks, accompanied by instruments from their homeland. Following the festival performance, the troupe went to Chicago, Washington D.C., and New York before touring the Soviet Union. The next year, Italian American flamenco dancer and choreographer José Greco performed. Other top dance troupes to grace the SIUE stage were Yugoslavia's Abrasevic Dancers, the Erick Hawkins Dance Company, James Cunningham & the ACME Dance Company, the Murray Louis Dance Company, the Phyllis Lamhut Dance Company, and the Kathryn Posin Dance Company.

Most notable from a local standpoint was the 1973 performance by the Katherine Dunham Dance Company. Born in Chicago in 1909, Dunham began learning modern dance in high school, and before she moved on to college, she had opened a private dance school for young Black children. A historic dance career followed, including the opening of the Katherine Dunham School of Dance and Theatre in New York City in 1945. Alumni included James Dean, Sidney Poitier, Shirley MacLaine, and Warren Beatty. The *New York Times* described Dunham as "a major pioneer in Black theatrical dance . . . ahead of her time."

Dunham settled in East St. Louis in 1964, becoming artist-in-residence at the Southern Illinois University residence center. There, she created a liberal arts curriculum focused on anthropology, sociology, and other areas. Dunham's Performing Arts Training Center in East St. Louis opened in 1967, and she received the Kennedy Center Honor in 1983 and a star on the St. Louis Walk of Fame in 1989.

Bluegrass
St. Louis native John Hartford and the Earl Scruggs Revue were not the only bluegrass artists to appear at the MRF. A 1974 show featuring Bryan Bowers, J.D. Crowe & The New South, New Grass Revival, and the Country Gentlemen attracted nearly two thousand fans.

Ragtime
Also in 1974, the New England Conservatory Ragtime Ensemble arrived

on campus at the perfect time. The chart-topping Scott Joplin-heavy soundtrack to the hit movie *The Sting* was attracting new devotees to ragtime, and the MRF show featuring a group of Boston-area students produced several standing ovations.

Barbershop

Yes, even a few concerts featuring barbershop quartets were scheduled at the festival! The first came in 1975 and drew more than 1,700 people. The next year, a trio of barbershop groups celebrated the coming bicentennial with a show packed with American-themed songs. In 1977, three more barbershop ensembles came to town, including the all-female Front Office Four from Michigan.

Family-Friendly

The Sunday pops concert on August 5, 1973, was something magical. Composer Carmen Dragon (father of two-time MRF performer Daryl Dragon of Captain and Tennille fame) led the St. Louis Symphony in a Disney-themed concert, complete with plenty of Disney characters (Mickey Mouse, Goofy, Snow White, Mary Poppins, and more) roaming the tent and lawn. Commemorating the fiftieth anniversary of Walt Disney Productions, the show attracted three thousand fans of all ages who enjoyed music from Disney films.

On this night, Rick Haydon made the jump from *Alestle* reporter to performer. "I was in the university choir to earn my ensemble credit for my degree, and they had a combined chorus performance with the symphony," he says. "We performed the music of *Fantasia*. The Disney characters were all there. That was an incredible experience. It was spectacular looking out through the tent after being on the other side all this time. I had never really been on the stage, and to stand there and look back up in the bowl and see all those people – it was just beautiful. There was nothing like it."

Big Band

One of the more popular musical styles that breezed through the festival from time to time was big band, a big hit with the parents of those who sat on the lawn for The Who, Chicago, and The Doobie Brothers. Musicians who starred in the Glenn Miller, Jimmy Dorsey, and Tommy Dorsey orchestras brought their talents to Edwardsville, including clarinetist Buddy De Franco. At a 1972 show, one female fan in a wheelchair asked a student usher to deliver a note to De Franco asking to meet him. Lyle Ward heard about the request, facilitated a meeting, and obtained an autographed picture for the fan. "This place is outstanding," De Franco said of the festival site. "The people, the tent—everything."[138]

Swing music veteran Buddy Moreno served as host of a 1975 show titled "Big Band Sounds from the Summer of '42." A familiar face locally, Moreno had moved to St. Louis in the 1950s, hosting television and radio shows and performing regularly at the Chase Park Plaza Hotel. Saxophonist Tex Beneke was on hand, showcasing his talents on Glenn Miller's hits "In the Mood" and "Chattanooga Choo Choo." Vocalists Helen O'Connell and Bob Eberly from Jimmy Dorsey's band performed solo and together on a number of standards such as "All of Me," "Embraceable You", and the show-closing "Don't Sit Under the Apple Tree."

Another World War II era act that graced the festival stage was the King Family. Dubbed "America's First Family of Song," the act began with the Grammy-nominated King Sisters and added dozens of extended family members to create one of the era's traditional wholesome acts. Performing in 1969 (the night before Janis Joplin), the King Sisters gave World War II veteran Charlie Cox a moment he would never forget, courtesy of a song played on Armed Forces Radio every night before "lights out."

"During rehearsal, Dad went up to them and said, 'I remember seeing you when I was in the army during the war—you came and did a show for us,' Doug Cox says. "Their big hit was called 'Nighty Night.' That night at the show, as they were introducing the song, they brought Dad up on stage and sang it to him. You could tell he was embarrassed, but really kind of thrilled, too."

Many of the same fans who sat on the lawn for big band shows also enjoyed a pair of festival visits from one of the era's top comedians, actors, and humanitarians.

"It's the only time that I allowed myself to pick up one of the artists"
Bob Hope and the Festival's One Millionth Fan

Remember when we noted that Lyle Ward only allowed one artist to exceed his self-imposed maximum guaranteed payday of $15,000? "That was Bob Hope," he says, "and I have to admit, there was some personal bias on my part for that one. His manager would not discuss anything other than $20,000, and, of course, I went with it. I even brought him back a second time. It was not a problem. We did not make money on his two concerts, but we did OK. It got lots of attention, and we had a lot of people who just loved it."

An American icon. An entertainer whose time had passed. Both could be said about Bob Hope when he played his first MRF show. Vaudeville, Broadway, radio, films, and television—Hope had done it all. And his 57 tours for the United Service Organizations (USO) to the South Pacific, Korea, and Vietnam had cemented his status as one of the nation's most beloved entertainers of the twentieth century.

But this was 1975. To many regular MRF attendees, Hope was a symbol of their parents' (or grandparents') time. The Civil Rights and Women's Liberation movements had changed the national conversation. Watergate and the fall of the Nixon presidency had altered how millions of Americans viewed their elected leaders. Times had changed dramatically, and Bob Hope was trying to find his place.

Hope was picked up at the airport by Ward, who personally drove him to Edwardsville. "Bob Hope was the consummate professional, and it's the only time in nine years that I allowed myself to go to the airport to pick up one of the artists," he says. "I was amazed that from the time he got in the car, he started asking me all kinds of questions about the campus, about the people who lived in our community, and particularly about John Rendleman—he wanted to know about the university president. He was really engaging in conversation. Well, a couple hours later, he walked on stage, and everything we spoke of became part of his act. He was doing jokes on John Rendleman. And it showed me how much of a professional he was to create his material on the spot."

Hope made his entrance into the tent in his familiar golf cart, nearly running over photographer Charlie Cox on the way. "I was told to get a picture of him in the golf cart, so I stationed myself in the aisle," he said. "Well, he entered the tent in the golf cart, and there I was in front of him. He started shouting at me, 'Get out of the way! Get out of the way!' But I wasn't about to move until I got the picture that I wanted. I got the picture and stepped aside, and he drove by me, got out of the golf cart, and went on stage."

The legendary comedian surveyed the MRF lawn and told the crowd it was the first time he had performed for so many people on grass. Fans enjoyed the show, but MRF officials had to be shocked at the low turnout— Bob Hope drawing just 3,400 people could not have been predicted back in the spring. Plus, the crowd was padded by about three hundred downstate legislators invited to attend a free party and the show. Those who turned out seemed to enjoy the familiar jokes, some targeted at minority groups and various ethnicities that, viewed through the prism of 2023, could now be considered offensive. In the *Alton Telegraph*, Doug Thompson wrote that Hope "is an institution in an age when we are fast learning institutions are mostly illusions."[139]

Perhaps the evening's highlight was Hope's presentation of a commemorative plaque to John Hugger, a 42-year-old Granite City resident who was recognized as the Mississippi River Festival's one-millionth customer. Hugger attended the show with his wife and two of his children.

Two years later, Hope returned to the MRF. On this occasion, he kicked off his visit by providing Jim Grandone with a glimpse into how a celebrity cultivates his fanbase. "I met Bob Hope at Lambert with a white limousine," he says. "We went through tremendous tactical maneuvers to get that limousine in position so he could get from the plane to the limo without having to go through a crowd of people. But when he landed, he didn't go into the limo—he went up the jetway. I reach to shake his hand, and he hands me his briefcase. I said, 'Why didn't you go into the limo?' He goes, 'Are you kidding? I want people to know I'm here.' So, we went through the entire airport, both escalators, and people were pointing and saying, 'Isn't that Bob Hope?!' And he loved it. He just loved it."

A crowd of three thousand fans watched as the 74-year-old star exhibited all the energy of a man half his age, delivering jokes at a breakneck pace, and moving around the stage briskly for 90 minutes. "I was in 196 performances last year and have more planned for this year," he told the crowd. "That is what I call slowing down."[140]

Closing the evening by singing "Happy Birthday" to America four days after the nation's 201st birthday, Hope exited to a rousing ovation. Still in town the next day, the comedian called the *St. Louis Post-Dispatch* sports department. "This is Bob Hope. Can you tell me who won the British Open?" "Tom Watson," the reporter answered. "Ah, you're kidding," Hope said, not knowing that Watson had birdied the last two holes to edge Jack Nicklaus by a stroke. "Oh, well, the suspense was killing me," Hope responded. "I know both of them personally, and I just couldn't wait for television."[141]

Fans of Bob Hope likely turned out for shows headlined by two other legends of the era. The "King of Swing"—Benny Goodman—visited in 1976, bringing his legendary clarinet skills to the MRF stage at the ripe old age of 67. Goodman's band was one of the most popular swing music acts during the World War II era and one of the first to be racially integrated. He arrived in Edwardsville a day early to meet with officials and share colorful stories from his storied career. The day of the show, Goodman had a long lunch with SIUE administrators and actually offered to help the MRF crew set up. "I've never had an entertainer offer to do that before," Ward said.[142] It was clear Benny Goodman made many friends during his visit. And a few weeks later, the university announced that Goodman would be awarded the honorary degree of Doctor of Music at summer commencement exercises in September.

Music of the 1940s was celebrated that same summer of '76, allowing Cab Calloway the opportunity to steal the show. The 69-year-old singer/conductor came from Harlem's Cotton Club and established himself as one of the iconic figures of swing music. His 1931 hit, "Minnie the Moocher," would become his signature song (complete with the call and response "Hi De Hi De Ho" section). Calloway performed the song for a new generation in the 1980 film, *The Blues Brothers.*

"He was a great addition to the MRF and brought a touch of what the East Coast entertainers were all about," Charlie Cox said. "He gave a great show. I remember he had on a white tuxedo. It was probably heavy material, and it was a hot night, so he was sweating profusely."

In his *St. Louis Post-Dispatch* review, Dick Richmond tossed bouquets in the legend's direction. "Calloway was amazing," he wrote. "There is no other word for it. He bounced onto the stage and gave the crowd of about 1,400 persons a show it probably won't forget."[143]

Calloway was also impressed by the MRF fans. "The thing that amazed me were the young people in the audience," he said. "They were out there digging that jazz."[144]

"We must have the freedom to tell people what is going on"
Folk Artists Bring Music and Message to the MRF

Quick trivia question: Who was the first "contemporary" music performer in MRF history? Even the most loyal festival attendee might have a hard time coming up with the name of Canadian folk singer Buffy Sainte-Marie. On June 23, 1969, the 28-year-old made history as she performed songs of her fifth album, *I'm Gonna Be a Country Girl Again*, which had been released a year earlier.

J'Deanna Twesten was there. "I had heard of Buffy Sainte-Marie but had never seen her before. She had a beautiful voice and was very entertaining. When she left the stage, she said hello to me."

Rich Dalton speculates that folk music was a logical way to begin taking things a step further at the MRF from the St. Louis Symphony concerts. "They started with the folkies because they were a little more adult," he says, "and I think they probably thought they were more compatible with the symphony crowd. But one of the things that ended up making the festival so great was that these weren't commercial people. It wasn't like Live Nation, you know? They really had no concert experience other than putting on these symphony shows. And they said, 'Well, let's try Judy

Collins. Joan Baez, she'd be good.' I don't know how Iron Butterfly got in there, but it did well. So, somewhere along the line, they started saying, 'Well, let's keep doing this.'"

Actually, in the festival's early days, the chasm between folk and rock music wasn't as wide as it may seem in hindsight. "They were playing Buffy Sainte-Marie a little bit on KSHE, so I knew her tunes," Dalton recalls. "Back in 1969, rock & roll was only about ten years old. So, they didn't have the plethora of music they would have later. So, at the same time as rock & roll, you'd be hearing Buffy Sainte-Marie, a little Joan Baez, and Gordon Lightfoot. Eventually, it all got pushed out. But yes, they definitely played folk at first."

In a way, it makes perfect sense that a folk artist would perform under the tent before a rock act. In the festival's early years, folk music played a prominent role on the music scene, in large part due to the highly charged political times of the late '60s and early '70s. Folk artists like Joan Baez, Joni Mitchell, Arlo Guthrie, and Pete Seeger were infusing their music with lyrics addressing the Vietnam War, the rights of women and minorities, corporate treatment of workers, environmentalism, and other social causes.

For Sainte-Marie, who made a return trip to SIUE in 1971, the message focused on the treatment of Native Americans in the U.S., as she herself was an Indigenous Canadian. Wearing red polka dot hot pants for her opening set and studded blue and white jeans after the intermission, Sainte-Marie made a tearful plea. "Now I'll sing something for you guys who go diggin' around in the (Cahokia) Mounds," she told the crowd. "I wonder what you'd do if some of us Alcatraz types showed up at the Episcopal Church with our shovels?"[145]

Guthrie appeared under the tent for the second time in August 1974, just days after the Watergate scandal ended with President Richard Nixon's resignation. The singer still had much to say on the subject. "I can't believe it. I saw Nixon go," he said after his second song, eliciting loud cheers from the crowd. "I don't know why I'm so happy. I lost a lot of money on that." The comments continued throughout the show. "Every time I think about Nixon, my guitar goes out of tune. So, I'll try to stay away from him tonight. It's hard. I'm so used to him."[146]

Guthrie performed his Watergate-themed song, "Presidential Rag," which included the lyrics, "You're the one we voted for, so you must take the blame for handing out authority to men who are insane."

Vietnam, inflation, poverty, hunger . . . all were laid at the feet of the now former president. After the show, while sipping a cold beer, Guthrie said he would afford the new president, Gerald Ford, a fair chance—"I'll give him some time to see what he is like"—but his attitude for Nixon would never change. "I hope they throw him in the can," Guthrie said. "Jail him. That would be great."[147]

The son of legendary folk artist Woody Guthrie would play two more festival shows, sharing the stage with his mentor and his late father's close friend, Pete Seeger. For folkies, watching Seeger perform the senior Guthrie's "This Land is Your Land" at the 1975 show must have been like watching the Beatles play Shea Stadium. Born in New York City, Seeger was active in left-wing politics and began setting his views to music before the dawn of World War II. Throughout the '40s and early '50s, Seeger enjoyed a stretch of popular records as a member of the Weavers. He was blacklisted during the McCarthy era but re-emerged in the 1960s as an activist against the Vietnam War.

Seeger's songs were staples on American radio throughout the '60s, with the Byrds ("Turn, Turn, Turn" and "The Bells of Rhymney"), Peter, Paul and Mary ("If I Had a Hammer"), the Kingston Trio ("Where Have All the Flowers Gone?") and others recording his works. Folk clubs popped up in major cities, and the next generation of folk stars (including MRF performers Bob Dylan, Joni Mitchell, and Joan Baez) created a renaissance in the art form.

As the clock approached midnight following the '75 show, Seeger sipped a beer and chatted with reporters. "We must have social change," he said. "We must have the freedom to tell people what is going on. The people are not being told what is going on. They are being told only what the television networks and the establishment want them to hear." When asked about the future, Seeger sounded a pessimistic tone. "It will be different from today, although I am not sure it will be any better."[148]

Two years later, the Guthrie-Seeger tandem returned during a period when folk was beginning to fade—rock and disco were now dominating the airwaves. Following their pre-concert sound check, Guthrie and Seeger hung out on the wooden runway leading from the stage to the dressing room area. As Guthrie nursed a beer, Seeger took a deep breath. "Smells good," he said. "This must be a good place. Tell me about the Mississippi River. Is it still the same? Someone is picking me up tomorrow to take me to the airport and I told him that I wanted to leave early enough so that I could go down and walk along the river. Can it still be done?"[149]

The relaxing vibe didn't extend to a handful of boisterous fans who whistled, hooted, and hollered their way through the show. The peacenik Guthrie was triggered, halting the show and blurting out, "Shut up, you turkeys. I've got enough to worry about up here without worrying about you, too."[150]

Baez—a performer from the festival's first summer—came back in 1975, six years after her Vietnam-charged first appearance. With the war now in the rearview mirror, the barefoot, blue-jeaned singer turned her attention to other topics, including the plight of a Soviet political prisoner and the United Farm Workers in California.

Mitchell also appeared in 1969 and followed it up with shows in 1974 and 1979. Unlike some other folk stars, she found a way to cross over into the contemporary charts and remain relevant. Between her first two MRF shows, Mitchell released one of her signature songs, "Big Yellow Taxi," and followed it up with perhaps her finest album, 1971's *Blue*. The LP reached No. 15 on the chart but has garnered greater respect in the ensuing years, ranking third in *Rolling Stone's* 2020 list of the "500 Greatest Albums of All Time." " Shortly before the '74 show, Mitchell's biggest hit, "Help Me," reached the Top 10. Mitchell's visit came amidst a critically-acclaimed tour featuring Tom Scott & The LA Express as her opening act and backing group.

A power failure at the MRF site caused a one-hour delay in starting the show. But those in attendance didn't seem to mind the wait, and Mitchell told the fans that the outage was nothing compared to the multiple rainouts she and the band had recently experienced. Opening with "Free

Man in Paris" and cruising through a set that included "Big Yellow Taxi" and "Woodstock," Mitchell put on a stellar show. At one point, a man from the crowd yelled, "I love you, Joni!" Another fan in the front row handed Mitchell a bouquet of flowers, which the singer placed on her microphone stand.[151]

In 1979, Mitchell was embracing a more jazz-oriented sound with her latest album, *Mingus*, which was a tribute to the late jazz bassist Charlie Mingus, with whom Mitchell had written music before his death. For this tour, Mitchell had assembled some of the greatest jazz musicians of the era, including bassist Jaco Pastorius, guitarist Pat Metheny, and saxophonist Michael Brecker. Bryan Erdmann was pumped for the show.

"I was a big fan of Joni Mitchell, and I was looking forward to her concert because she was also bringing along these heavy hitters," he says. "I worked in the University Center, which had a really nice, well-equipped craft department in which people could make and print their own T-shirts. So I printed one that said on one side 'God Must Be a Boogie Man,' which was one of her songs, and on the other side it said 'Joni Mitchell.' It was green with white lettering, and, of course, I wore that for Joni's show. She really liked it, and I asked if she would sign it for me. She said, 'Sure!' So, I went into her dressing room and pulled the T-shirt off and laid it on the table. She got a *Magic Marker* and signed her name. I don't think that T-shirt has ever been washed since."

Perhaps the most historic folk concert in MRF history occurred on August 11, 1978, when Peter, Paul and Mary kicked off their 18-city reunion tour after eight years of separation. Travers had performed a solo show at SIUE in 1972 and appeared in a Muny Opera production of *South Pacific*. "My daughter, Alicia, loved it there," Travers said. "She learned to high dive in the hotel swimming pool. She's always asking about coming back. I think it's in her genes. My mother was born in St. Louis.[152]

The trio's first reunion show was a hot ticket, with fans traveling to Edwardsville from throughout the Midwest. "We started seriously talking about doing this last December," Travers said at the time. "We had discussed it before, but the status had been, 'One of these days, let's do it.' We decided we would do it this year."[153]

Peter, Paul and Mary received a standing ovation before ever singing a note. "This is our first concert in eight years," Yarrow said, eliciting more loud cheers.[154] The set list brought back all the favorites ("Leaving on a Jet Plane," "Puff the Magic Dragon, " "If I Had a Hammer," and many more), as well as new songs from the upcoming *Reunion* album. But as this was 1978, not 1968, the trio was supported by an electric band—even Peter Yarrow and Paul Stookey plugged their acoustic guitars into amplifiers.

Emotions ran high in the crowd of around ten thousand and among the performers, who seemed moved to be performing together again. They closed with a new song called "Like the First Time" that contained the lyrics, "We're a song that must be sung together, like the first time, only this time could it be forever?"

"We want Donny!!!"
Teen Idols of the '70s Send Young Girls Over the Edge

David Cassidy. Donny Osmond. Andy Gibb. The mere mention of those names to girls of a certain age in the 1970s would cause screams, tears, and other hysterical emotional outbursts. And on four occasions at the Mississippi River Festival, that's just what transpired.

Teen idols have been a fixture on the American scene for as long as there have been American teens. Frank Sinatra and the Beatles did the trick for previous generations, and 21st-century kids swooned for the Backstreet Boys, NSYNC, and One Direction. But the decade of the '70s brought its own steady stream of heartthrobs, whose pictures dotted bedroom walls from coast to coast.

Best known as Keith Partridge on the television show *The Partridge Family*, David Cassidy was quickly outgrowing the box he was living in and struggling to come to terms with Beatle-esque levels of teen adoration in 1972. Cassidy wanted to break free from the teen idol label and be viewed as a serious musician. Four months before his MRF appearance, Cassidy appeared nude on the cover of *Rolling Stone*, with the accompanying article disclosing his drug and alcohol use. Still, Cassidy's career was at its peak, with a pair of sellout crowds at the Houston Astrodome and a sold-out show at Madison Square Garden.

The SIUE attendance was much smaller (4,863), but no less spirited. Preteen screams filled the Edwardsville night, with some of the more excitable trying to rush the stage to get a piece of their hero.

Cassidy was accompanied by a loud, aggressive band of merchandise vendors who sold a wide array of souvenirs—programs and buttons for $1, posters for $2—from a table in the site's food service area. The large quantity of items for sale exceeded traditional MRF protocols, which allowed programs to be sold by festival staff. "I made a mistake allowing this," Ward said. "This is the last time I make an exception. This is not the type of thing we want at the festival."[155]

Despite a markup of 500 percent or more per item, the hawkers were disappointed. "We didn't do too well," said John Fowlkes, a vendor from Alabama. "The crowd was too small. A larger crowd and we could have sold some stuff."[156]

By 1975, a family act from Utah had stepped into the teen idol spotlight. The Osmonds were originally a barbershop quartet consisting of brothers Alan, Wayne, Merrill, and Jay. When younger brothers Donny and Jimmy climbed aboard, the act became a phenomenon. Donny emerged as the star, performing with his brothers and as a duo with his sister, Marie (the *Donny & Marie* television variety show would debut months after the act's first festival show).

All seven Osmonds performed at the MRF's '75 finale, presenting a "flashy show of sugar-coated rock" complete with glitter outfits, choreography, and family-friendly humor.[157] Donny elicited screams by singing "Go Away Little Girl" and "Puppy Love."

Following the concert, which drew a crowd of nearly 4,500, scores of fans gathered near the dressing room entrance, most hoping to interact for just a minute with one member of the family in particular. "We want Donny" some yelled, while others chanted "D-O-N-N-Y."[158] Gary Kochan worked MRF security from 1974 to '76, and through all of the hard rock acts and large crowds he experienced, this was the night that stood out. "As strange as it may sound, in terms of security, that was one of the toughest ones," he said. "It was all these parents with all these kids. They basically took over the backstage area. The kids and the parents were making up stories trying to get to meet Donny and Marie. You know, things like, 'I'm their cousin.' I'd have to say that was one of the hardest nights."[159]

The next year, the Osmonds returned and topped 5,000 fans. Donny and Marie expressed the kind of emotion you might expect from the wholesome brother-sister act when told that the concert had sold out its reserved seats under the tent two months in advance. "Wow!" Marie said. "That's neat!" Donny exclaimed.[160]

The scene was a repeat of the year before, with preteens running rampant across the MRF site. The Osmond siblings emerged on stage from a sea of dry-ice smoke and immediately made a statement with their choreographed dance moves and harmonies. The most popular moments were duets between Donny and Marie, whose TV variety show was now a smash hit. Their "A Little Bit Country, A Little Bit Rock 'N Roll" segment drove the kids wild.

Shari Faltus, 24 years old on this night, was in attendance. And to her great surprise, she would become the envy of thousands of young girls. "I was not even a fan of the Osmonds, but I got front-row tickets for my girlfriends' nieces," she said. "I was the only adult in the front row. Donny was singing 'Puppy Love' on our side, and I winked at him. I don't know why."

What happened next? Osmond leapt from the stage and kissed Faltus on the cheek. "All these girls were screaming," she said. "I know it was because I was the oldest one in the row, and he wasn't scared that I'd attack him."[161]

Another senior Osmonds fan went to greater lengths to meet her heroes. "Some of us were standing in the backstage area after the show," Rick Stankoven says. "There was a bus waiting for the musicians, but not the Osmonds themselves. They had already left in cars. But there was a woman in her forties or fifties who didn't know that. She had somehow managed to get past security, worked her way around the maze of things, and next thing you know, she pops out of the door right behind us. I can still picture it. She looked this way. She looked that way. She saw the bus, and she leapt off the balcony and into the shrubs. The shrubs are shaking, and she pops out the other side and throws herself at the doors of the bus.

We didn't take pictures of it because we were kind of in shock."

As the disco era exploded and changed the musical landscape, Andy Gibb took his seat on the teen idol throne. In 1978, the Bee Gees ruled the world after the meteoric success of the *Saturday Night Fever* film soundtrack. Younger brother Andy was just 20 years old that summer, but he already had two No. 1 songs to his credit—"I Just Want to Be Your Everything" and "(Love is) Thicker Than Water." His third, "Shadow Dancing," would hit the top spot within days of his MRF concert and become Billboard's No. 1 song of the year.

Scores of young fans chanted, "We want Andy! We want Andy!" in the moments leading up to Gibb's arrival on stage.[162] Each song brought waves of shrieks from the crowd, and, just before the encore, some of the more excited fans rushed the stage and tangled with security. One of the captivated young fans was Katy (Krchniak) Katzenberger, who was seated under the tent. "There were a lot of girls my age and a lot of women," she recalls. "I guess I wasn't sitting that close, but I was close enough to where I thought he was staring at me. I really loved him!"

SECTION 4
CHALLENGES
1976-77

"Most of us consider John to be the patron saint of the festival"
The Death of John Rendleman

After the disappointing 1974 season, SIUE partnered with a local advertising agency to create a campaign designed to entice groups and individuals within a fifty-mile radius to attend the festival. Posters, signs, and other touchpoints would showcase the first-ever MRF theme, "Where the stars come out at night."

"I had a student job in the Bursar's office, and I was approached by a campus photographer to pose in the new T-shirt designed to feature the theme for the MRF season," Terry Twesten remembers. "I have that photo, and a button, but only wish I still had the shirt."

The hard work paid off, as the 1975 season turned a slight profit of $1,521 and attracted 225,000 fans. "The programming was superb," John Rendleman said. "It had great appeal for a wide variety of musical and artistic tastes. I am not surprised that the average attendance was up in nearly every category. I think we have proven that the university can produce and manage the festival with success. And I believe that our seven years of experience and growing expertise in this field will enable us to develop even greater festivals in the future."[163]

A *St. Louis Post-Dispatch* editorial summed up the post-1975 air of confidence. "There is now renewed hope that the tent on the SIUE campus will continue to glow for many more summers."[164]

But behind the scenes, a tragedy was playing out that would have serious repercussions for the university and the festival. In January 1976, Rendleman was honored by the MRF board of directors for his "dynamic leadership and spirit of enthusiasm on behalf of the Mississippi River Festival." Rendleman was presented with a plaque by board member Dr.

Albert W. Trtanj, who said, "The history of the festival is known to all of us. We recognize that its success is mostly due to one individual's effort."[165]

The board knew something most of the public did not. The previous year, Rendleman learned that he had lung cancer, and despite treatment, the disease progressed rapidly. Aware of the situation, festival staff collectively signed a card for Rendleman and sent it to him during the summer of 1975. Rendleman thanked the workers through a letter to Lyle Ward. "Since the card asks how I am, just let me say that my spirits were lifted immeasurably when I received it," Rendleman wrote. "To know that I am in the thoughts of so many fine, dedicated people is rich comfort indeed. This also gives me the chance to congratulate everyone who has done so much to make the festival a success this summer. The splendid job you are doing more than justifies my confidence that the university could accept full responsibility for this great challenge. The way that you all have responded has been a grand inspiration indeed."

On March 4, 1976, John Rendleman died at the age of forty-eight. "This is a tremendous loss to the Southern Illinois University system," SIU Carbondale President Warren Brandt told the *Southern Illinoisan*. "John Rendleman's individual contributions to the development of SIU-Edwardsville have been nothing short of fantastic . . . His death represents a substantial loss to the educational world."[166]

Illinois Gov. Dan Walker added, "It is tragic news for Southern Illinois and especially for SIUE. John Rendleman really fought for the university . . . It is a real loss."[167]

During Rendleman's seven years at the helm, SIUE grew to become the largest public university in the St. Louis metropolitan area, and the Mississippi River Festival established itself as an important cultural jewel in the region's crown. On March 9, the SIUE campus was closed in Rendleman's memory, with a memorial service held that afternoon. Rendleman was survived by his wife, Lenora, and five children.

"Dad was a friendly guy—I've heard him described as avuncular," John S. Rendleman says. "He was wicked smart and had a great memory. And he was open in the sense that he wasn't afraid to show affection. As far as being the author of the MRF? I think there were several people that could claim its birthright. My Dad happened to be chancellor of the university at the time it went on, so I guess he got a lot of credit for it. But there were a lot of people working really hard to make the MRF happen. And if dad did anything right, he knew when to stand out of the way and let people do the things they were good at doing. He was a very good administrator because he recognized that if he were to have any success, it was because of the people who worked with him and for him."

Lyle Ward was one of those people. "John Rendleman always brings a smile to my face," he says. "Most of us consider John to be the patron saint of the festival. It's clear that the festival would've been discontinued as early as 1970 without his absolute support. John was the one who dealt with the legislature; he was responsible for dealing with the faculty who had concerns. He was a remarkable man and such a positive person. I was blessed to have him as a mentor so young in my life."

With Rendleman gone, SIUE Vice President and Provost Andrew J. Kochman stepped in as interim president, irrevocably altering the trajectory of the Mississippi River Festival. Within two years, the university would cede management of the MRF to an outside company. Within five years, the festival would be history.

"If John had remained healthy, it would have been a very different ending for the festival," Ward says. "Number one, he had great ownership of it. He was very proud of it, and he knew the value of it. We would have continued to have a very diverse program under some kind of management, whether it was internal or hiring someone to do it. But it would've gone on."

Jim Grandone adds, "John's reputation was riding on this festival. It was his baby and I think he made it happen as long as he was still with us."

"I guess it will be tiring, but we wanted to get to that part of the country"
Tony Award Winners Hit the Stage

Music legends weren't the only superstars to play the MRF. On a few occasions, some of the biggest names in theater made the trip to Edwardsville.

During the 1976 and 1977 seasons, the Mississippi River Festival presented four theatrical events, another example of the broad diversity the summer series offered area residents. The final show of 1976 was *Mark Twain Tonight!*, a one-man show starring Hal Holbrook.

First performed in 1954, the show featured Holbrook's depiction of Twain reciting some of the writer's beloved dramatic and comedic works. *Mark Twain Tonight!* debuted on Broadway in 1966, with Holbrook winning a Tony for the role in 1967 and earning an Emmy nomination the same year for a televised version of the show.

While in town, Holbrook spoke with SIUE drama students for two hours the evening before the performance. But on show day, Holbrook's dedication to the process was astounding—six hours of makeup, the vocal inflections, the body movements . . . at times, you would think Mark Twain was actually speaking on the stage. "There is no point here in saying that Holbrook as Twain is very good," wrote Robert Sanford in the *St. Louis Post-Dispatch*. "Everybody knows that. All there is to report is that Holbrook is still that good."[168]

The actor would remain in the role for decades, performing the show on Broadway for the final time in 2006 and retiring it in 2017. Holbrook pointed out that he had performed under the name "Mark Twain" longer than Samuel Clemens had.

The next year, real-life mother and son Viveca Lindfors and Kristoffer Tabori presented *My Mother, My Son*, a play focused on difficult familial relationships, in the Communications Building Theater. Tabori was the product of Lindfors' five-year marriage to Don Siegel, who directed five films with Clint Eastwood (including 1971's *Dirty Harry*) and John Wayne's last film, 1976's *The Shootist*.

Also, in 1977, a leading portrayer of Shakespeare's works came to town. Sir Michael Redgrave had been a fixture on the British stage since the 1930s, making his debut at London's Old Vic Theater in 1936 and performing in *Hamlet* the next year alongside Sir Laurence Olivier. Over the next 40 years, Redgrave became one of the world's foremost Shakespearean actors, receiving his knighthood in 1959.

Presented under the tent for three nights, *Shakespeare's People* included segments from numerous plays (including *Hamlet*, *King Lear*, and *Romeo and Juliet*) performed by Redgrave and actors from the American Conservatory Theatre of San Francisco. The MRF events marked the American premiere of the show and served as warm-ups before the production headed for Broadway. But the combined crowd of less than 1,400 for the three nights was a disappointment. "How often do Midwesterners get the chance to see a talented group of Shakespearean actors present vignettes from the Bard's works?" asked the *Alton Telegraph's* Doug Thompson. "Not often enough. With crowds like the three hundred who turned out Thursday night . . . it's no wonder. It is a comment on the community when shows like *Shakespeare's People* can't draw enough paying customers to even pay the utility bills."[169]

Aside from Redgrave, the biggest star of the weekend may have been SIUE theater department scenery artist Larry Bogdan. Hours before Thursday's opening show, a 12ft. x 12ft. linen backdrop featuring Shakespeare and some of his best-known characters was stolen from the MRF site. A substitute carpet filled the space for Thursday's show, but, by Friday night, Bogdan and three students—Sue McKinna of Edwardsville, Rodney Masinelli of St. Louis, and Ken Bryant of Belleville—had painted a replica backdrop for the final two shows. "Fortunately, I had a four-color photograph of the tapestry, which I very rarely carry with me," said Bernard Jay, co-producer of *Shakespeare's People*. "The (SIUE theater) art department unbelievably quickly had an excellent copy painted."[170]

In fact, Bogdan and his team worked Thursday afternoon and all Friday to complete the piece. "We didn't even take a lunch break," Bogdan said. "We worked on straight through 'til it was finished."[171]

Things got even more complicated when Bogdan received a phone call from his wife. "When the actors were talking to me (about the original), my wife called and said she had to go to the hospital, but said it wasn't that serious, and she told me, 'Go on and finish the backdrop,' he said. "It was a day of days![172]

Despite the intense effort, Bogdan felt the result was less than perfect. But it did the job. "A couple of the road people said it looked better than the original," he said. "I didn't see the original, so I couldn't say."[173]

If an award for MRF dedication was presented to a headliner, it might go to American actress Julie Harris, who went to monumental lengths to bring her one-woman play, *The Belle of Amherst*, to Edwardsville in 1976.

Producers had been striving to bring *The Belle of Amherst* to St. Louis but had run into logistical issues finding a theater. Harris was performing the show on Broadway, with an open date on June 28. As fate would have it, a scheduled MRF show on that date was postponed. Now, the stars had aligned. "We could have worked for 12 months to get this here, and it happened in three days," Concert Manager Vicky Holt said.[174]

A replica of the show's Broadway set was constructed on the festival stage as Harris prepared to travel from New York to Edwardsville and back to New York. "I guess it will be tiring," she said in advance of the trek. "But we wanted to get to that part of the country."[175]

Written by William Luce and directed by *Match Game* regular Charles Nelson Reilly, the play centered on the life and works of poet Emily Dickinson and was set in her Amherst, Massachusetts, home. The role would earn Harris one of her five Tony Awards.

Through his obvious connection as son of the director of University Food Services, Bill Craft had a unique perch for the evening's events—he was tabbed to serve dinner to the Broadway legend. "She had been in a movie our family liked called *The Hiding Place*," Craft recalls. "My father asked if I wanted to take the food to her dressing room. I did get paid, but it probably wasn't much, and I did have to put on a penguin suit.

"I knocked on the door and said, 'Miss Harris, I've got your supper. Where would you like it?' She asked for it to be placed on a table, so I did, and I said, 'Well, if there's nothing else, I guess I'll go.' And she said, 'No, you can stay.' I'm standing by the door, not sure what to do, so I said, 'I saw you in *The Hiding Place*; you did a good job.' She said, 'Thank you.' I said, 'What did you think about doing that part?' And she said, 'Well, I realized that it's terrible the way human beings can treat each other,' because that movie was about a concentration camp. I waited while she ate, and when she was done, I took her plate and flatware. She said, 'Thank you,' and I left. No one else was there—just her and me. The whole encounter was 20 to 30 minutes, tops."

During the play, Harris (as Dickinson) shared the recipe for a cake. And on the Broadway stage, the role of the cake was played by a prop. But the MRF took things up a notch with an actual cake. "Can you imagine they baked it from Emily's own recipe?" Harris told a reporter backstage before an early-morning flight back to the Big Apple. "On Broadway, we just use a Sara Lee cake, but this is a real fruitcake; I'm so glad I came."[176]

Craft was unaware of that detail. "My dad probably had that done," he says. "He was a stickler for details when it came to food, and he had a professional baker working for him. I don't remember if my dad told me about that; I don't think I knew."

The clock ticked past midnight. With the interview completed, Harris gave the bouquets of flowers in her dressing room to festival staff and headed off to catch a few hours of sleep before flying back to Broadway.

"I get a little miffed because he's rarely mentioned"
Bill Crabb and University Food Services

No matter the event, be it Grateful Dead, the St. Louis Symphony, Buck Owens, or the National Dance Troupe of Zambia, there was a common thread among all MRF events—refreshments. The staff of SIUE Food Services—along with students from SIUE and area high schools—worked diligently to supervise, prepare, and serve food and beverages on the festival grounds.

This was a task of staggering proportions. For example, more than 67,000 cups of soda were sold during the 1971 season. Food options that summer included box dinners of chicken, fish, shrimp, roast beef, or ribeye steak, which sold for between $1.30 and $1.75 apiece. Each box included cole slaw, French fries, and a roll. Individual items such as hamburgers, hot dogs, sandwiches, and barbecue beef were available, as were snacks like peanuts, popcorn, and watermelon. And for those with a sweet tooth, the list of dessert options was a long one: ice cream sundaes, cupcakes, caramel corn, candy apples, Twinkies, and Cracker Jack (the university was reported to be the largest single retail outlet in the U.S. for Cracker Jack one MRF summer).

Food Services Director Bill Crabb noted the difference in eating habits between popular music fans and classical aficionados. "On rock nights, we sell more hamburgers, hot dogs, and Cracker Jack," he said. "On symphony nights, we sell more box meals and sandwiches."[177]

Ward adds, "Food was seen as part of the evening's experience. We had a great Food Service Director, Bill Crabb, who had been with the university from its inception. He could present the wide variety of food we wanted—from nights with the symphony and major picnic functions we did, to the popcorn and hot dogs that the young people wanted. He was very important."

In addition, particularly on symphony nights, it was common to see couples spread out on blankets on the lawn with bottles of wine, cheese, and other upscale snacks brought from home. But The Who's 1971 visit was definitely not a Brie and crackers sort of night. Back on the lawn that evening was 15-year-old Bill Craft, a student at Edwardsville High School and Crabb's son. "On some nights, I would work for an hour or so and then he'd let me wander around and watch the concert," Craft says. "I didn't make any money, but I got in. That night, we were just pouring soft drinks as fast as we could."

Since this was an evening when roles and responsibilities were tossed out the window, Crabb was sent to perform a very non-food service task. "There were a lot of gate crashers that night," Craft recalls. "I was helping out at the food service tent, handing out food and packing boxes. One of the administrators came in and said, 'We think we're going to have a rush on one of the fences. If we can get enough of us men to stand on the other side, maybe it will deter them.' So, my dad and a couple of his managers went over and stood in front of this section of fence. All of these guys were massing behind it, and they finally pushed forward, knocked down a section of fence, and came running in. They just ran past my dad and all the other guys. There was nothing they could do. My dad laughed about it when he was telling me. I said, 'Were you able to stop anybody?' He said, 'No, I tripped a few, but that's it.'"

As noted in the Julie Harris story, another responsibility for University Food Service was to feed the stars, a job that may seem daunting but usually wasn't. "People fantasize that touring rock bands, actors and actresses, and singers have terribly exotic tastes in terms of food," Concert Manager Vicky Holt said during the '76 season. "Actually, we haven't had any unusual requests from our performers for way-out food."[178]

Holt said performers were viewed as guests, and therefore, officials would go to great lengths to get them what they wanted—aside from beer or liquor. Standard beverages for artists and their crews included soft drinks, juice, coffee, and mineral water, while some requested tea with honey and lemon. A buffet, directed by MRF Food Manager Eleanor Alexander, included turkey, ham, roast beef, cheeses, bread, salads, potato chips, cole slaw, and fresh fruit. A few artists, including Todd Rundgren and the Winter Brothers (Johnny and Edgar), requested vegetarian dinners.

Feedback was generally positive. "We got the greatest compliments from Miss Harris, Benny Goodman, the Spinners, and Emmylou Harris," Holt said. "They all said they want to come back here and perform again because the atmosphere and food were excellent. It makes it worth all of the time and effort to get such appreciation."[179]

"My dad did a fantastic job," Craft adds. "I get a little miffed because whenever I read these histories of SIU, he's rarely mentioned. The school had many different administrators and lots of professors, but there was only one food service director (from 1965 to 1992). Everybody that went to college there probably set foot in the dining room, but his job also included vending machines, sports venues, the University Club restaurant, banquets, and catering . . . everything on campus. And my dad was there for just about every MRF event. He wouldn't get home until midnight. It was extra work, but he never complained. I never heard him say, 'Oh, I gotta go to the MRF tonight.' That was just the job."

"It still makes the hair stand up on the back of my neck"
Marshall Tucker Leads a Southern Invasion as Unruly Behavior Increases

The back half of the '70s was a time when artists from south of the Mason-Dixon line stormed northward to sell millions of records and play live before enormous audiences. Likely because of its geographic location in the nation's center, St. Louis-area rock fans have always had a soft spot for rock artists who infuse their sound with a tinge of country. Groups that couldn't get noticed in certain parts of the country would sell out large venues in the Midwest.

Several of the most prominent southern rock bands made stops at SIUE. Large crowds followed, but often, increased rowdiness came along as well. "That southern music—people get really rowdy for southern music," said fan and Washington University student Mike McCleod in 1979. Fellow attendee Denise Balazic of Columbia, Missouri, agreed. "I think it has a lot to do with the particular message of the music. That's like 'get drunk' music."[180]

Spartanburg, South Carolina's Marshall Tucker Band, was an MRF favorite, playing three well-attended festival shows that were some of the most boisterous in the festival's 12 seasons. Led by brothers Tommy and Toy Caldwell and lead vocalist Doug Gray, the band emerged in 1973 with a gold debut album and the hit "Can't You See." Tireless road warriors, Marshall Tucker toured the world and built a loyal following. Shortly after their first MRF show in 1976, the band would release *Carolina Dreams*, which would quickly go platinum and introduce the Top 20 hit, "Heard it in a Love Song."

It was a stormy night, and the lightning flashing across the summer sky was accompanied by the thunder of one of the MRF's louder performances. Tucker favorites such as "Fire on the Mountain" and "Take the Highway" brought big cheers, and the band closed with an encore of "Will the Circle be Unbroken?" Though the concert was a success by most indications, Marshall Tucker drummer Paul Riddle wasn't satisfied. "I really had a terrible night," he said.[181]

It was also a terrible night for festival staff and a few attendees. One fan from St. Louis was stabbed and hospitalized at St. Elizabeth's Hospital in Granite City, while Dan Buck, son of St. Louis Cardinals broadcaster Jack Buck, was beaten by a large group of men and required 12 stitches to his face. Gary Gunter, Director of University Police, said the incidents were the worst he had seen in the festival's eight seasons.[182]

The "Tucker boys"—as Charlie Daniels immortalized them in song—
returned in 1978, the first show under post-SIUE management, and a crowd
estimated at twenty thousand turned out. Their final MRF concerts the
next summer were held on consecutive nights, the first such arrangement
in festival history. Shortly before going on stage the first night, Gray was
asked if his group would still be playing together 10 years from now. "Yeah,"
he said. "A real big yeah. 'Cuz hell, I don't know how to do anything else."[183]
Gray was right—the band would continue, with multiple lineup changes,
well into the 21st century.

A visit from Southern rockers such as the Marshall Tucker Band, the
Allman Brothers, the Outlaws, or the Charlie Daniels Band was sure to
draw a big crowd. And it was a virtual certainty that John S. Rendleman
and his group of friends would be sitting on the lawn, right of the stage, in
an area locals referred to as the "Edwardsville Side."

"As I got into high school and started really appreciating the music that
was being played at MRF, I may have had some residual pride that my
father was a part of it, but mostly, I was trying to find friends who would
want to go to the concerts with me," Rendleman says. "I found a regular
group who were interested in the fact that I could get tickets and, more
importantly, parking passes so you could drive in the back and park easily
and just walk up to your seats.

"We would all pile into my mother's big Chrysler New Yorker. I never
thought it was a good idea to try to pull rank on anybody, but we had my
mother's car so we could park in back because the parking lots in front were
filled. We rolled up to the gate one time, and the guy stops me and says,
'Who are you?' I said, 'Well, I'm John Rendleman, Jr.' He didn't believe it. I
said, 'Well, look at the license plates.' My mother's license plates were 'JSR
1' because my dad had a little vanity. The guy looked and realized, 'Yep, this
is the president's kid. Better let him through.' I didn't generally do that, and
it was a little awkward. But I'll tell you what, if it meant parking within a
hundred yards of backstage or going around two miles to the parking lot, I
got over that pretty quickly."

Michael Hammonds was a member of Rendleman's group, and those
festival shows with his friends opened the door to new experiences and

lifelong memories. "My uncles used to listen to blues and that kind of stuff, but I never did go to any concerts," Hammonds recalls. "I would listen to KSLQ, which was kind of a pop station because they played both Black and white music, but I would never go to concerts. Then, around my sophomore year in high school, we'd go to parties, and they would play Marshall Tucker and bands like that. Well, it was great music. All of a sudden, they started showing up at the MRF, so we would all go for $3 to sit on the lawn."

As a young Black man, Hammonds estimates he was outnumbered "about two thousand to one" at the southern rock shows. "There were a couple other Black guys who would go to the rock concerts, but we were in the minority," he says. "But I would go with my group of friends, and I knew they would protect me with their lives. Nobody would say anything nine times out of ten. Every now and then, somebody would say, 'Man, what are you doing here? Why are you here?' You know, they'd throw an 'N bomb' out a couple times, sure. But then I would do a risk assessment—'OK, if I jump on him, I'm sure he's got five or six people around that are going to do something.' So yeah, I just dealt with it. My personality is not the kind to jump on somebody anyway. But my memories are good. It didn't stop me from going."

Another member of the group, Andy Kovarik, reflects on one moment in particular—a perfect summation of his teenage years at the MRF. "There's one thing I can remember like it was yesterday," he says. "We all had lawn tickets for Marshall Tucker, but one of us had a single tent seat. So, we alternated going down there to listen to a couple songs each, and then the next person would go down. As soon as it was my turn, I went down and they started playing '24 Hours at a Time,' which was one of my favorite songs. It was a perfect night—there was a nice, cool breeze blowing through the tent, just blowing your hair a little bit, and Toy and Tommy Caldwell were just cranking up there. It was just awesome. I'll never forget it. It still makes the hair stand up on the back of my neck."

Today, some forty-five years later, Hammonds is still friends with Rendleman and Kovarik, and he still listens to southern rock. "I know all those bands," Hammonds says. "Even to this day, on my iPod, I have the southern rock and the '70s stuff that I listened to. People at work say, 'Man, what are you listening to? What is that?' I say, 'Man, this is the best music of all time. What are you talking about?' I listen to everything—I think I'm just well-rounded. But that time was just magical."

Musically, maybe. But from a crowd behavior standpoint, it was clear times were changing. By the mid-to-late 1970s, the "peace and love" days were a distant memory. A new audience was coming to the MRF, with a small segment interested in causing trouble. "The responsibility of that generation in 1969 and the early '70s seemed to shift a little bit," Ward notes.

To be fair, minor unrest at the MRF wasn't a new phenomenon. Thousands of people gathering for a night of revelry—often fueled by alcohol and drugs—created the perfect blend for the occasional brawl or car break-in. As early as 1971, university officials were growing concerned with the use of drugs on-site during certain events. Before the 1973 season, tough new rules were implemented, designed to discourage alcohol consumption on festival grounds. The MRF board passed a clampdown on guests bringing their own alcohol, especially beverages in disposable containers. Signs were posted at parking lots and shuttle bus stops notifying fans of the new guidance, and additional verbiage was added to tickets. Those attempting to circumvent the rules were stopped at the front gate. "What we want to do is curtail the use of alcohol and stop the possibility of injuries at the same time," Ward said.[184]

The first '73 crowd to top ten thousand was headlined by Sha Na Na, and the new guidance was met with mixed reviews. "This ruins the whole thing," one fan told Merrill Brown of the *St. Louis Post-Dispatch*. "People come out here to have a good time. The more rules they have, the less people feel at ease." Another crowd member asked, "If you're old enough to buy it, why can't you come here and have a few beers?"[185]

The clampdown may have kept some beer and wine bottles out of the venue, but resourceful fans still found creative ways to sneak in their contraband. Brown reported that one fan stuffed a bottle of wine into a whole chicken, while a girl hid a bottle in her jeans. Others just poured liquor into soda bottles. "I shouldn't tell you or everybody will start doing it," one fan admitted.[186]

Working the crowd on most popular concert evenings was the Crisis Intervention Unit. Based on St. Louis' Acid Rescue group, this team of volunteers dressed in white T-shirts adorned with a green peace symbol and a red cross assisted overserved fans who needed help. "Sometimes we tripped over a kid," one of the volunteers said after the 1973 Manassas show. "If they didn't move or cuss us out, then we knew they were really out of it and needed some help."[187]

On a busy evening, a few dozen fans could be treated by the unit, whose members were trained in first aid and knowledgeable about the effects of various substances. More serious cases were transferred to St. Elizabeth's Hospital in Granite City. SIUE students Larry Richie and Randy Thompson started the group in time for the 1973 season, and by 1974, the CIU had been formally recognized as a student campus organization. "Our general feeling is everyone has the right to help, and everyone has a right to a friend," said Kristina Madison, CIU Secretary. "The stand we take is not so much one against drug use but against drug abuse."[188]

Greg Drexelius, who saw his share of inebriated fans over five summers working under the tent, compliments the CIU's work. "If someone was impaired by drugs or alcohol, we were told to help them however we could and keep them safe," he says. "If we knew they had friends there, we would get them back to their friends so they could take care of them. But if it went beyond that, the Crisis Intervention team was great. They really handled things well out there, and they didn't get all the credit they deserved for what they did. That was really a thankless job in some ways, but they really did a great job."

In an effort to boost attendance, festival officials tweaked the alcohol guidelines again prior to the 1975 season, allowing alcoholic beverages provided they were in plastic containers or thermos bottles—no glass allowed. "It certainly will increase our attendance," Ward said. "Last year, people who wanted to have a picnic were offended by not being able to bring a bottle of wine into the site. We want to get that type of image out of the festival this year."[189]

Jack Twesten was working at the front gate that summer. "We had a bunch of empty milk cartons, and as security stopped people, we would pour their alcohol into empty milk cartons so they could bring it in," he remembers.

But occasional incidents continued to pop up, particularly over a four-week stretch during the summer of 1976. Concerts by Johnny and Edgar Winter, the Doobie Brothers and Heart, and the Nitty Gritty Dirt Band saw arrests for underage drinking and disorderly conduct, and a few injuries from fights and thrown bottles. Interim SIUE President Andrew Kochman, Security Chief Gary Gunter, and Ward met to determine how large concerts could be made safer. Within days, security and police patrols were stepped up at select festival events.

The situation was becoming a hot topic throughout the Metro East. In its Citizen Sound-Off section, the *Belleville News-Democrat* asked its readers to call in, vote, and leave comments on the question, "Should rock concerts be discontinued at the Mississippi River Festival?" On July 22, the results were published, and it was a landslide: more than eighty-eight percent of respondents voted "No." Among those voting "Yes" for canceling the rock concerts, comments included: "Rock music and drugs go together," "I think the drug-taking kids have ruined the MRF for everybody," and "We have enough trouble raising our kids without having something like that."

"No" comments included: "That's the only way the MRF makes any money," "A mountain has been made out of a molehill," "Young people need some form of entertainment, too," and "If anyone looks for trouble, he can find it anywhere."[190]

In response to the shifting environment, festival officials instituted big changes for the 1977 season—fewer big-name artists would be on the schedule and alcohol was banned. "Our biggest problem is the image the festival now has with the community," Kochman said. "We have to change that image to bring the people back. I think the changes we are making will help do that. I have great hopes for what will happen this season. I don't make it a habit to associate myself with failures. I may have had some personal failures in my career, but the projects I work on are successes. I don't intend for this to be my first failure."[191]

By 1978, SIUE was no longer running the festival, but some of these same issues remained for their successor to deal with. Today, Ward reflects on one of the very few negative facets of the Mississippi River Festival. "When you have as many as thirty thousand people, you naturally have a different kind of crowd, and they're bringing different kinds of alcohol. It created more and more problems as the crowds grew and the number of events grew. So, as time went on, we first had to eliminate people bringing in certain containers of alcohol and then, finally, alcoholic beverages of all kinds. That was unfortunate, but it was a reflection of what was going on from 1969 through the mid-70s."

It's important to keep things in perspective—despite the troubling incidents of violent behavior, the vast majority of attendees at an MRF rock show were there for a good time and returned home safe and sound. "I know in 1978, when I started driving, me and my friends would go out there all the time," Buddy Fendler says. "We probably were on the lawn for every good show that summer. Crime? I never saw anything like that. Everybody was always partying, you know? We all sat around and had a good old time. I'm sure there was a fight or two here and there that I never really paid attention to, but it was probably just two drunk guys. It wasn't any big brawls or people pulling out guns and knives and shooting and killing each other."

Andy Kovarik agrees. "Oh, there were a few fistfights here and there. That just gave the critics something to jump on and say the MRF was a den of iniquity."

"I felt like David Freese hitting that home run in the World Series"
Michael "Supe" Granda Goes from Lawn to Stage

Mississippi River Festival experiences could vary greatly depending on what side of the fence you were on. Those who sat on the lawn had a different perspective from those who performed on the stage. But a St. Louis native named Michael "Supe" Granda is one of the few who can relate to both ends of the spectrum.

"Growing up in St. Louis and being a music nut, I'd been to Kiel and the Checkerdome and maybe the Fox, but the sound usually wasn't very good,"

Granda recalls. "But then they said, 'We're gonna have this thing called the River Festival on the campus over in Edwardsville, Illinois.' I was like, 'Put me in coach! Count me in!'"

Granda was an MRF regular from the very first season, enjoying nights on the lawn with friends and seeing Paul Butterfield, The Who, Grateful Dead, and many others over the festival's first few summers. "We were outside, there were stars in the sky, and we could just put blankets on the hillside and hear music," he says. "When I walked in the first time I said, 'I've died and gone to heaven.' When I left that night, I just couldn't wait until the next concert."

A few years later, Granda moved from St. Louis, settling in Springfield, Missouri, picking up the bass, and co-founding the Ozark Mountain Daredevils. By 1976, the band was established, with a pair of successful singles—"If You Wanna Get to Heaven" and the No. 3 hit, "Jackie Blue." They were ready to headline at the MRF before a crowd of nearly eleven thousand.

"The first time I played the Mississippi River Festival, it was like I was on acid or something because I'd been going for so many years walking in the front gate. This time, when I went around through the back and got out, I went, 'Man, this is actually happening. I'm actually going to play the river festival,'" Granda recalls. "For years, I'd been telling my bandmates about this festival. To receive an invitation to play it was an absolute dream come true. It was the thrill of a lifetime for a kid from St. Louis. I felt like David Freese, hitting that home run in the World Series at Busch Stadium—'Hometown kid fulfills boyhood dream.'"

Granda and the Daredevils would return to the festival three more times. "Each time, the thrill was immense, just like the first time," Granda says. "One magical moment when we played the MRF? There wasn't one, there were four. After you play there a couple times, you go, 'Oh boy, we're gonna play the MRF. Oh, we're playing the MRF in September.' You start gearing up for it in July. Then, all of a sudden, it's August. Then it's two weeks away. 'I just can't wait. We're gonna play, we're gonna play.' These other gigs? We're just gonna play those until we get to the MRF. The MRF was the absolute pinnacle of every one of those Daredevil tours. It compelled me to play my ass off. It compelled all of us to play our asses off. Nothing will ever replace the Mississippi River Festival."

"I'll get the tape rolling. You guys do whatever the hell you wanna do" Tales from the Holiday Inn

It may not have been a five-star hotel with all the bells and whistles the nation's top entertainers were accustomed to. But if you were playing the Mississippi River Festival, more often than not, your home in Edwardsville would be the Holiday Inn.

Although Bob Hope was famous enough to stay at the Chase Park Plaza in St. Louis, he didn't miss the chance to have a little fun at the local hotel's expense during his 1977 MRF performance. "Bob Hope said, 'I've been to a lot of hotels where you can hear the couple in the next room through the walls. But I've never been in one with walls so thin you can see through them,'" Jim Grandone says. "He was talking about the Holiday Inn."

Located at 3080 State Route 157, high on a bluff adjacent to the SIUE campus, the Holiday Inn looms large in the festival's history for many reasons. But none is more notable than the August 17-18, 1977, stay of Jackson Browne.

Browne made his MRF debut in 1972, opening for Yes. The relative newcomer from Southern California had just released his self-titled debut album after getting his start writing songs for other artists. Hits "Doctor My Eyes" and "Rock Me on the Water" garnered radio airplay and introduced an integral figure of what would become the California Sound later in the decade. The next year, Browne returned to the festival on a bill fronted by America, playing songs from his second album *For Everyman*. The first LP to feature longtime Browne sidekick David Lindley, the album kicked off with "Take It Easy," a song co-written by Browne and Glenn Frey that had been a No. 12 hit for the Eagles in 1972. At SIUE, Browne dedicated his song "Redneck Friend" to local fundamentalist Bill Mars, who was making waves at the time by calling rock music the work of the devil. "What (Mars) is doing is so totally ridiculous," Browne said after the concert. "I thought

I should do something."[192]

Then came the 1977 visit. In the annals of the MRF, there are a few specific moments that stand above the rest. This was certainly one, although not for anything that happened on stage. While touring the U.S. that summer, Browne was creating something unique for his fifth album. Focused on the theme of life on the road, the album—later named *Running on Empty*—would feature songs recorded live in concert, as well as on buses, in hotel rooms, and in other locations on tour. This brings us back to the Edwardsville Holiday Inn.

Following his August 17 MRF show, Browne and crew decided the hotel would be the perfect place to record a couple of songs for the new album. Backed by Lindley and the ace session musicians from the Section, Browne settled into room 124 and recorded the songs "Cocaine" and "Shaky Town" before leaving town the next day. Right there in the album's liner notes, memorialized forever, is Edwardsville's most famous hotel:

5. Cocaine (4:55)
(Rev. Gary Davis)
Recorded in room 124 at the Holiday Inn, Edwardsville, Illinois – 8/17/77. Additional lyrics by Jackson Browne and Glenn Frey.

6. Shakey Town (3:36)
(Daniel Kortchmar)
Recorded in room 124 at the Holiday Inn, Edwardsville, Illinois – 8/18/77. The author sings harmony.

A third song recorded during Browne's stay, "Edwardsville Room 124," was included as a bonus track on a 2005 remastered version of the album.

Rance Caldwell, audio engineer for touring services provider Showco, was on the road with Browne that summer and worked the MRF show. But because of the nature of Browne's new album, he knew he would never be completely off the clock. "It was a rather lengthy call because when we were not performing, we were actually tracking stuff for this album," Caldwell said. "We went out in the woods behind the pavilion and recorded crickets and lizards and tree frogs and all kinds of things, you know, just to have some background and ambient noises."

And when the scene shifted to the Holiday Inn, the work continued. "We set up a couple of adjoining rooms—mine being one—with recording equipment in one room and a rehearsal space or tracking space in the other," Caldwell said. "We took the beds and turned them up against the wall and put the drum kit in there and a couple of guitars for Jackson. We ran all the wires and cables and the microphone snakes and everything back into my room, where it was my job to keep it rolling and make sure it all was tracked and recorded. That was my job, whether I wanted it or not—whenever they were in the room noodling around or playing or whatever, it was my job to make sure all that stuff was captured on tape, which was a full-time job.

"It was really a labor of love. I'm in the shower. 'Yeah. Yeah. I'll get it, I'll get the tape rolling. You guys just do whatever the hell you want to do,' you know? But, at the end of it, when it finally came out, and it was a million-selling record, to realize that some of that stuff that I captured in my hotel room was on there was kind of a gratifying thing. There's a lot of magical moments that I can say, 'I put my fingers on that knob at that moment,' you know, and that's kind of a little timepiece."

Also viewing the proceedings was J'Deanna Twesten. "They all went in the hotel rooms, and I was pretty outgoing, so I'm like, 'Oh, I'll go in there with you,'" she remembers with a laugh. "They moved the stuff around in the room, and I sat there watching. The recording equipment was set up, and they placed the mattresses against the wall to make more space for the many people and instruments in the crowded room. By being there, I realized how recording songs is very different from hearing a performance on stage, with the starting, stopping, and refinements. I felt like I was a witness to their creative process."

Released in December 1977, *Running on Empty* would reach No. 3 on the album chart and receive a Grammy nomination for Album of the Year. Browne's best-selling album, it would reach the level of seven-times platinum.

Poco lead singer Rusty Young had memories of the Holiday Inn, too.

But his were less celebratory and more bittersweet. "I remember pulling up to the Holiday Inn in August 1973 and seeing 'Welcome Poco' on the large sign out front. We thought, 'Oh, this is gonna be fun because now everyone knows where we're staying. This will be really fun tonight!'"

It was during this stay, hours before a festival concert with Loggins and Messina and Jim Croce, that Young would have a poignant dinner he would never forget. "I have one vivid memory of the festival," he said. "We had done a number of shows with Jim, and he was a real sweet guy. If you look at pictures, he looked rough, but he was just a sweetheart. And I remember Jim and I met up for dinner at the Holiday Inn. We talked about what he was going to do and where he was going. He was having all these hit records, but he was a little frustrated because he was still opening shows for bands. We just had a great time. And then, it was maybe a month later that he was in that plane crash and died. I felt really fortunate that I got to have an hour where Jim and I could sit there, just the two of us, and have dinner and talk and really get close before he had that plane wreck, which has killed so many rock and rollers. That's what I remember most about the festival."

The Holiday Inn was ground zero for post-concert revelry, and, not surprisingly, the party following The Who concert was one of the most notorious. "There were fleets of limousines, and we all just jumped into whatever limousine was available and zoomed off to the hotel," Andy Powell of Wishbone Ash remembered. "We were on the second floor hanging out with Pete (Townshend), and he thought it was really strange that I brought my wife along on the tour. I remember him leaping over the railing, running across the lawn, and diving into the pool fully clothed. There was just mayhem at the hotel. I mean, Moon was blowing up toilets! Then, we were back in the rooms drinking cognac. I can remember that lots of women were around. John Entwistle was walking around filming everything, probably with a Super 8 camera."

Bryan Erdmann says the Holiday Inn was notorious among MRF staff as the place to be for post-concert merriment. "Most of the time, the road crews wanted to rest because they had another long night ahead of them. But they really liked to party after the load out, and there were a lot of parties out at Holiday Inn. That's where most of the MRF partying was done. I never went to one. I was told that I should have gone to the one for Jackson Browne. If I had heard about it at the time, I'd have gone."

The hotel was also a site for impromptu fan interactions. In 1975, university employee Connie Schmidt and her mother met Mac Davis as he departed for his next gig in Philadelphia. "We found out he was staying at the Holiday Inn, so we went there to have him sign an autograph," Schmidt said. "We just waited outside his room. They were getting ready to leave, but he stopped and talked to us anyway. He was very nice."[193]

One night after America had played under the tent, Michael Hammonds was attending a post-concert party at the hotel when he headed to the restroom to answer nature's call. "I was standing at the urinal, and the guy from America who wore glasses (Gerry Beckley) was at the next urinal," he says. "I didn't know much about America, but I said, 'Man, you look familiar.' He said he was so and so from America and that they had played that night." Hammonds laughs, "I was looking up, not down!"

J'Deanna Twesten also met America at the Holiday Inn. "I was often at the swimming pool, and some of the band members were sitting around the pool. I recognized them from photos. They seemed like nice guys, and we started talking music and about the St. Louis area. After a while, one of the guys asked if I could drive them to pick up some cigarette papers because they didn't have a car available to them. So, the four of us jumped into my Buick, and I drove them to Ballweg's Drug Store at Montclaire shopping center."

Also visiting the Holiday Inn pool was Daryl Dragon, the "Captain" of Captain and Tennille fame. "He seemed like a light-hearted, funny guy," Twesten says. "He smiled a lot, and he wore his trademark captain's hat that he wore on stage as he sat by the pool."

Rick Haydon spent a memorable afternoon at the Holiday Inn pool with George Benson. "I went to the concert and hung out backstage with him and his band, and they invited me to the hotel the next day," he says. "I went, and the whole band was sitting around the pool. I sat and talked to George Benson for two hours at the Holiday Inn, right here in my backyard. That's what I tell people. That all came to me right here. I was a poor kid from

East Alton. There was no way I was going to get to New York. It was hard for me to get to St. Louis to see a show. For folks here, we were country, you know? We were isolated. And for all that to come here, I'll be forever thankful that it happened."

On a few occasions, the Holiday Inn played host to disorderly—and even criminal—behavior. Virgil Fox was one of the most acclaimed organists of all time, best known for his Heavy Organ act that consisted of a bombastic performance of Bach compositions played on the organ accompanied by a psychedelic "Revelation Lights" show. But those in the house for the 1973 performance almost didn't get to enjoy the experience. Two nights before the concert, a truck containing $30,000 in special effects equipment was stolen from the parking lot of the Holiday Inn. The truck was later discovered in the Bellefontaine Neighbors section of North St. Louis County, some 20 miles away, minus a projection screen and a briefcase.

The Allman Brothers' well-earned reputation as a marauding band of miscreants was on full display at the Holiday Inn in 1979. The band and its crew had booked 23 rooms at the hotel, and guests in six of those rooms had not checked out by the noon deadline. A disturbance ensued, with Gregg Allman and the band's road manager at the center of it, scuffling with hotel staff. Madison County Sheriff's deputies were called, everything was sorted out, and the Allman Brothers entourage finally checked out of the remaining rooms and boarded the bus for their next show in Ohio.

J'Deanna Twesten had a much more civil interaction with Gregg Allman at the hotel. "I walked into the bar and saw him sitting alone at the bar having a drink. I walked up and sat next to him to see if he might speak with me. He said hi, and we talked about music. At 18, I saw myself as a kid. I didn't expect he would give me his time and attention."

What became of the Edwardsville Holiday Inn? When the MRF drifted into history in 1980, the hotel began to fade. After becoming a Knights Inn, the building was torn down on November 15, 1993. Today, a hotel still sits on the site of the Holiday Inn, but now it's a Comfort Inn.

Mississippi
River
Festival

SECTION 5
DEMISE
1978-80

"We will become a valuable part of this community"
SIUE Hands Festival Management to Nederlander, Inc.

Since the death of John Rendleman, the financial picture of the Mississippi River Festival had changed very little. The deficit from the 1976 season was estimated at $178,617—about $104,000 owed to the university and $74,000 owed in bills and other services. Lyle Ward pointed to five canceled shows, bad weather, competition from large rock shows in St. Louis, and disorderly incidents as factors in the disappointing financial picture. While he expressed optimism that financial backing would soon be found, it seemed clear that, without a new strategy, the MRF's future was bleak.[194]

Should a 1977 season come to fruition, Ward said the policy of having pop and rock concerts subsidize lower-attended fine arts programming and shows should be discontinued. "Now is the time to define our level of programming—how much fine arts we can realistically afford to support with the resources we have available. Rock concerts are no longer the golden egg they were in earlier years. If we continue the festival, a number of changes have to be made."[195]

The plan to save the festival included fewer shows and fewer "contemporary" concerts. Acts that might attract larger crowds would not be booked. Lesser-known artists would be brought in based on merit, not their ability to sell tickets. In reflecting the new path forward, organizers cut the MRF's budget in half and put a cap on crowd size at 17,000. "It is unusual to be in a situation of limiting attendance," Ward admitted.[196]

In the opinion of the *Alton Telegraph's* Doug Thompson, the changes were for the better. "MRF '77 is shorter, quieter, and less innovative than previous seasons, but the management has managed to maintain some balance between the quest for quality and the realities of financing," he wrote. "In making the sacrifices, the MRF has come closer to establishing an identity and appears to have given up any pretensions as either a serious music festival or a multi-faceted entertainment extravaganza. What's left is an attractive, and far more promising, season."[197]

But back at the *Belleville News-Democrat* Citizen Sound-Off, the changes were not as warmly embraced. Responding to the question, "Do you think the lineup of artists for the Mississippi River Festival is a good one?" More than 86 percent of those who called to register their opinion voted "No." The responses were all over the map: "They need more women." "They should have some easy listening groups." "They have no groups that appeal to the older generation." "They should have a few more good rock groups."[198]

The alterations didn't work as hoped. Yes, attendance was down in '77—but it was much lower than expected. One MRF board member sounded a portentous note. "We will have to make the big decision: Can we afford to go on? I can't speak for the other members of the board, but I'm pretty sick of trying. I don't know if it is worth it anymore."[199]

October brought the painful truth—the 1977 season ran $118,000 in debt, and now the MRF owed SIUE more than $270,000 in total. This marked seven of nine festival seasons ending in the red. Attendance was 103,475, lower than the projected 135,000. The timing couldn't have been worse, as a new character in the MRF story was now sitting in the most important seat at the table. In January 1977, Edwardsville native Kenneth "Buzz" Shaw, Vice President at Towson State University in Maryland, took the reins as SIUE president. He didn't like what he saw from his first festival season. "I think we have clearly demonstrated that the festival cannot support itself," Shaw said. "What we have to do now is determine the festival's priority in the university community."[200]

As a student member of the SIU board of trustees, Jim Grandone had access to the MRF's financials and was well aware of the precarious situation. "The festival was heavily subsidized by rock & roll," he says. "The symphony was a loser as far as money is concerned, but a winner as far as bringing in people from St. Louis to enjoy and discover SIUE. That said, the MRF was not fading in any way in '77. It was still running hard, running strong. It's just the financials weren't there. When people started hearing rumors that the MRF was in trouble, they were totally in denial—'Oh no, they can't do that.'"

"My dad died in March of 1976, and I was a grief-stricken high school kid who wasn't paying attention to a lot of things," John S. Rendleman adds. "But by 1977, when the rumors of the MRF's decline were being discussed openly, it was a sad thing because my family had an interest in the festival for all kinds of reasons. There was some understanding that the management of the festival was being shopped out, so we know it wasn't going to just be in the hands of the people at the university."

Shaw brought in J. Christopher Fahlman, manager of the Cleveland Orchestra's Blossum Music Center, to conduct an extensive festival audit. Fahlman's work led Shaw to create a position paper shortly before Christmas that spelled out possible changes that could be implemented over a three-year trial period. One of the key points was a subsidy request of $50,000 a year from the SIUE Student Government. The Student Senate balked at the three-year commitment requested by the president, instead offering a conditional one-year subsidy. Shaw, who had said in December that it was unlikely the festival could continue without the three-year commitment, told the board of trustees the situation was "negotiable."

That said, the president was looking at alternatives. On February 9, Shaw announced the formation of an ad hoc Mississippi River Festival committee to make recommendations for a possible 1978 season. Chaired by university Vice President Ralph Ruffner, the committee consisted of two administrators, five students, two faculty members, and two community representatives. What turned out to be the pivotal direction from Shaw to the committee was this: Explore the possibility of bringing in talent buyers, booking agencies, and independent promoters to lease the festival site and produce the MRF themselves. Ruffner said he hadn't the "slightest notion" whether a '78 season could be organized at this late date. "That's what the committee is supposed to find out."[201]

Should an outside entity come in and run the festival, the university had conditions, including a continuation of the alcohol ban, a positive festival image, a balance in the genres of entertainment offered, and the continued hiring of SIUE students in roles such as concessions, ticket takers, ushers, and parking attendants. One local promoter contacted by the *Alton Telegraph* said the MRF situation was an attractive one, even with the university's conditions. "There's a lot of promoters in the Midwest," he said. "We'd be very interested in the MRF, and I'm sure a lot of others would be, too."[202]

In March, the committee met with and received presentations from several promoters, including Feyline of Denver; Reggae and Contemporary Productions, Inc., of St. Louis; Jam Productions, Ltd. of Chicago; Concerts West of Beverly Hills; and Nederlander, Inc., of New York City.

With no time to lose, a quick decision was needed. And on April 6, at a hastily called press conference, Shaw announced that Nederlander had been awarded a 10-year contract to assume all MRF responsibilities. Calling the agreement a "no risk, some gain" proposition, Shaw said the promoter would pay the university for any services provided and SIUE would receive a percentage of gross receipts (later identified as 1.5 percent).[203] Any profit the university saw would be reinvested back into the MRF. In addition, Nederlander had agreed to the university's conditions—no alcohol, employing students, crowd control measures, etc. "The MRF does have a future," Shaw said. "Indeed, a bright and stable one. The Nederlander name has the kind of expertise and clout to get our association off to a good start. The Nederlander name stands for good taste."

Founded in Detroit in 1912, Nederlander was then, and remains today, one of the largest operators of live theater and music venues in the U.S. In 1978, Nederlander was run by five brothers, and owned and operated three New York City theaters, the Greek Theater in Los Angeles, the Garden State Art Center in New Jersey, the Pink Knob Music Center in Detroit, and numerous other notable sites around the country. "This is the first time we have gone into an opportunity without a lot of apprehension," said co-owner Joseph Nederlander, adding that the group "always tries to present a cross-section of entertainment. We will become a valuable part of this community."[204]

The Nederlander deal was only solidified after a vote by Grandone and the rest of the university's board of trustees. "When that came to me as an agenda item, I was torn," he remembers. "I found it very hard to believe that the university would give this giant PR machine up, but I understood financially that they couldn't continue to subsidize it. Those were some serious numbers. So, here comes Nederlander, the white knight from New York, saying, 'We'll do it for you.' I vividly remember watching the signing of the contract thinking the end of the MRF had been postponed."[205]

Obviously, time to put on a summer music series in 1978 was growing short. But co-owner Wayne Nederlander dropped a few names at the press conference, teasing that the Marshall Tucker Band and the Doobie Brothers would be coming back to town.

It was clear that Nederlander's arrival would spell the end of the St. Louis Symphony and other high-minded acts under the tent. Popular music would rule the roost for the remainder of the MRF's run. "The Mississippi River Festival, it appears, has abandoned its original reason for being: Serious music," read an *Alton Telegraph* editorial. "Obviously the followers of the more serious phases of music have lost a battle to maintain the prestige reflected from support of such attractions."[206]

"The MRF was not conceived to be just a series of rock & roll performances," adds John S. Rendleman. "It was conceived to be cultural performances and a little bit of everything for everyone. In the later years, when the only driving force for the MRF was the rock & roll, it lost a little bit of its elan. There was a sense of loss at the university that really we'd lost a gem."

All things considered, the MRF had accomplished a great deal—probably more than anyone could have imagined—in its first nine seasons with a patchwork organization assembled by the university, the symphony, and local benefactors. But now, for the first time, the Mississippi River Festival would be operated by a professional organization with actual real-world experience running entertainment events and facilities. This meant higher ticket prices ("comparable to the St. Louis market") and fewer shows.[207] But Nederlander also committed to employing about 450 individuals (mostly students) and constructing a permanent structure to cover the stage and a portion of the seating area that would replace the tent. An eight-year Nederlander employee, 29-year-old Peggy Wells, was appointed festival general manager. After nine seasons, Skip Manley's days at the festival were over. Lyle Ward's association with the MRF also officially ended; he remained in his post as assistant director of the University Center.

"(In early 1978), there was no given, or even optimism, that it would go on," Ward recalls. "The first possible solution they came up with was to hire professionals to do it and to change the programming. I was angry. I was disappointed. I felt like the rug had been pulled from underneath me. I thought it was a terrible mistake for the university and it cost me a job that I loved, valued, and felt I had done all I could do with. I never attended another show and didn't go back to the festival site for several years."

It only took about a month for the full 1978 lineup to be announced—obviously, Nederlander had the connections and the juice to put together a schedule quickly. On May 5, area fans learned that, in addition to Marshall Tucker and the Doobies, big names such as Dolly Parton, the Charlie Daniels Band, Kenny Loggins, Harry Chapin, and the reunited Peter, Paul and Mary would be coming to town. Ticket prices, as expected, jumped to $5 for the lawn and $7.50 under the tent. "This is the first time we've put together a program in this short a time," Wayne Nederlander said. "We are already booking for the 1979 season."[208]

The season would begin with the Marshall Tucker Band on June 3. When told that a previous MRF performance by the band elicited one of the wildest nights in festival history, Wayne Nederlander said, "Rowdiness will not be tolerated. We do not put up with any rowdiness."[209]

Nederlander's first MRF show was a big one. While official attendance figures for festival events were no longer reported, estimates put the crowd close to twenty thousand for Tucker's second visit to SIUE, making this the best-attended opening night in MRF history. There were a few growing pains for the new festival managers—specifically, parking issues and disorganization among security officers, now dressed in bright red shirts. But all in all, it was a promising start for the Nederlander-SIUE partnership. "Sure, there are problems, but we'll get them worked out during the first few concerts," Wayne Nederlander said.[210]

Bryan Erdmann says that from a stagehand perspective, it was standard operating procedure when Nederlander came onto the scene. "The business is pretty much the business," he says. "I think there may have been a little resentment among some of the road managers because Nederlander had probably run over them a couple of times. But other than that, everything was pretty much the same as it had been for us."

But among the larger SIUE community, the vibe was much more pessimistic. It was still the Mississippi River Festival, and it was still held on campus. But things had forever changed.

"When it changed over to Nederlander, the sense of the people that I knew was sad, because the memories of the MRF when we were students were golden memories," Grandone says. "Even though we didn't know the scope of the festival's impact on the region, we knew it was special."

"Nederlander brought in some Eastern ideas that maybe would have been better left in the East," Charlie Cox said. "I think it would have been wiser to use a Midwestern production company to manage the festival. Some company like Contemporary Productions in St. Louis perhaps could have done a better job because it wasn't too long before you could read into the way things were going . . . that the MRF was going to end its run."

"You just wanted to see if those wigs were as big as everybody was saying"
Dolly, Willie, and the Burgeoning Country Scene

We've covered just about every popular music form of the 1970s—except one. Country music always had a festival presence, but as artists such as Willie Nelson, Waylon Jennings, and Dolly Parton became superstars in the latter half of the decade, MRF country shows grew much larger.

The first country star to play the festival was Buck Owens in 1970. Owens' career was at its zenith that summer, as he and his band, the Buckeroos, had been voted the top country act in the U.S. for the past five years. Owens had performed for President Lyndon Johnson at the White House in 1968, one year after a successful tour of Japan (rare for a country music artist). In the year before appearing at the MRF, the pioneer of the rock-tinged Bakersfield Sound gained greater attention through a CBS variety show called *Hee Haw*. Chock full of country music legends and cornpone humor, *Hee Haw* was co-hosted by Owens and guitarist/vocalist Roy Clark. Striking a chord with rural viewers (and probably more than a few urbanites who secretly enjoyed the music and gags), the show would move to syndication in 1971 and air for 22 more seasons.

Urged on by an announcer who shouted, "Make some noise! The more noise you make, the harder they work," fans of all ages—but predominately of the over-thirty set—responded with 'Yee Haws' and 'Yahoos.' On this night, the long hair was worn by the ladies, and the smell of beer permeated the tent instead of the preferred weed on rock concert evenings. The show was "smooth and professional" and full of "down-home twang and toe-tapping beat," according to the *St. Louis Post-Dispatch*.[211]

In 1972, one of the most multi-faceted performers to ever play SIUE graced the tent for the first time. Few entertainers could match the diverse resume of Kris Kristofferson. A Rhodes Scholar who studied at Oxford University. An Army Ranger. The career paths available to the young Texan were seemingly endless. But his passion was songwriting, which led to a 1965 break with his disappointed military family.

Before long, Kristofferson was in Nashville, writing songs that weren't selling and sweeping floors at Columbia Recording Studios. He slipped a tape of his work to June Carter and asked her to pass it on to her husband, Johnny Cash, to no avail. It wasn't until 1970 that Cash discovered the Kristofferson-penned ode to waking up alone and hungover, "Sunday Morning Coming Down." The song would top the Billboard Country chart, be named Song of the Year by the Country Music Association, and launch a lifelong friendship between the pair.

Suddenly, Kristofferson's songs were in great demand. At the 1972 Grammys, three were nominated for awards—Janis Joplin's version of "Me and Bobby McGee," Ray Price's "For the Good Times," and the Grammy winner for Song of the Year, Sammi Smith's "Help Me Make it Through the Night." In addition to writing for other artists, Kristofferson was now recording his own albums as a singer. But he had not yet grown confident in his voice. "I know I ain't no singer," Kristofferson said backstage before the MRF show. "I just go out there and do what I can and hope they like it."[212]

Kristofferson opened with a set of his own songs before bringing his soon-to-be wife, Rita Coolidge, on stage after intermission. Dressed in purple jeans, a tank top, and cowboy boots, Coolidge—fresh off stints with top artists like Bob Dylan, Jimi Hendrix, Eric Clapton, and Stephen Stills—performed several songs before the duo closed with "Help Me Make it Through the Night" and an encore of "Me and Bobby McGee."

"We've never been before a crowd this large," Kristofferson said of the attendance approaching six thousand. "I'm used to country fairs and country theaters with about seven hundred to one thousand people."[213]

Five years after their first festival appearance, the team of Kristofferson and Coolidge returned to campus. In the period between shows, Kristofferson's fame had grown immensely through his acting endeavors. Most notably, he starred opposite Barbra Streisand in the 1976 film, *A Star Is Born*, earning a Golden Globe nomination.

The crowd, smaller than expected due to threatening skies, was a bit subdued, causing Kristofferson to question himself backstage after the show. "I keep thinkin' there might be somebody out in that audience who has driven six hundred miles just to hear me sing," he said. "And by God, I owe it to that person to do the best job possible."[214]

Coolidge, who was featured during the second half of the show, was experiencing a career zenith in the summer of '77. Her hits "(Your Love Has Lifted Me) Higher and Higher" and "We're All Alone" both cracked the Top Ten. She and Kristofferson would divorce in 1980.

In 1974, Tom T. Hall and Melba Montgomery came to town. Hall had made a splash by writing Jeannie C. Riley's 1968 No. 1 crossover hit, "Harper Valley PTA." Following that breakthrough, Hall's recording career took flight, with country hits such as "(Old Dogs, Children and) Watermelon Wine" and "I Like Beer." Montgomery went from singing duets with George Jones to a solo career in the 1970s, highlighted by the 1974 No. 1 country hit, "No Charge."

Emmylou Harris made her first festival appearance in 1976, opening for ex-Youngbloods' lead singer Jesse Colin Young. Harris was part of the New York City coffeehouse scene in the late '60s before joining forces with former Byrds and Flying Burrito Brothers country-rock trailblazer Gram Parsons. Harris contributed to Parsons' *GP* and *Grievous Angel* albums before Parsons died of a drug overdose in 1973. Harris embarked on a solo career and formed the Hot Band, which featured former Elvis Presley band members James Burton and Glen Hardin. Their 1975 album, *Elite Hotel*, won a Grammy. Harris continued collaborating with some of the biggest names in music, including Bob Dylan, Neil Young, and Linda Ronstadt, and appeared in the Band's documentary film, *The Last Waltz*.

Mention the name Mel Tillis, and most people will think, "Oh yeah, the guy who stuttered." While true, Tillis' credentials as a country music singer/songwriter far exceeded his peculiar speech affect. Writing hits for others since the late 1950s, Tillis emerged in his own right at the dawn of the '70s, and during the decade, he placed 24 songs in the Country Top Ten.

Backed by his longtime band, the Statesiders, Tillis sprinkled humorous anecdotes and stories between songs during his 1977 MRF show. Before his death in 2017, Tillis received numerous honors, including the National Medal of Arts and induction into the Grand Ole Opry and the Nashville Songwriters and Country Music Halls of Fame.

By 1978, country was booming, and one of the biggest names in the business was Dolly Parton, who fought off a bronchial infection to keep her date with Edwardsville fans.

Parton was born in a small Tennessee cabin, the fourth of 12 children, and began appearing on local radio and TV programs as a youth. By age 13, Parton was performing at the Grand Ole Opry, and, after graduating from high school, she moved to Nashville to become a songwriter. When country star Porter Wagoner offered her a spot in his act and on his weekly syndicated TV program, it was the big break she needed. A run of successful duets followed, but it wasn't until 1973's No. 1 country hit "Jolene" that Parton experienced solo success. The next year, Parton wrote and recorded "I Will Always Love You," a song about her musical "divorce" from Wagoner that also topped the country chart. Now on her own, Parton was ruling the country and pop airwaves, with a successful career on the silver screen lying just over the horizon.

Braving the elements on a hot summer night, Parton peppered her set with plenty of fan favorites and colorful stories. She even acknowledged what some in the audience had come out to see for themselves, albeit with a humorous twist. "I know that a whole lot of you brought binoculars out here tonight, and I know what you're looking at," she said. "You just wanted to see if those wigs were as big as everybody was saying."[215]

Parton has won 11 Grammys, sold more than one hundred million records, and recorded 25 country No. 1 singles. Her Hollywood resume includes the films *9 to 5*, *The Best Little Whorehouse in Texas*, *Rhinestone*, and *Steel Magnolias*. And, in 2022, she was inducted into the Rock & Roll Hall of Fame.

That same summer of '78, the legendary Willie Nelson appeared at the festival. The long road to success for Nelson has been well-documented. A struggling songwriter reduced to selling vacuum cleaners door to door, Nelson finally tasted success in the early 1960s when a few of his songs were recorded by other artists, including "Pretty Paper" by Roy Orbison and "Crazy" by Patsy Cline. But his own recording career stalled. In 1972, Nelson made the wise decision to relocate from Nashville to Austin, Texas, joining the city's exploding and more progressive music scene. Along with artists such as Waylon Jennings and Kris Kristofferson, Nelson was a pioneer of what became known as "outlaw country," and his 1975 *Red Headed Stranger* album was a classic of the genre. Finally, with his eighteenth album, Willie Nelson was a star.

Three months before his MRF concert, Nelson had taken a bit of a left turn with the release of *Stardust*, an album of pop standards such as "Blue Skies," "All of Me," and the Grammy-winning "Georgia on my Mind." Nelson gave his all to the Edwardsville crowd, kicking off as always with "Whiskey River" and playing an exhaustive set covering his long, diverse career and culminating with "Mammas, Don't Let Your Babies Grow Up to Be Cowboys," a duet with Jennings that had topped the Country chart the previous spring.

"Willie Nelson was a quiet person," Charlie Cox said. "I remember his guitar had a hole in it that he had scratched from his fingernails playing it so many times, and he had autographs all over the guitar." That Martin N-20 nylon-string acoustic guitar, dubbed *Trigger*, had been Nelson's main guitar since 1969, and it continues to be his trusted companion today more than 50 years later.

Willie Nelson fans are among the most loyal in the business, and the response under the tent and on the lawn reflected it. Comments such as "Willie is fantastic," "He's tough," and "He's so neat, I just love him," could be heard around the festival site.[216]

Troy's Paul Jarvis was within a few feet of his idol but let opportunity pass him by. "He walked right in front of me," he said. "I was going to say hi and shake his hand, but he was talking to someone, so I didn't interrupt him. I missed my chance." Jarvis went on to become a Willie Nelson impersonator.[217]

Emmylou Harris opened the show, wearing pink satin sneakers while performing her own set and then joining Nelson for several songs during his portion of the show. One fan, Lynda Nowell of Mount Olive, Illinois, was highly impressed. "She can really rock & roll," she said. "She gets down and does it. I think music is naturally dominated by males. I can really dig it when a chick comes out and wails it like Emmylou."[218]

Nelson's partner in outlaw country crime was Waylon Jennings, who played one of the MRF's final shows in 1980. The evening served as a "This Is Your Life" event for Jennings, a Texas native who got his big break in 1958 when he was hired to play bass by the legendary Buddy Holly on his upcoming Winter Dance Party Tour.

Tragically, on the night of February 2, 1959, after a concert in Clear Lake, Iowa, Holly and his band (Jennings and Tommy Allsup) were planning to fly to the next show in Moorhead, Minnesota. Other musicians on the tour were traveling by bus. Allsup lost his seat to teen singer Ritchie Valens in a coin toss. Jennings voluntarily gave his seat to singer J.P. Richardson, performing under the stage name The Big Bopper, who was sick with the flu and wanted to avoid riding on the cold bus. Shortly after takeoff, the plane crashed into a cornfield in rural Iowa, killing all on board.

Jennings scuffled through the 1960s, seeking success as a member of the rockabilly band, The Waylors, and on his own with the Waylors as his longtime backing band. It wasn't until the country music winds changed in the '70s that Jennings found stardom working alongside Nelson, Kristofferson, Cash, one-time wife Jessi Colter, and others. His recording of the theme song for the hit TV show *The Dukes of Hazzard* was a No. 1

country song in 1980.

The Waylors received a shot as the opening act on this night, followed by a set from members of Holly's former band, the Crickets (Jerry Allison, Joe B. Mauldin, and Sonny Curtis). Jennings joined the Crickets before his own set to sing Holly classics "Peggy Sue" and "That'll Be the Day."

"'The Picasso of our Profession' and the 'Queen of Disco'"
Pryor Paints Edwardsville Blue, while Summer
Romances the Crowd

In the festival's final years, two entertainers stood above the rest in terms of dominating their art forms. The hottest name in American comedy circa 1978 was Peoria, Illinois, native Richard Pryor. In addition to being one of the most electrifying stand-up comics in the business, Pryor was branching into movies through appearances in *Lady Sings the Blues*, *Uptown Saturday Night*, and *The Bingo Long Traveling All-Stars & Motor Kings*.

No doubt, Pryor specialized in "blue" humor, and his lone MRF appearance was no exception. He found humor in tales of his rough upbringing as the son of an alcoholic prostitute growing up in a brothel run by his grandmother. Pryor relayed a story about his mother catching him with $1,600 worth of cocaine, which he flushed down the toilet. "My mother said, 'I told you that stuff would make you stupid. Why didn't you sell it back to the man you bought it from?'"[219]

But it was a popular bit the comedian refused to do that led to an awkward moment for Michael Hammonds. "I had second row for Richard Pryor," he says. "When the schedule came out every spring, you would look to see what concerts you wanted to go to. I was a high school kid, so I was buying lawn tickets. But Richard Pryor was one of my favorites—he was red hot at that time. So, I spent like fifteen bucks per ticket for that one to get in the second row. My dad didn't want to go. He was a working man, you know? He really didn't care. So, I went to a friend of mine I played football with, and he couldn't go. But his dad wanted to go, so he went with me.

"The album before, (Pryor) had done a character called Mudbone, who was like an old Black man that would say things like, 'Where you from?'

'Tupelo.' 'Where's that next to? One below?' So, I'm in the second row, and I yell, 'Richard, do Mudbone!' He looks at me and says, 'Shut up! I'm not talking to you. I'm not doing Mudbone. That was the last album.' I just sat back and shut up because I didn't want him on me at all! But people around us started laughing and giving me a hard time—I got heckled. But it's a good story. I knew I was stepping into the fire when I said something to him. It was a good time. He was hilarious."

In 1979, the disco craze was polarizing American music fans. For those who embraced the glitz and glamour of the mirror ball, one artist reigned supreme. Donna Summer launched her career in 1968, but it wasn't until seven years later that she tasted success with the No. 2 hit, "Love to Love You Baby." By 1978, Summer was a household name, cranking out a string of eight Top Five hits over an eighteen-month period. Weeks before her two-night MRF stand, Summer boasted the No. 1 single ("Hot Stuff") and album (*Bad Girls*) in the U.S. The week after the concerts, "Bad Girls" would be the No. 1 single. Illustrating disco's dominance in the summer of '79, slots two through six on the chart were also disco songs.

To properly capture the spectacle that was disco, Summer chose to wait until the sun was all the way set before coming on stage, adorned in a purple sequined dress (and later a leopard-pattern dress) and descending a stairway lined with silver lame. Yes, she looked every bit the Disco Queen. During the second night's show, after a steamy version of "Love to Love You Baby," Summer told the fans, "I do love you. I mean, without you I wouldn't be here. Right? So, I must love you."[220]

Shouts of encouragement got the fans up and dancing, but it was Summer's vocal prowess that opened some eyes. "I didn't know she could sing like that," one fan said. "She's just powerful."[221]

Dancing along to Summer's disco classics certainly beat the "entertainment" playing out on area TVs. On the evening of the second show, President Carter gave a televised address regarding the nation's "crisis in confidence"—it would be immortalized as Carter's "national malaise" speech.

"*If there is not a pronounced change, we'll be moving on a collision course*"
The Tent Comes Down as the Relationship Between SIUE and Nederlander Frays

Nederlander expressed satisfaction with the initial batch of shows in 1978 and began thinking long-term about festival revisions. "We're looking for improvements that can be made in the facility," Wayne Nederlander said. "We've been surveying area residents to keep in touch with their feelings on the festival. Suggestions have been made concerning such things as who they would like to see appearing at the MRF, traffic, sound, etc."[222]

Toward the end of the season, GM Peggy Wells was teasing an expansion in the number of events from the twenty-four of the current summer to more than one hundred in 1979. "Next year, we definitely want to have something almost every night," Wells said. "Most of our summer theaters do."[223]

Site improvements such as permanent seats and a larger, covered stage were also possible. Wells said the 1978 season had been planned at the "twelfth hour," leaving little time for major changes. "I thought I was going to be busy with hard work but that it would be simple," she added. "I didn't realize I would be inheriting the problems of other years. There were a lot of minor problems, but there was a lot of goodwill from other years, too."[224]

From a bottom-line perspective, the 1978 season was the most successful in three years. The festival made money and attendance approached two hundred thousand, although Nederlander and the university didn't want to go into further detail. Shaw said he was pleased with the first summer under Nederlander's management but that he would be soon discussing contract adjustments with the organization. "I don't think it's wise to talk about what we'd like to change before we go into negotiations," he said.[225]

But in 1979, something changed. Nederlander went radio silent. The promoters and university brass went months without speaking. Shaw's assistant James Buck was beginning to wonder if Nederlander even wanted to present a summer festival in '79. The attendance boost was a win from the SIUE perspective, but it seemed Nederlander was disappointed. "They do have some concern as it relates to attendance," Buck said. "They really didn't have such a good season here compared with other sites where they're flooded with people."[226]

Was he worried Nederlander might try to pull out of the MRF contract? "I'm not concerned that they might, but they might," Buck said.[227]

In addition, Nederlander calculated the university's 1.5 percent take for 1978 at $13,935 but sent a check for just $6,095, holding the rest for "capital improvements" the organization said it had previously made. Buck went public with his concerns, which served to smoke Nederlander out of hiding. Representatives soon reached out to university leadership. "We very forcefully stuck to the position that they have no right to use that money at their discretion," Buck said. "They're sending a check for the difference."[228]

While Nederlander said they had already booked about twenty acts for the 1979 season, there was no progress on the promised permanent facility. The only renovation for the upcoming summer would be the removal of one of the festival's most iconic elements—the tent. "The university has no desire to force them into erecting the tent," Buck said. "It costs $25,000 to put up, maintain and take down. They will have to measure that cost in relation to the people who might not come because of inclement weather."[229]

"Nederlander did a bunch of stuff that was terrible," Rick Stankoven adds. "The worst thing, in my opinion, was getting rid of the tent. When they got rid of the tent, it wasn't the MRF anymore. The tent made it iconic. When they took over, it went south quickly. They reduced the number of concerts, raised ticket prices. But the biggest for me was the tent. You take away the tent and you take away a lot of the atmosphere."

Other issues were being negotiated, including the university's expectation that Nederlander would provide for a standard number of police based on crowd size, and a clarification on division of labor that would ensure less involvement by SIUE. But it was becoming clear that communication between Nederlander and SIUE was dimming, bordering on non-existent.

When the 1979 schedule was announced in May, it fell well short of the one hundred shows Wells had teased the month before. Nederlander also raised prices to an average of $9 per show for reserved seats (sans tent) and

$7 for lawn seats. Festival ticket prices, once in the ballpark of $1.50 to $3, now exceeded base prices at the Checkerdome and Kiel Auditorium in St. Louis.

"People started saying that the town didn't want it here and kids were getting rowdy," Rick Haydon says. "But I think what changed was people started figuring out you could make a lot of money doing this. I think that probably had more to do with it. Now, you go to the concerts I was seeing for a buck and a half and three bucks, and you pay a hundred dollars for a ticket. So, it became big money, and when that changed, all the other stuff sort of came with it."

The high-minded mission of the MRF had turned into a money-making venture, with no room for the cultural aims originally intended by the university and the symphony. Dance companies, chamber musicians, and theatrical performances had been replaced by a steady stream of rock and pop shows. In response, the *Alton Telegraph* ran an editorial critical of the types of entertainment Nederlander was bringing to town—the kinds SIUE had tried to run away from in 1977. "The university apparently has subscribed to a liberality in choosing attractions which lets the bars down for those highly attractive to and stimulative of the violent and unruly elements. No matter how much we try to pass the responsibility for peace maintenance back and forth between the university and Nederlander, the source, we believe, lies in the types of crowds attracted."[230]

Meanwhile, members of the ad hoc committee that recommended Nederlander the year before were now expressing disappointment that the promoter was not sticking to its promises. "One of the strong bases on which we voted for the Nederlanders is that we felt they would bring to [the] MRF a range of cultural programming, as well as the rock and popular music that the other organizations (that expressed interest in running the festival) would be more limited to," said committee member Alfred Kahn. "In other words, we expected a lot more of them. When they distributed sample programs from the other festivals, we were led to believe we would be getting a similar range of programming here."[231]

Directly or indirectly, disturbances on site ticked back up in 1979. At a Charlie Daniels Band show, a Lake St. Louis youth was stabbed in the abdomen and chest, sending him to the intensive care unit at Wood River Township Hospital. This marked the second stabbing of the season, and, when combined with numerous other incidents at the Daniels' show, local authorities were motivated to express their concern for the lack of security at festival shows. Madison County Sherriff Emil Toffant said county deputies would no longer work the MRF unless Nederlander increased its number of security officers. Fred Bright, director of operations for the sheriff's department, said there were just eight officers at the Charlie Daniels Band show. Under police guidelines, there should have been at least 25—one for every 1,000 attendees.[232]

"The company is not, in my opinion, living up to their obligation," Bright said. He added that, before the season began, Nederlander officials had informed the sheriff's department, Edwardsville police, and campus police that adequate security would be provided at festival events. "We would be very remiss if we did not sit back and say a problem is brewing."[233]

Sheriff's department officials scheduled a meeting with Nederlander to discuss the situation, and Bright issued a threat. "If the Nederlanders don't live up to their obligation to the people of Madison County . . . we won't provide people with a false sense of security."[234]

Following the meeting, it was announced that Madison County Sheriff's deputies would continue providing security for the remainder of the 1979 schedule, but only in emergency situations or when too few campus officers were available. Off-duty deputies—who worked as security at some MRF shows and had not yet been paid for 1978 services—would no longer be provided after the current season ended.[235]

"We informed them we want to get out of the business of being at (SIUE for concerts) even on an off-duty basis," Bright said. "We certainly are not pleased with the situation, and we do not intend to become involved in any long-term agreement to provide security."[236]

Student volunteers were also increasingly frustrated by the sketchy conditions at some festival shows. "It's unbelievable around here some nights," one said, asking to remain anonymous. "People try to rush the stage. They punch you out if you try to stop them. They get drunk, or stoned, or both and start fighting. They carry knives and chains and guns.

It's just incredible."[237]

Madison County Board member William R. Haine of Alton called for a court order shutting down the MRF until better crowd control could be guaranteed. Haine also called on Shaw to take another look at the university's contract with Nederlander. "The entire thing has become a nuisance," Haine said. "These rock concerts have become a danger to the health and welfare of the people of Madison County. It besmirches the name of Southern Illinois University. The Nederlanders should be told if they can't uphold order, they shouldn't schedule rock concerts. If they don't want to do that they should be shut down."[238]

Trouble was coming from all sides. SIUE's Student Senate voted to support a festival boycott, declaring that students were being cheated by Nederlander. Senate President Michael Stern said the promoter should be providing discounted tickets for students, better-trained security guards, improved working conditions for student employees, and more restrooms. "We felt that, as a campus constituency group, we had to make a statement about the students being ripped off," Stern said, adding if the festival was going to be a completely private enterprise, "take it to Kiel Auditorium, take it to the Checkerdome."[239] Stern added that Wayne Nederlander had refused to meet with him or discuss the senate's concerns.

Jim Grandone watched the situation play out from afar, having transferred to the University of Illinois-Springfield to complete his degree. "I heard that it was pretty well chopped down," he says. "It was just basically to make money and not really to be an event for the region. It was just a moneymaker. I was saddened by that, and a lot of people that I talked to were bummed out about it and said it just wasn't the same. Seeing those last three seasons and knowing that it was changing and it wasn't the same as when Lyle and the others ran it—it was heartbreaking."

The end of the 1979 season brought nothing more than crickets. Unlike years when SIUE controlled the festival and the annual postmortem of profits, deficits, and attendance figures played out in area newspapers, Nederlander and the university remained silent. It took until mid-May for Wayne Nederlander to publicly declare that a 1980 season would be held, although it would start late. Questions related to security, the kinds of acts to be scheduled, and other important festival topics went unanswered.

In his *St. Louis Post-Dispatch* column, Joe Pollack summed it up: "The Nederlander Organization may be a major production force in the American theatrical world, but it sure has a talent for losing friends and confusing issues, along with one for making lots of money."[240]

It was obvious to all that tensions were rising. And in the midst of the fragile situation, university leadership was changing again. Shaw was named the first chancellor of the SIU system and Earl Lazerson stepped in as president.

Clearly, the Mississippi River Festival was not the same summer music series many fans remembered so warmly. By early 1980, the MRF was clouded in mistrust on all sides—university officials, SIUE students, area law enforcement, and supporters of the fine arts, to name a few—and the common enemy for all was Nederlander. The promised permanent facility had not been constructed. Communication was virtually non-existent. For the first time, there was talk that SIUE would back out of the contract after the 1980 season by alleging breach of contract.

"If there is not a pronounced change in the way the Nederlanders handle the situation—both in attitude and operation—then we'll be moving on a collision course," an unnamed university official said. "The festival began with a bang (the cannon fire of the St. Louis Symphony's performance of the '1812 Overture'). It may well end with a battle in court—or everyone saying, 'To hell with it.'"[241]

Lazerson said SIUE would be exploring "all options," adding, "I think the university will look very carefully at what happens this summer."[242] Wayne Nederlander fired back, holding a press conference in Edwardsville to defend his organization from "misrepresentative reports," declaring that criticism of how Nederlander handled MRF security and programming was unjustified. "It is a community site. We are operating it. We want community input. We want to be part of the community."[243]

Regarding the acts being booked at the festival, Nederlander turned the tables on his critics. "The public dictates what we present," he said, before promising the promoter would work with local non-profit organizations to bring in cultural presentations.[244]

Finally, Nederlander said a renegotiation with SIUE was not on his radar. "We have signed a contract for the site. We plan to uphold it, and we think the university will too.[245] There have been no violations of the contract. We are here for the long run."[246]

"Yeah, well, it's a religion for us, too"
A Decade Later, the Grateful Dead Return

Two nights after President Jimmy Carter was nominated for a second term at the Democratic National Convention, one of his favorite bands, the Grateful Dead, returned to the MRF after a 10-year absence.

What a long, strange trip it had been since the Dead's 1970 festival appearance. A series of albums and tours kept the band in front of its fans on an almost-constant basis. Keyboardist Ron "Pigpen" McKernan died in 1973 from complications of liver damage and was replaced by Keith Godchaux on keys, and by his wife, Donna Jean Godchaux, on backing vocals. The Godchauxs left the band in 1979 and Brent Mydland moved in for 1980s *Go to Heaven* album. Notable for the hit, "Alabama Getaway," the LP disappointed in terms of sales, with the cover photo of band members wearing white suits coming across as a little too "disco" for some longtime fans. "The cover, featuring us in *Saturday Night Fever* disco suits against a white background, reinforced the impression that we were 'going commercial,'" said bassist Phil Lesh.[247]

In an interview shortly before the show, Jerry Garcia was asked about the passion of the band's "Dead Heads" fan base, which bordered on a form of religion. "Yeah, well, it's a religion for us, too," Garcia said. "Our commitment is as deep as any Dead Head's. I know I'd feel hypocritical if I wasn't. We're providing an experience that a certain kind of person wants in their life, and that's good, I guess. Doesn't seem to be hurting anyone too badly."[248]

The Grateful Dead entertained a crowd estimated at 10,500 with two sets on what was the opening night of their 1980 tour's summer leg. The first set was more straightforward, including songs from the new album. But the second portion of the concert was experimental, and, as expected, extended jams were a centerpiece. A storm rolled through campus while the band was jamming on "Ship of Fools," but Garcia and Weir kept noodling and exploring on their guitars, seemingly oblivious to the raindrops.

"I went to both Grateful Dead concerts at the MRF," says J'Deanna Twesten. "I remember dad talking about extra security being brought in for the first concert. The second time they came, I was more familiar with their music and liked it better. I remember thinking how Jerry Garcia reminded me of Grizzly Adams!"

In the summer of 1980, John S. Rendleman was an SIUE student on a path that would lead to a successful career as an attorney in Carbondale. He attended the Dead's show, and then found himself up close and personal with the legendary band. "While the band was in town, they went to a local house called the Farm Crib that was occupied by people from National Town Meeting, which was kind of a forerunner to Ralph Nader's public interest research groups. That house happened to be across a farm field from the apartment in ESIC where I lived. So my roommate and I walked across this field to the Farm Crib to meet the Grateful Dead. And there they were—Jerry Garcia was sitting in an overstuffed chair on a porch. I was sitting on a couch, you know, five feet from him as he played guitar. And that had nothing to do with me being the son of the chancellor or anything. It just happened to be that they came and played at the Farm Crib across the field from where I was living."

The Dead continued as a working band until Garcia's death in 1995, although group members continued to play in various combinations for many years after.

"The Last Waltz"
ZZ Top Plays the Final MRF Show

Did anyone in attendance on August 23, 1980, know that this would be the 353rd and final event in the 12-year history of the Mississippi River Festival? Maybe a few university officials had an inkling of what was to come. But there was no way for fans to know for sure that ZZ Top would be the last band to play the MRF.

The "Little Ol' Band from Texas" made for quite a ruckus, playing loudly and wearing baseball caps and Hawaiian shirts along with their long beards (guitarist/vocalist Billy Gibbons and bassist Dusty Hill anyway; drummer Frank Beard stopped with just a mustache). Formed in 1969, the three musicians performed together for more than half a century, achieving their greatest success in the '80s through the albums *Eliminator* and *Afterburner* and the accompanying music videos that were huge MTV hits.

In the summer of 1980, ZZ Top was touring behind their sixth studio album, *Deguello*, which went platinum and launched the favorites "I Thank You," "I'm Bad, I'm Nationwide," and "Cheap Sunglasses." The band was inducted into the Rock & Roll Hall of Fame in 2004. Hill died in 2021.

The show ended. ZZ Top left town. The festival site was cleared. It was again time to wait and see. What would the university do? Would SIUE officials pull the plug on the MRF? Or would they find a way to improve the situation with Nederlander and keep the festival alive in 1981 and beyond? The remaining months of 1980 would give no indication. Silence reigned again.

Mississippi River Festival

SECTION 6
END OF THE ROAD
1981

"Is the MRF dead? You can look at it that way, I suppose"
The 1981 Season Is Canceled

While Nederlander remained mum on the future of the Mississippi River Festival, the organization continued operating its many other businesses and even tried to add a new one. James Nederlander made a pitch to purchase Major League Baseball's Cleveland Indians during the winter of 1980-81, but the deal fell through.

In a February 1981 wire service report, James Nederlander said the promoter would be ending its affiliation with the MRF, citing a 50 percent drop in festival receipts from 1979 to 1980. Buck said this was news to him. "We talk periodically, and everything appears to be proceeding as it has in past years," he said. "We don't presume there will be any change from actions in the past."[249] Nederlander representatives were expected to visit Edwardsville soon for discussions about the festival's future. Buck said any attempt by Nederlander to break its contract could be met by legal action.

After a follow-up discussion with Wayne Nederlander, Buck seemed confident that the festival would continue. He did, however, ask the promoter to make the permanent site renovations it had promised (including sheltered seats) and to broaden the programming. As usual, Nederlander was unavailable for comment. But according to Buck, counter to earlier reports, Wayne Nederlander told him no final decision had been made on festival plans for 1981.

Several weeks of silence followed, and in this case, no news was certainly not good news. On May 22, 1981, after two days of meetings, officials from the university and Nederlander issued a joint announcement: The 1981 Mississippi River Festival season had been canceled. The reason given was the need for major improvements to the MRF site. Buck said he had toured Nederlander's Poplar Creek Theater near Chicago, which offered roofed seating for seven thousand seats and thirteen thousand lawn seats, and felt the facility was "spectacular." He added that he and Nederlander representatives would continue meeting to develop a plan for the festival's future.[250]

So, was the MRF dead? "You can look at it that way, I suppose," Buck said. "But I look at it on the positive side. This is the thing we've been waiting for—a final look at site improvements . . . It's the image (of the site) that has been keeping people away, and it's a physical change that's needed." But money would be a major issue, as a project to get the MRF site close to Poplar Creek would cost "in the plural millions as opposed to a few hundred thousand," Buck added.[251]

The *St. Louis Post-Dispatch* sang a sad song upon the news, lamenting the festival's decline under Nederlander. "The something-for-everyone appeal has slipped away during the past three years. The festival, the offering of a variety of cultural events, may have died when the university decided it could no longer afford to subsidize it and signed over control to the New York promoters."[252]

The *Post's* Dick Richmond was aligned. "The friendly atmosphere disappeared. The Nederlander Organization entered the picture to run the program. In three years, (the MRF) has gone from marvelous to an afterthought."[253]

And that was it. No headlines were forthcoming. No press conferences announcing construction projects. No updates from SIUE or Nederlander. The festival just disappeared. "The MRF didn't so much die as fade away," wrote Pat Gauen in the *Post-Dispatch*.[254]

Time has eased some of the pain Ward felt back in the late '70s. Today, he's more objective about the festival's demise. "Part of it was a cultural thing," he says. "It's funny. I think we collectively, at least me and my group, tend to blame a lot on the Nederlander organization because things were starting to fall apart. It just seemed like when they came in, it was the beginning of the end. But you know, in their defense, probably a lot of that was a cultural thing. The culture was changing, times were changing. So yeah, it really was a different time."

John S. Rendleman takes a similar stance. "I don't know if hindsight has any value for us in these things, but by the early '80s, open-air concerts might have been on the decline anyway. Nederlander was a business and a promoter, which made them distinctly different from a bunch of people who were altruistic and wanted the MRF to succeed because it was a great thing. Nederlander wanted to make a buck. There is a clear distinction. Whether somebody other than Nederlander would have allowed the MRF to live longer than its lifespan, I don't know. I remember there being a lot of complaints about Nederlander, but I remember there being some pretty good acts that came during the time they ran the MRF, too."

By early 1982, there were only a few questions floating around regarding the MRF's possible return. Those were put to rest in April when Buck said contact between the university and Nederlander had been minimal, and no progress had been made toward solving the challenges that led to the cancellation a year before. The university would not be fronting any money for site improvement projects. "Since we're not intending to go partners on this, there's not much we can do right now," Buck said.[255]

Buck sent a letter to Nederlander urging the two sides to reconnect and sharing letters he had received from fans in remote locations such as Ohio and Maine seeking information on the '82 season's schedule. "I told him that if we're getting inquiries from places like that, he can imagine the interest there is locally for it." He added that, technically, Nederlander could erect the tent and bring in some performers without much lead time. "But I suspect they still want the site improvements before they will do anything."[256]

Instead of seeing construction vehicles and hearing hammering at the MRF site, students and locals driving past the area began to notice that weeds were growing higher and higher, beginning to overtake the area.

Now it really was over. The 12-year journey of the Mississippi River Festival had reached its end. "I didn't frequent the place as much toward the end, but it never left me," says Michael "Supe" Granda. "It was a sad day when it went down, although I knew it was coming. And when it came, I just said, 'Oh Lord, Lord, Lord.'"

Mississippi River Festival

SECTION 7
EPILOGUE

"Long Time Gone"
After More Than Four Decades,
the Mississippi River Festival Lives On

In the summer of 1983, a reporter and photographer from the *Alton Telegraph* ventured to the Mississippi River Festival site, now vacant for nearly three years, to get the lay of the land. "The golden wheat-like weeds are chest-high in the parking lot, once crowded on mid-summer nights," wrote Carol Clarkin. "Green vines entwine the turnstiles at the entrance. The stage and dressing rooms—all the backstage area—has been raped by vandals. The once-neatly mown grassy knolls which sloped down to the 'big tent' stage area are thick with undergrowth."[257]

Buck said SIUE lacked the manpower to keep the site tidy. And with the new multi-purpose sports building (the Vadalabene Center) being constructed, the MRF site would no longer be in play for any events or performances.[258]

That same year, Jim Grandone walked the MRF site with Lyle Ward. Having returned to SIUE to pursue a Journalism degree, Grandone was working for *The Alestle*. "I asked Lyle if the MRF was really over, and he said it was, and it wouldn't be coming back. My story ran on the front page—'MRF Dies.' That put it to rest."

In 1985, a proposal to construct an outdoor amphitheater on the East St. Louis riverfront was introduced. Lazerson said should a facility be created the university might have interest in rebooting the MRF in its original form. "It would certainly not be a rock festival," he said. "It would be a true Mississippi River Festival."[259] The amphitheater was never built.

Meanwhile, back at the festival site, a radio control aircraft club was using the site to fly its planes, helicopters, and gliders. "For all of us who worked here and spent a number of years on the site, it's kind of a sacred place, a place we still hold dear in our memories," Bob Gill said at the time.

"But it's good to see other people still enjoying the site. The cross-country runners come through here, the bicycle riders, the stargazers, the airplane guys – they're all enjoying the site today, like we did, just for different purposes. But it's still kind of sad to think how many people used to be here and how few come into this area today."

By 1989, the university was toying with the idea of placing an eighteen-hole golf course somewhere on campus, with the MRF site proposed as one of the possible locations. The idea was met with stiff opposition from those who didn't want campus land to be cleared for a profit-making venture. The golf course was never constructed.

By the 1990s, the Mississippi River Festival had drifted into local folklore. Newspapers asked their readers to share their memories for articles commemorating the twenty-fifth anniversary of the festival's launch. The university created an MRF Retrospective exhibit in the Morris University Center Gallery to commemorate the festival's thirtieth anniversary in 1999. The presentation included more than five hundred photographs, signed contracts, posters, and artwork—much of it supplied by Lyle Ward. That fall, the St. Louis Symphony Orchestra returned to campus for a performance in the Meridian Ballroom. "The symphony was for many years an integral part of summers on the SIUE campus," said administrator Richard Walker. "It is a thrill to have them back with us."[260]

As the new century dawned, another proposal for a new amphitheater was rolled out, this time a 7,000-seater in Collinsville to be named the Mississippi River Festival. As with the East St. Louis project sixteen years before, SIUE was supportive of the idea. And as with the East St. Louis project, it never happened.

In 2006, another amphitheater project in the Metro East was introduced, this time in Alton. And this time, it would come to fruition. The 4,000-seat Liberty Bank Amphitheater is still booked regularly today during the summer months.

To commemorate the fortieth anniversary of the festival in 2009, a university committee paid $1,000 for an Illinois State Historical Society marker to be erected near the concert site. The 44 x 51-inch cast aluminum plaque now resides on a pole off North University Drive near the festival's parking area. "(The festival is) the kind of thing that our generation—I'm talking about baby boomers—needs to recognize," said Historical Society Executive Director William Furry, a patron at several MRF events himself. "It was one of those places that brought them into the larger world culture."[261]

With her perspective as a local historian and member of the Madison County Historical Society board—as well as an MRF regular—Cindy Reinhardt says the festival is an important part of the area's cultural heritage. "Nearly everyone who was around at that time had some kind of experience with the MRF," she says. "In addition, think of the hotels and the restaurants in this area that benefited, because people came from everywhere to go to the MRF. You would run across people who came from California or New York for a concert. It really put us on the map."

Former festival stalwarts Joan Baez, Judy Collins, Arlo Guthrie, and Poco would return to SIUE for concerts in the 21st century. And a 2016 MRF Revisited series brought back the Nitty Gritty Dirt Band, Ozark Mountain Daredevils, and Pure Prairie League. Meanwhile, the refurbished Wildey Theater in Edwardsville has hosted shows featuring Wishbone Ash, Brewer & Shipley, and other festival entertainers. But there is no tent. There is no lawn. There are no stars glimmering above.

"It was a different time," Cindy Reinhardt says. "There were so many different things that were happening at that time. And that natural amphitheater would be very difficult to replace. It all just came together as a package and created something that was kind of magical. They've had MRF nights on campus in the Meridian Ballroom, but it's not quite the same."

She laughs. "I'm sitting on a blanket on a hard floor! This is not the MRF!"

Smaller events and concert series have popped up from time to time in the Edwardsville area using the "Mississippi River Festival" name, and a few brief attempts have been made to resurrect the inspiration of the original festival and start it up again. But it always becomes clear that nothing will ever replicate the original.

"I remember when my daughter was taking a music appreciation class in college and she called me and asked, 'Dad, have you ever heard of anybody called the Allman Brothers?' That kind of took me back to the days when we were at the MRF as high school kids, having a big time," John S. Rendleman says. "When I come back to Edwardsville, if I'm anywhere near the site, the memories flood back. Or if I'm with friends who remember the MRF during its golden years, we can share stories and talk about things that happened. Those were the glory days. We were kids with no great responsibilities. We could just enjoy ourselves, and we sure did. It wasn't just the summer home for the St. Louis Symphony. It became the summer home for everybody in Edwardsville."

SECTION 8
IN THEIR OWN WORDS

"This is the only concert in the country tonight"
Why Artists Loved to Play the MRF

Michael "Supe" Granda, Ozark Mountain Daredevils
"The buzz was all over the country—well, actually, I think all over the world—about this venue in Edwardsville, Illinois, called the Mississippi River Festival."

Tom Shipley, Brewer & Shipley
"You have to understand that we were traveling all the time and we were on the bill with other acts. The musical community was fairly tight. You were always banging into one another. I heard about it because everybody was playing it. People were talking, you know, 'Oh, we just played the Mississippi River Festival.' They were saying what a great time they had."

John McEuen, Nitty Gritty Dirt Band
"We'd heard about the Mississippi River Festival, but none of us thought we'd get lucky enough to get booked on it. When we did, it was like, 'Okay, we're really valid now.' Not that we didn't feel valid, especially in Missouri—we had the Cowtown Ballroom in Kansas City, and we played the Fox Theater in St. Louis. But finally getting the Mississippi River Festival was a real mark in our career. It was like playing the Carnegie Hall of the Midwest."

Mike Reilly, Pure Prairie League
"When we started doing a heavy tour schedule around 1973, we were at Carbondale, we were at Kiel Auditorium in St. Louis. We were everywhere, and we played with a lot of bands. Everybody was always talking about the Mississippi River Festival. You know, 'You guys playing there this year? No, but you know, we're scheduled to play there next year in June.' So that was always a big treat. We looked forward to it because, after the first time we

played there, it was one of those things - like Woodstock."

Rusty Young, Poco
"That was the era of festivals after Woodstock. Everybody wanted to have a festival—the Atlanta Pop Festival, Newport Pop Festival—there were at least one or two of those big outdoor shows every month. I remember I was surprised because the MRF seemed like it was so far out in the country for such a big, beautiful venue. That was a pleasant surprise."

Andy Powell, Wishbone Ash
"We had played some of the festivals in England, but when we stepped into that natural amphitheater there by the river, that was one of the largest spaces we had seen turned over to a rock concert. It was just awe-inspiring. It was like taking off in a jet plane when you started to fire up the guitars—everything was just massive. And to see that many people, you really did feel there was a youth movement starting up then. We started to do many, many tours of the United States after that, and we got a real sense of the mood of American youth at that time. It was out with the old, in with the new, and the River Festival was definitely a symbol of that."

Richie Furay, Hillman-Souther-Furay
"What was special about the MRF was just the history of Missouri and the Mark Twain thing, and just being out here on the Mississippi River. It was a neat event for us. These festivals that were happening at that time were just absolutely a scene in and of themselves."

Jeff Hanna, Nitty Gritty Dirt Band
"It was one of the first giant rock shows that we ever played, and it was great. This part of the world, especially in the '70s, was really a big part of our fan base. I remember there were a lot of people there and we were looking at each other going, 'Why are all these folks here?!' We were playing a lot of Fillmore Auditorium-sized venues, a lot of ballrooms. So, to see that many folks outside gathered there to hear the Dirt Band play was really exciting and pretty scary for us, too."

John McEuen

"It was even better the second time we played there. We could see the people coming in. Oh my God, there's like five thousand . . . there's seven thousand. Oh, there's like nine thousand, you know?! So, we're really feeling pretty cocky. But this slowly crumbled because we couldn't get the fiddle to go into the house audio. We'd been doing this a long time. We knew what we were doing. And I'm up on stage with the road manager going, 'Why can't we get the dang fiddle to work?' The roadie tried, we changed every line, changed batteries . . . we did everything we could. Finally, we're standing there in front of the amp, and I say, 'Hey, Leonard, the light's burned down on the amp. That's why we don't see it.' He looks at me and goes, 'I don't think so.' (*laughs*). We had to turn the amp on. That was a real indication of how nervous we were. We didn't turn on the amplifier! It was the biggest gross the band had ever had to that point in our career. We were happy, scared, nervous, confident, and unknowing."

Andy Powell

"'To walk out on the stage there was quite overwhelming. You could not fail to be elated by the vibe in the audience. For a band like us, it was a huge inspiration in terms of what we could do in America—that we could get on these kinds of shows with a major headliner."

Bob Heil, Audio Engineer

"One of the interesting things that I noted about the festival is that you'd take people like Arlo Guthrie and Joni Mitchell. A lot of people never heard of them. They would appear there and blow everybody away. Like, 'Who are these guys?' And of course, they became legends, many of them inducted into the Rock Hall. They were just amazing when you heard them in their infancy at the MRF. And they enjoyed playing there because the facility was so good. You'd see them come off the stage with a big smile because the MRF was such a special place. They were treated so much better than they got treated everywhere else."

Bryan Erdmann, Student Worker

"We never heard anyone say, 'Oh, I don't want to play. It's too dusty out here. It might rain.' I never saw that. Everybody thought it was worthwhile. When the crowd was good, it literally felt good on stage because the sound was focused back. So, happy crowd, happy stage."

"Supe" Granda

"Every performer had a magic moment when they went there because the place was so perfect. The place was set up so together that when you walked out there, boom, the performer was going, 'Oh my God, this is heaven.' And that helped make good performances. That's why there were so many cool performances there. That sound was just kind of rolling around the bowl, that little valley there."

Jeff Hanna

"It was this amazing venue carved out of a natural setting. It seems like when you're in a natural setting like that, it's all the better. I mean, man can do pretty good work, but God does a lot better job of putting these things together. It was just astounding, that audience coming straight up from the stage, kind of that eye-level landscape out there."

Richie Furay

"I count the Mississippi River Festival right up there with other shows that were special and unique. When Poco played Carnegie Hall the first time, it was awesome. To play Madison Square Garden . . . those places are just unique. The setting was one of the most beautiful places that I ever played. With the natural amphitheater, it was just unique unto itself. It was really, really neat."

"Supe" Granda

"Every time we see Jimmy Buffett, we say, 'Man, remember that night we had such a great time at the River Festival?' I mean, everybody, when they were passing through, stopped at the River Festival. We just happened to live here. Yeah, the memories are just so great. Just good feelings, good vibes, and good art.'"

Rick Haydon, *Alestle* Reporter/SIUE Professor
"Three of my best friends are Roger Guth, Peter Mayer, and Jim Mayer of Jimmy Buffett's Coral Reefer Band. They asked me to come out to Aspen one time for a golf benefit. I played this little bar in downtown Aspen and ran the PA at the benefit. That's where I met Jimmy for the first time. He asked me what I did, and I said I was a college professor. He asked where I taught, and when I said Southern Illinois University Edwardsville, he said, 'The MRF!' To this day, he remembers playing here and sitting in with the band at the Stagger Inn.'"

Bob Heil
"You get around a Jackson Browne, a Joe Walsh, and all these performers who are friends of ours, and every once in a while, they'll talk about the MRF. Of course, we'll get into a long dissertation. It was just really something to be able to be a part of this.'"

Rance Caldwell, Audio Engineer
"Being a touring engineer, we'd been to a lot of festivals, and this one was right up there with everything we expected it to be and more. The lovely ladies, the starry nights, and when the music wasn't playing, obviously you had the serenade of the crickets. If I knew I was going to be on a tour that came there, I was looking forward to it. I always had such a good time here. After you go around touring for so long, you think of a venue and you go, 'Oh, I know this guy, I know that guy.' So, it's good to see people that you've made contact with, not just on a professional basis, but as friends. I have fond memories of it. I wish to hell it hadn't gone away.'"

Tom Shipley
"I cannot tell you how many times Michael (Brewer) and I will be playing, and somebody will come up and say, 'I saw you at the Mississippi River Festival.' That just happens over and over again. So, it made an impression on the musicians, but it also made an impression on the community, the

fans, the people that enjoyed good music."

Rance Caldwell

"Catering was always excellent. The security wasn't like the Gestapo. You had the feeling that people were always glad for you to come and really appreciated the music that you brought to them. That's one reason why the Mississippi River Festival holds a special place in my heart. I've still got two MRF T-shirts in a drawer. My wife keeps telling me I need to get rid of all these things, but they're like my memories. I can look at a T-shirt and go, 'Oh, the Mississippi River Festival. I remember that. I got that when I played here with James Taylor or with Jackson Browne or with Stephen Stills.' That's how old dogs like me have our memories; not by what we remember, but what we've collected and the people we know."

Mike Reilly

"When you came into a big gig, usually it was in a van, and you came around the perimeter and you didn't really get to see what was going on. But we came in on the main road at the MRF. You came over this little sort of rise, and you could see the top of the stage, and then you looked down and you saw this natural bowl in the hillside. It was just breathtaking. This was big time for us. Those are the gigs you remember all your life."

John McEuen

"You really felt like you were in the space that you belonged that night. When you were standing on that stage, and you had the Mississippi River behind you and all that tradition of America . . . it just felt like the sun is going down, the audience is gathering, it's a beautiful space, and this is the only concert in the country tonight. It really felt that way. It was perfect."

"It was a hell of an experience"
Why Locals Loved the MRF

Gary Kochan, Student Worker

"It was a really special thing for those of us who worked there. It was a family kind of atmosphere."[262]

Shari Faltus, Fan

"I thought the MRF was really peaceful. It was just such a happy time and innocent. The great thing about the MRF was that it was never a commitment. It was like, 'If I'm not busy, I'll bring my blanket.'"[263]

Joseph Biro, Fan

"It's a flashback of good times, real good times. Meeting people, good music, just laying back, no one bothering you. I think a lot of people miss that."[264]

Tim Crawford, Fan

"It was a wonderful venue. It was just beautiful out there. It seemed like the performers who came there really enjoyed it. Some of them would visit local establishments like the Stagger Inn and the old Corner Tavern and just mingle with the locals. It was great."[265]

Jim Muffo, Fan

"You would go through the turnstiles and it was flat. Then, all of a sudden, you came to this place and it started sloping down. People would be walking in from all around. The tent was down there. You just walked down into the bowl, and you could find a place anywhere you wanted to sit. Naturally, people went toward the front, especially if you were lawn sitters because you had to stake your claim. So, you put your huge blanket out and you'd think, 'This is all mine.' And before it's over, there's blankets infringing on your blanket—you're butt to butt, man! But it was just great. And then the next day, you'd hear the reports once you got to school. It was a hell of an experience."

Bryan Erdmann, Student Worker

"The first time I walked the site, it was daylight, and nobody was there aside from some workers. I just thought, 'Wow, this is great.' I hadn't seen a natural amphitheater that big. If you were lucky enough to travel to Italy or

Greece or maybe Spain, they had these outdoor arenas that are a thousand years old, and every one of those places is in a natural bowl like the MRF site. I thought SIUE and the area were lucky to have a place like that. I still think they were lucky . . . *we* were lucky."

Katy Katzenberger, Fan

"We lived right in the backyard of it, so it was always a big deal for us. We used to sit in our backyard in lawn chairs and just look at the stars and listen to the shows. We used to ride our bikes out to University Drive and watch the people come in. When Marshall Tucker came, I remember watching all the people with the flags and thinking that was a big deal. I was completely into music—even at that young age, I had a huge 45 collection, so it was a real cool thing to have in Edwardsville. I mean, my God!"

John Jarvis, Fan

"I can remember seeing the sea of white lights coming off of 157 after a concert. It was unbelievable. Just car after car, so you knew that the concert had just ended. You wondered who played that night, you know? Some of those big ones, the traffic jam would take hours to get out of campus. It was just unbelievable how many cars came out of there!"

Andy Kovarik, Fan

"It was one of my favorite high school memories. It was the thing you centered your entire summer schedule around. It was a time in your life when you didn't have kids, you weren't married, you didn't have a career yet, and you didn't have a lot of real important responsibilities. It was fun going out there with your friends and doing whatever you wanted. And the other part of it is you could pay $3 to sit on the lawn and then roll in a little red wagon with a pony keg in it."

Katy Katzenberger

"The funny thing is, we have something out here (in California) called the Shoreline Amphitheater, which is down in Silicon Valley. They have the same tenting they had at the MRF. It's a bit nicer, but it always reminds me of the MRF when I go. I love sitting under the tent."

Buddy Fendler, Fan

"I live in California now. Sometimes at the beach, I'll talk to people and find out that they're from the St. Louis area and that they went to the MRF. We'll go, 'How cool was the MRF?!'"

Gene Haffner, Student Worker

"I have met people from the St. Louis area that have moved out here to Colorado, and I always ask, 'Have you ever heard of the Mississippi River Festival?' And so often, they say, 'I went to the MRF! It was the greatest thing.' It was just magical. Somewhere along the line, I bought a copy of the MRF photo book the university put out. Over the years, some of the acts who played the festival have come through the Greeley area, and I always connect with the personal manager or the road manager, tell them the story, and usually, the artist will remember the MRF. I started collecting autographs of artists in that book. I've got Judy Collins, John McEuen of the Nitty Gritty Dirt Band, and all these people who have come through this area."

Doug Cox, Fan

"I was in Edwardsville maybe three or four years ago at the Artisan Bakery. I was standing in line and the guy behind me was wearing an MRF shirt. I said, 'Well, that's an old shirt.' And he said, "No, it's for the 50th anniversary.' I said, 'My dad probably took the picture on the back of that shirt.' We got to talking and he sent me some T-shirts."

Jim Muffo

"I go up to the campus every once in a while. I love going up there. I can't go back to my high school. I can't go back to my old neighborhood where I grew up. My neighborhood isn't even there anymore. The house that we lived in burned down. It's gone. I can't go back to that, but I can go back to SIUE."

Rick Stankoven, Student Worker

"I was really sad when it ended. To this day, when I ride my bike, one of my routes is through campus, through the parking lots, and then over to the MRF site. And I always play Harry Chapin while I ride through there."

Rick Haydon

"About ten years ago, I was walking at the MRF site with my wife. There was a mast from the tent lying on the ground. I walked up alongside the mast, just kind of reminiscing, catching the vibe again, and I looked over and saw one of the turnbuckles that set the tension for the cable on the main mast. It was like four feet tall and still had about two feet of cable on it. I had a student who was into weightlifting, and he came into my office one day and said he had bench pressed 450 pounds. I said, 'That's awesome. You want to put that to practical application?' I took him out to the site and pointed to the turnbuckle, and I said, 'When you feel like lifting weights again, come out here and pick that up and carry it over and put it next to my garage.' I live right by the MRF site. So, I came home from school two weeks later and saw something on the side of the garage. I went over, and it was that turnbuckle. I bounded it in concrete, and now it looks like a piece of modern art. It's sitting in my backyard as my reminder of how the MRF changed my life."

Greg Drexelius, Student Worker

"If you go back out to the MRF site today and listen very, very carefully, the music is still there. By the laws of physics, it doesn't go away. It spreads out, and it just gets lighter and lighter. If you listen very carefully, you can still hear it. And there was just such wonderful music."

Jim Grandone, Student Worker

"Part of the reason I kept my production supervisor badge was to prove that I worked there because it's hard to believe it happened if you weren't there. So, I show that to people to prove I was in the heart of it. Looking back, it was perfect. I wouldn't have changed a thing. I'm humbled and honored that I was a part of it. I enjoyed every moment."

John S. Rendleman, Fan

"Today, when I think of the MRF, I remember a lot of good times. It brought me together with a lot of friends that I wasn't necessarily close to in high school. We all had different things to do, but we all enjoyed the concerts at the MRF—and the after-parties here and there. Now, we talk about the MRF as a big part of our life as young adults. It's awfully nice to have the MRF as something we can point to and say, 'We were there. We were a part of that.' It's part of our identity. Even today, if I'm around people who don't really know where Southern Illinois is, I can say I saw The Who, or I saw this band or that band. I think there's a little bit of pride in the fact that, yes, I'm from Southern Illinois, but I'm also from the MRF."

"You should have been at the Mississippi River Festival, man!" Why the MRF Was Special

Bob Heil

"It will never be duplicated—never. It was a different time, different feeling. The financial things. I mean, what was it? Two bucks to get onto the grounds and lay back and hear some of the best music ever? No matter what you wanted—it could be anything from classical to The Who or Joe Walsh to Peter, Paul and Mary. It didn't make any difference what your music was, it was always at the Mississippi River Festival. Just wait a couple of weeks and it'll come back with something that you like for two bucks. Could you do that today? You can't park your car for that. You can't buy a soda for that."

"Supe" Granda

"The Mississippi River Festival was before it's time. I mean, those people had such a clear, perfect idea, and they built it in such a perfect location. See, that was the '60s and '70s, and that's when music hadn't become corporate; that's before music had become marketing. You know, when music was art. So, when we went to the MRF, we didn't go to see *Budweiser* presents the *so and so*, we went to see these people making their art. They came onto the stage, and they played whatever they wanted. They were making art directly from the heart and from the soul. The people who sat in the audience were able to have that art just washing over them."

Rance Caldwell
"The Mississippi River Festival had a notoriety for the simple fact that it was a loose environment where you could go and have fun and not feel like you were going to be some kind of merchandising victim. Things were reasonable there. I always walked around, and I found it was a very open non-commercial environment. That's where they've got you nowadays. The magic is lost when the greed factor comes in and it becomes a money game rather than let's go play in the woods, hang out, and have a great time playing music. I mean, I didn't get into this for the money."

Billy Peek, Musician
"I played a lot of big festivals with Rod Stewart. We did a lot of outdoor things in Australia and New Zealand with at least 35,000—as many as 50,000 people at one event. I think the difference between those and the MRF is the commercialism because it's pretty much about the money today. The MRF didn't charge exorbitant amounts of money. They usually had more than one act on the show; I mean, they had a proper show, like the show I did had four top names. A lot of companies sponsor shows now; I guess it's just a necessary evil. But in those days, it was about the art, it was about the music—it was about people really enjoying themselves and having a good time."

Richie Furay
"I just think times have changed. I'm not saying it's better or worse, but back then, I think the bottom line was the music."

Tom Shipley
"The MRF was more like a happening. It wasn't like the shows at the big outdoor amphitheaters now that are well promoted by the record companies, and you've got the management companies and everybody putting a lot of money into it. These tended to feel like happenings. I

suspect that's why there were so many people there and why they were having such a good time."

"Supe" Granda

"The MRF was the embryo—the very first, you know? The venue, like the artists and the music back then, was so much freer. We didn't know what we were doing. We were just making it up, man. Let's try this. Okay. Let's see. Oh, that doesn't work? Let's try this. Oh, that's great! Ideas were just flying through the air like that, like that, like that. It was the same way with the MRF."

Bob Heil

"We had no script. We had nothing to guide us because this had never been done before, not like this. I think what I take away from the Mississippi River Festival, more than anything, was all of that great camaraderie we had and how much we learned from each other—being able to trust in the system and say, 'Here, go do it.' And you know what? We all did our part, and it was magnificent. I don't think you could do that today. People don't work together like that anymore. Egos are too high. We didn't have any of that with the festival. The whole synergy thing was just so hot there. It was great. And that could never be duplicated ever again."

"Supe" Granda

"They're trying to replicate it now. The theaters today are modeled after the Mississippi River Festival. The technology is forty years progressed. The sight lines may be better. They may be more efficient. They may be better able to handle bigger crowds. But there was no greater feeling than there was at the Mississippi River Festival for both the audience, as well as the performer."

Bob Heil

"Every once in a while, somebody will call me. 'Hey, you did the sound at the River Festival. We're going to do it again, and we're gonna do it better. You know, my uncle's got fifty acres down here in southern Missouri.' 'Oh,

OK.' There hasn't been a lot of thought put into it. At the MRF, major bands would show up in a couple of Volkswagen vans. Today, bands have sixteen fifty-five-foot semis. How are you going to haul in all these acts today when they're not gonna come in Volkswagen vans anymore? They're gonna fly in on their own private jet and their own helicopters and all this. I mean, they haven't been spoiled, but that's what the standard is today."

Lyle Ward

"The Mississippi River Festival was really unique to that time, and I honestly don't think it could be recreated today. All the pieces of it could be recreated and done as well or better with the kinds of facilities that are available now. But when you take the total scope of the product and the goals of the institution, I think it would be very difficult to do that. The rock performers who become the income generators for it are enormously expensive. Their productions are almost unbelievable in terms of the size and quantity of things that they need. So, no, in my opinion, to try to recreate it is not a realistic possibility."

Charlie Cox, SIUE Photographer

"Everything changes. The MRF had its time, and it provided a spot in history that will long be remembered by everybody who attended it. It left a mark on the region, and we can all be proud of what it did for us."

"Supe" Granda

"Now, because it's been gone for so long, a lot of people don't remember it. All they know is, you know, the Intel Cellular One Pavilion. Oh yeah? Well, you should have been at the Mississippi River Festival, man!"

Rick Haydon

"My students are stunned when I point in the direction of the MRF site and say, 'Guys, I saw Cannonball and Nat Adderley there. Freddie Hubbard, Chick Corea. All right there.' They're pretty shocked, and they ask, 'Why isn't that still going on here?!'"

John S. Rendleman

"The MRF was really about the artists who performed, be it symphony, rock & roll, or dancers. There may be a time when future generations want that kind of thing because, once the MRF started, it was the art that drove it. It was sincere, and people recognized that it was authentic, and that caused it to grow quickly and fully. There will be a time when my kids will be thirsting for performance art like that. So, perhaps an MRF can happen again. It may not be monetized or commercialized the same way. It may be different, but there will be a place where art can grow again."

Mark Rogers, Fan

"Nothing close comes to the MRF. It was the definition of a once-in-a-lifetime venue. And no polish needed. It was all true."

Greg Drexelius

"Some people have said we should bring it back. I think we just need to remember it for what it was, which was a unique experience, and let it be. It was perfect as it was."

Rich Dalton, Fan

"It was a magic moment, and I was glad to be there and glad to be part of it. What's better than seeing music in a good situation with good companionship? It was serendipity, and it was inspired. It just all came together. Perfect time, perfect place. It can't be duplicated, but it happened then, and that's enough. And we're still sitting here in 2022, talking about it."

"A Life of Its Own"

"It grew to have a life of its own . . . the offspring of a strained relationship . . . two independent parents sometimes struggling to insure their own bright futures. There was no marriage, just an affair which seemed at the time to be both glamorous and mutually beneficial.

So, it was a bastard of sorts. And all who came to love it and nurture it . . . and try to save it . . . were treated like illegitimate parents. But we also were privileged to experience the excitement firsthand. Neither family fully accepted it . . . not really. Yet few had more admirers. They came from everywhere to this place few had heard of before. They laughed with us, sang, and danced and performed with us. They wrote about us and sometimes cried with us. We grew up together for a while.

It was well-conceived. Those of us at the table watched the joyous birth, sometimes tenuous development, and the wonderful early years. Then we watched the child grow and change dramatically as all children do. We were all amazed by it all.

And then with the strains of adolescence . . . along with growing disenchantment between the parents and a home environment tiring of change, it began to question itself and be questioned. Too big, too small . . . too popular, too elitist. Was it asking too much from the families? Was it worth all the effort? What about the secrets, what about the press? Was it becoming too dangerous?

And so, the parents and so many who had provided it support for its early years turned their backs. They let it struggle . . . gave it little nourishment or direction and finally told it to go away.

It was allowed to die . . . to just go away to be forgotten. But it never did . . . and it never was."

Lyle Ward
Feb. 24, 1998

In Memory Of . . .

Neil "Buzzy" Butler
Charlie Cox
Bob Gill
Bill and Bettie Hudgens
Rusty Young

ACKNOWLEDGMENTS

First and foremost, this project would not have been possible without the countless contributions of Lyle Ward and Jack Twesten.

Lyle had considered writing a book about his MRF experiences for many years. Although it didn't come to fruition, many of the documents, photos, memorabilia, and personal connections he accumulated in anticipation of his own project were invaluable to the completion of this one. Thank you, Lyle, for trusting me with this subject that is so dear to you. I hope you walk away feeling that the MRF's story has now been told. You truly are the keeper of the festival's flame.

Jack has been interviewing MRF performers and officials since the 1980s with a goal of creating a documentary on the festival (coming soon!). Those interviews elicited many of the stories and quotes in this book—notably those from Linda Ruth Brubaker, Rance Caldwell, Charlie Cox, Richie Furay, Bob Gill, Michael "Supe" Granda, Jeff Hanna, Bob Heil, John McEuen, Larry Medlin, Billy Peek, Tom Shipley, and Rusty Young. Besides that, Jack knows just about everyone who ever played a role in the MRF story. Jack, thank you for being so generous with your resources and knowledge. I hope I have helped you as well.

Ultimately, it's all about archiving the stories and memories of those for whom the MRF is such a special part of their lives. By working together, Lyle, Jack, and I were able to accelerate and greatly enhance our individual efforts. I feel blessed to have played a role in shining a spotlight on this amazing tale.

Heartfelt thanks to Joe Clote, Olivia Orman, Rebekah Icenesse, and the team at Publishing Concepts, LLC, for their guidance and for believing in a first-time author writing about a subject from decades ago. Special thanks to Lacy McDonald from the Hayner Library in Alton and Ronald DeBrock of the *Alton Telegraph* for the use of their archival photos; and Cindy Reinhardt and Mary Rose from the Madison County Historical Society for the *Edwardsville Intelligencer* archival photos.

A big dose of gratitude to Rick Stankoven, who combed through decades of his photo archives to find scores of photos he shot at the MRF over the years that had never seen the light of day—until now. Thanks, Rick!

Special thanks to all of the individuals and venues that helped make the interviews possible, including Dale Benz, Bob Bell, Scott Nienhaus, Terry Jones Rogers, Terry Perkins, David Thomason, Rivers Edge Entertainment, The Sheldon Concert Hall, The Stagger Inn, The Wildey Theatre, and The Wildwood Springs Lodge.

Last but certainly not least, a big "thank you" to all who shared their Mississippi River Festival remembrances with me. While I never attended an MRF event, I hope I have captured the feeling of sitting on the lawn on a summer night and enjoying the music with friends. I wish I could have been there with you.

ABOUT THE AUTHOR

Mark Pierce

Mark Pierce has been a journalist and corporate communications leader in the St. Louis area for more than 30 years. A graduate of Southern Illinois University Edwardsville, Mark's love of music and connections with many who played pivotal roles in the Mississippi River Festival story served as inspiration to write the first book that truly tells the MRF's story. Mark lives in Glen Carbon with his wife, Sara.

PHOTO GALLERY

Delyte W. Morris, SIU President (1948–70)
Courtesy of the *Alton Telegraph*

John S. Rendleman
SIUE Chancellor (1968-71) and President (1971-76)
Courtesy of the *Alton Telegraph*

An early map of the MRF site
Courtesy of Jack Twesten

Aerial photo of the MRF site during the 1973 Chicago concert
Courtesy of the *Alton Telegraph*

The colorful sails that greeted fans at the MRF main entrance
Courtesy of Jack Twesten

Fans make their way down the slope from the entrance toward the lawn and tent
Courtesy of the *Alton Telegraph*

Fans line up to purchase tickets at the main entrance
Courtesy of Jack Twesten

The festival tent at dusk
Courtesy of the *Alton Telegraph*

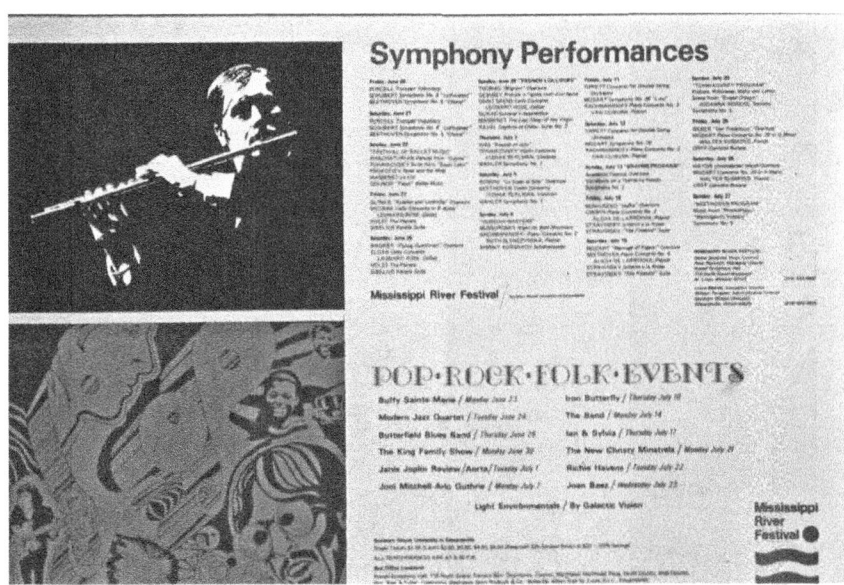

A marketing piece promoting the festival's 1969 lineup

Courtesy of Lyle Ward

The St. Louis Symphony Orchestra performs on the festival's opening night, June 20, 1969

Courtesy of the *Alton Telegraph*

 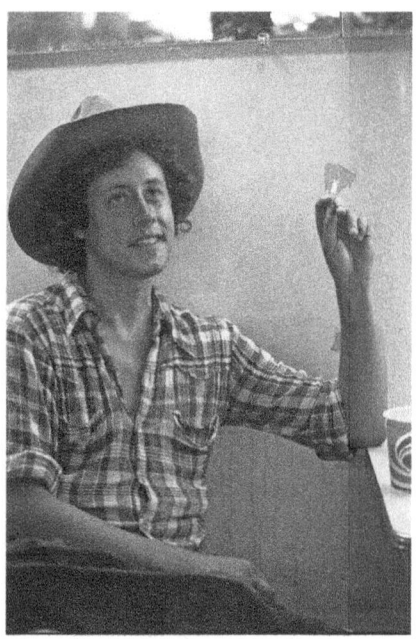

SLSO Conductor Walter Susskind
on opening night
Courtesy of the *Alton Telegraph*

Arlo Guthrie chats backstage
before his 1974 show
Courtesy of the *Alton Telegraph*

SIUE Photographer Charlie Cox
Courtesy of Rick Stankoven

Joan Baez discusses the Vietnam War
with reporters in 1969
Courtesy of the *Alton Telegraph*

Bob Heil and the MRF mixing board
Courtesy of Jack Twesten

Heil Sound's MRF mixing board under the tent
Courtesy of Jack Twesten

Peter Cetera of Chicago, 1974
Courtesy of the *Alton Telegraph*

Tent Master Skip Manley, 1971
Courtesy of the Madison County Historical Society,
Edwardsville Intelligencer Collection

Terry Kath of Chicago, 1974
Courtesy of the *Alton Telegraph*

The tent team raises the tent
Courtesy of the Madison County Historical Society, *Edwardsville Intelligencer* Collection

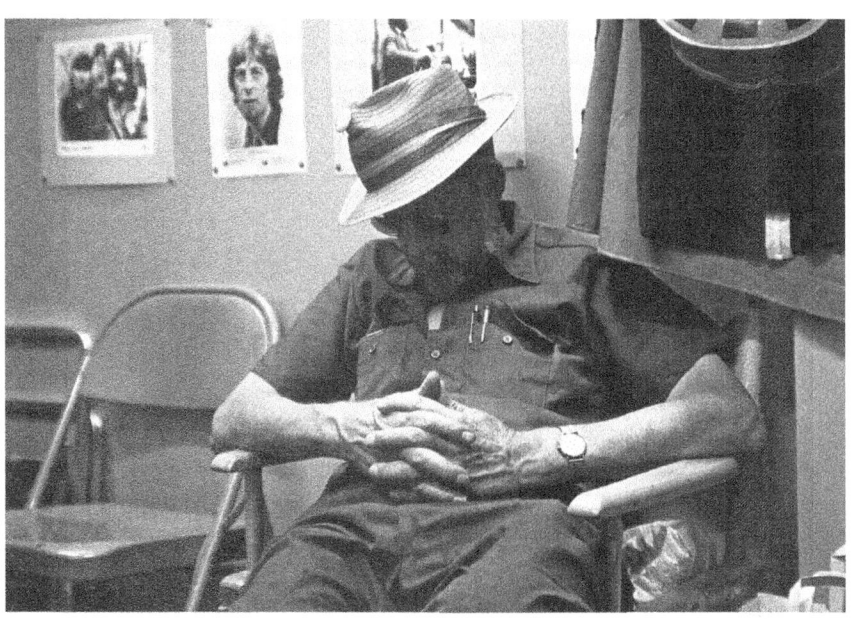

Skip Manley naps backstage
Courtesy of the *Alton Telegraph*

The damaged tent following the 1969 tornado
Courtesy of Jack Twesten

Greg Drexelius, far right, and other staffers present Skip Manley
with a "miniature Manley" figurine, 1974
Courtesy of Greg Drexelius

Local artist Billy Peek, far right in the
shadows, supports Chuck Berry, 1971
Courtesy of the *Alton Telegraph*

Chuck Berry, 1977
Courtesy of Rick Stankoven

Skip Manley's omnipresent hat
Courtesy of Lyle Ward

Wolfman Jack, 1976
Courtesy of Rick Stankoven

Lyle Ward backstage, 1973
Courtesy of the *Alton Telegraph*

Sha Na Na backstage, 1976
Courtesy of Rick Stankoven

Lyle Ward and Gene Haffner discuss
plans on stage
Courtesy of Gene Haffner

Dodie Ladd, the MRF's "Bell-Tree Ringer"
Courtesy of Jack Twesten

Student workers Jim Grandone and
Jody Weisenfeld discuss plans
Courtesy of Jim Grandone

Grace Slick of Jefferson Starship, 1975
Courtesy of the *Alton Telegraph*

Student worker Neil "Buzzy" Butler
Courtesy of the *Alton Telegraph*

Pete Townshend's guitar pic from
the 1971 show
Courtesy of Jack Twesten

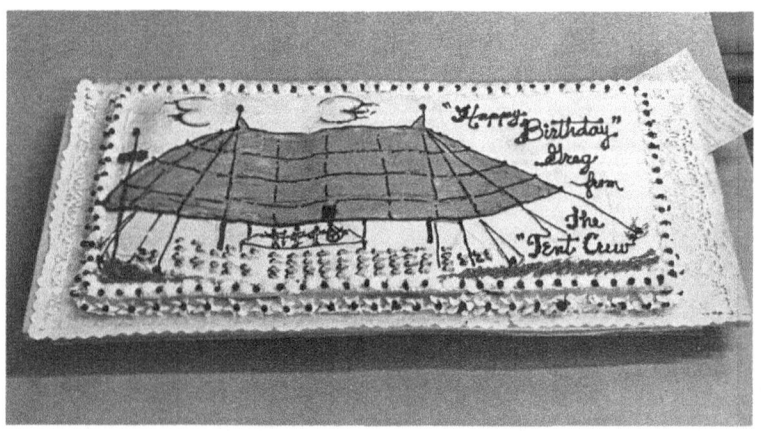

A tent-themed cake presented to student worker Greg Drexelius by the tent crew
Courtesy of Greg Drexelius

Pete Townshend shows off his legendary windmill technique, 1971
Courtesy of the *Alton Telegraph*

Keith Moon and Pete Townshend of the Who, 1971
Courtesy of the *Alton Telegraph*

Autographs from Jimmy Buffett
and his band obtained by Mary Kay Leach
after the '77 show
Courtesy of stlmusicyesterdays.com

Jimmy Buffett, 1977
Courtesy of Rick Stankoven

MRF student worker Bob Gill sits behind the Nitty Gritty Dirt Band's John McEuen
as he records music backstage, 1973
Courtesy of the *Alton Telegraph*

Mac Davis plays golf with Bill Hudgens and Larry Hepler, 1975
Courtesy of Jack Twesten

Autographed photo of a 1972 golf outing including John Rendleman (left),
Bill Hudgens (second from right) and John Denver
Courtesy of Jack Twesten

Emmylou Harris, 1978
Courtesy of the *Alton Telegraph*

Toy Caldwell of the Marshall Tucker
Band, 1978
Courtesy of the *Alton Telegraph*

Mike Love of the Beach Boys, 1977
Courtesy of Rick Stankoven

Brian Wilson of the Beach Boys, 1977
Courtesy of the *Alton Telegraph*

Carl Wilson of the Beach Boys, 1977
Courtesy of Rick Stankoven

Fans sing along with the Beach Boys under the tent, 1977
Courtesy of Rick Stankoven

Fans under the tent watch the St. Louis Symphony perform
Courtesy of the *Alton Telegraph*

Harry Chapin, 1976
Courtesy of Rick Stankoven

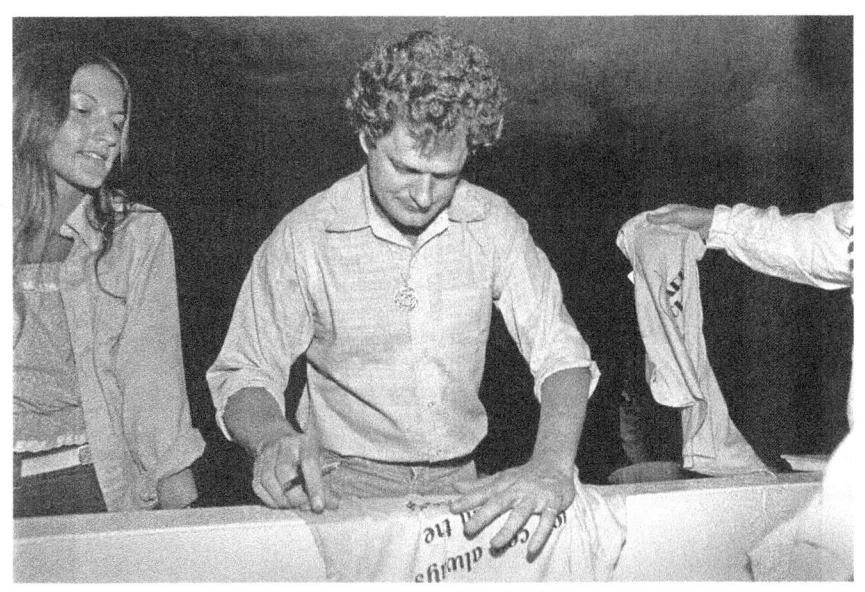

Harry Chapin signs T-shirts for fans, 1979
Courtesy of Rick Stankoven

Harry Chapin shakes hands with a fan, 1979
Courtesy of Rick Stankoven

Harry Chapin chats backstage, 1979
Courtesy of Rick Stankoven

Harry Chapin greets fans in the
front row, 1976
Courtesy of Rick Stankoven

Andy Powell, left, and Martin Turner
of Wishbone Ash, 1971
Courtesy of the *Alton Telegraph*

Peoria native Dan Fogelberg, 1974
Courtesy of the *Alton Telegraph*

Gary Richrath of REO Speedwagon, 1975
Courtesy of the *Alton Telegraph*

Jeff "Skunk" Baxter of the Doobie
Brothers, 1976
Courtesy of the *Alton Telegraph*

Fans reach for a piece of REO Speedwagon's Gary Richrath, 1975
Courtesy of Rick Stankoven

Rainy nights were not uncommon at the MRF, leaving lawn fans
to be creative in finding shelter
Courtesy of Rick Stankoven

David Crosby and Graham Nash, 1976
Courtesy of Rick Stankoven

Tina Turner signs autographs
backstage, 1971
Courtesy of the *Alton Telegraph*

Stephen Stills, 1975
Courtesy of Rick Stankoven

Members of the Crisis Intervention Unit
Courtesy of Rick Stankoven

Doug Gray of the Marshall Tucker
Band, 1978
Courtesy of the Alton Telegraph

Bob Hope, 1975
Courtesy of Rick Stankoven

Bob Hope entertains staffers
backstage, 1977
Courtesy of the *Alton Telegraph*

Bob Hope presents a plaque honoring
John Hugger as the MRF's One
Millionth Fan, 1975
Courtesy of Rick Stankoven

Bob Hope is interviewed by KSD-TV's John Auble, 1975
Courtesy of Rick Stankoven

View from the lawn before a show
Courtesy of Rick Stankoven

Donny and Marie Osmond, 1976
Courtesy of Rick Stankoven

Fans of the Osmonds gather backstage, 1976
Courtesy of the *Alton Telegraph*

SIUE Food Services Director Bill Crabb
Courtesy of Jack Twesten

MRF Food Service workers, 1975
Courtesy of Rick Stankoven

University Police inspect coolers at the main entrance, 1973
Courtesy of the *Alton Telegraph*

Marshall Tucker Band fans were some of the most raucous in MRF history
Courtesy of the *Alton Telegraph*

Fans enter the lawn with their coolers and blankets
Courtesy of Rick Stankoven

Lawn fans gear up for the evening
Courtesy of Rick Stankoven

259

Fans on the lawn digging into a bucket of chicken
Courtesy of Rick Stankoven

Fueling up on the lawn for the evening's festivities
Courtesy of Rick Stankoven

Signs direct attendees toward food
areas at the site
Courtesy of the *Alton Telegraph*

Kris Kristofferson, 1977
Courtesy of Rick Stankoven

Michael "Supe" Granda of the Ozark
Mountain Daredevils, a St. Louis native,
attended many MRF concerts as a fan
before playing under the tent four times
Courtesy of the *Alton Telegraph*

Jackson Browne performs hours before
recording two songs for his *Running on
Empty* album at the Holiday Inn, 1977
Courtesy of Rick Stankoven

The Edwardsville Holiday Inn was the
site for numerous historic festival
moments over the years

MRF ticket stubs
Courtesy of Jack Twesten

Willie Nelson, 1978
Courtesy of Rick Stankoven

America, 1975
Courtesy of Rick Stankoven

From left, Bill Kreutzmann, Phil Lesh, Jerry Garcia and Bob Weir
of the Grateful Dead, 1980
Courtesy of Jack Twesten

The abandoned MRF stage, 1981
Courtesy of Rick Stankoven

Weeds begin to overtake the
MRF site, 1981
Courtesy of Rick Stankoven

The empty ticket booth, 1981
Courtesy of Rick Stankoven

MRF tent chairs on display in Andy
Kovarik's basement

Lyle Ward before a display of MRF photos at the Wood River, Illinois, Museum, 2022

Concert photos adorning the walls of Andy Kovarik's basement

The Eagles headline the schedule in a 1975 festival ad
Courtesy of Jack Twesten

Newspaper ad
highlighting
upcoming shows,
1978
Courtesy of Jack Twesten

1978 schedule
Courtesy of Jack Twesten

The MRF's 1977 schedule
Courtesy of Jack Twesten

MRF T-shirts from the 1974 and 1975 seasons
Courtesy of Lyle Ward

The MRF tent turnbuckle
on display in Rick Haydon's
backyard

A sign for the 50th anniversary exhibit
at SIUE, 2019
Courtesy of Lyle Ward

Endnotes

1 Kerber, Stephen. "The Mississippi River Festival at Edwardsville, 1969-1980." *Journal of the Illinois State Historical Society*, Fall 2006-Winter 2007

2 Sutin, Philip. "SIU Picks Outdoor Site for Symphony." *St. Louis Post-Dispatch*, November 24, 1968

3 Ibid

4 "Manley: Big Top to MRF." *SIUE News Service*, August 23, 1976

5 Peters, Frank. "Symphony Thinks Big About Summer at SIU." *St. Louis Post-Dispatch*, March 30, 1969

6 "Editorials . . . What we think about . . . Equipment Purchases . . . River Festival . . . " *Alton Telegraph*, March 19, 1969

7 "Mississippi River Festival." *St. Louis Post-Dispatch*, May 11, 1969

8 Caplan, Lois. "Women's World." *St. Louis Jewish Light*, June 4, 1969

9 "East, West Sides Meet at Festival." *Alton Telegraph*, June 6, 1969

10 Ibid

11 Willis, Thomas. "Mississippi River Festival Opens Friday at Edwardsville." *Chicago Tribune*, June 15, 1969

12 Peters, Frank. "Successful Opening for River Festival." *St. Louis Post-Dispatch*, June 21, 1969

13 Defty, Sally Bixby. "Symphony Beginning Series at SIU Tonight." *St. Louis Post-Dispatch*, June 20, 1969

14 Schaub, Robert C. "Festival Under Way." *Edwardsville Intelligencer*, June 21, 1969

15 Ibid

16 Barnes, Harper. "Janis Joplin's Rock and Roll Sends Huge Crowd – to Its Feet." *St. Louis Post-Dispatch*, July 2, 1969

17 Norrish, Dick. "Janis Joplin Is Smash Hit." *Edwardsville Intelligencer*, July 2, 1969

18 Barnes, Harper. "Janis Joplin's Rock and Roll Sends Huge Crowd – to Its Feet." *St. Louis Post-Dispatch*, July 2, 1969

19 Norrish, Dick. "Butterfield Blues Act Boring." *Edwardsville Intelligencer*, June 26, 1969

20 Lemcoe, Laura. "Havens Has a Gentle Approach." *Edwardsville Intelligencer*, July 23, 1969

21 *United Press International*, July 25, 1969

22 Ibid

23 Barnes, Harper. "Joan Baez At Festival." *St. Louis Post-Dispatch*, July 24, 1969

[24] "'Iron Butterfly,' Group With New Sound, to Be at Festival." *Alton Telegraph*, July 8, 1969

[25] Uhlenbrock, Tom. "Festival is getting record attendances." *UPI*, June 15, 1976.

[26] Barnes, Harper. "Crowd Soars With Iron Butterfly." *St. Louis Post-Dispatch*, July 11, 1969

[27] Ibid

[28] Walters, Ron. "Butterflies Bomb 'Beat' Generation." *Alton Telegraph*, July 18, 1969

[29] "'The Band' Will Be Featured At River Festival Tonight." *Alton Telegraph*, July 14, 1969

[30] Barnes, Harper. "Finding Pieces of Hate." *St. Louis Post-Dispatch*, May 23, 1980

[31] Ibid

[32] Helm, Levon; Davis, Stephen. *This Wheel's on Fire*. William Morrow, 1993.

[33] Barnes, Harper. "Bob Dylan Is Surprise Guest At Edwardsville Festival." *St. Louis Post-Dispatch*, July 15, 1969

[34] Weaver, Larry. "Christys Exhibit Magical Appeal." *Alton Telegraph*, July 22, 1969

[35] *United Press International*, July 25, 1969

[36] Weaver, Larry. "Audience Not 'Anti' to Baez." *Alton Telegraph*, July 24, 1969

[37] Rosenbaum, Connie. "Revival-Style Rock Moves River Festival Audience." *St. Louis Post-Dispatch*, July 30, 1970

[38] Ades, John J. "Songs of Wrightson, Lois Hunt sentimental, idealistic, moving." *Alton Telegraph*, July 27, 1970

[39] Mueller, Mary. "Grateful Dead Stirs Revival At SIU Campus." *Belleville News-Democrat*, July 14, 1970

[40] Thompson, Doug. "Lively 8,500 visit Grateful Dead." *Alton Telegraph*, July 9, 1970

[41] Ibid

[42] Richmond, Richard T. "Mancini At Festival." *St. Louis Post-Dispatch*, July 19, 1971

[43] Ibid

[44] O'Neill, Lillian. "Two symphony concerts enhance MRF." *Alton Telegraph*, August 15, 1977

[45] Mueller, Mary. "'Chicago' Rock Group Offers Original Sound." *Belleville News-Democrat*, July 17, 1970

[46] Ronzio, Judy. "Record MRF Crowd." *Edwardsville Intelligencer*, July 16, 1970

[47] Ibid

[48] Richmond, Dick. "Rock Band 'Chicago' To Be On TV Special." *St. Louis Post-Dispatch*, July 15, 1973.

[49] Maddox, Teri. "Traces of MRF." *Belleville News-Democrat*, January 13, 2009

[50] Cullinane, John. "Chicago Concert At River Festival." *St. Louis Post-Dispatch*, August 22, 1974.

[51] "Largest Crowd Of Season See Chicago at MRF." *Edwardsville Intelligencer*, August 22, 1974.

[52] Newsom, Thomas B. "Judy Collins Performs At River Festival." *St. Louis Post-Dispatch*, August 6, 1970

[53] Thompson, Doug. "Performs before 10,000." *Alton Telegraph*, July 16, 1971

[54] Ibid

[55] Landers, Jim. "Judy Collins is a start who doesn't act like it." *Alton Telegraph*, August 11, 1973

[56] Newmark, Judy J. "'I Am Going To Sit In Splendor.'" *St. Louis Post-Dispatch*, July 27, 1975

[57] Thompson, Doug. "Another good evening of mellow music at MRF . . ." *Alton Telegraph*, July 23, 1975

[58] Norris, Dick. "Cliburn Opens MRF." *Edwardsville Intelligencer*, July 12, 1971

[59] "Manley: Big Top to MRF." *SIUE News Service*, August 23, 1976

[60] "Meet the Festival Tentmaster." *Edwardsville Intelligencer*, March 18, 1969

[61] "Manley: Big Top to MRF." *SIUE News Service*, August 23, 1976

[62] Ibid

[63] Ibid

[64] Thompson, Doug. "'Shakes' entire MRF stage." *Alton Telegraph*, July 27, 1971

[65] Kelly, Robert J. "Midnight Ride Planned To Get Festival Tent." *St. Louis Post-Dispatch*, June 26, 1974.

[66] Thompson, Doug. "MRF 1974: a case of survival." *Alton Telegraph*, July 6, 1974.

[67] "Manley: Big Top to MRF." *SIUE News Service*, August 23, 1976.

[68] Thompson, Doug. "Robinson's crowd-evading tactics preserve life, limb after concert." *Alton Telegraph*, July 21, 1970

[69] Ibid

[70] Ibid

[71] Ibid

[72] Ibid

[73] Cullinane, John S. "Dick Clark And Vintage Rock At SIU." *St. Louis Post-Dispatch*, June 25, 1977

[74] Thompson, Doug. "13,000 cheer old rock 'n roll." *Alton Telegraph*." July 15, 1972

[75] Thompson, Doug. *Alton Telegraph*, July 31, 1976

[76] Richmond, Dick. "Sha Na Na Performs At Festival." *St. Louis Post-Dispatch*, July 19, 1973.

[77] Thompson, Doug. "New Sha Na Na routines thrill 11,900 at MRF." *Alton Telegraph*, July 19, 1973

[78] Thompson, Doug. "Rockin' the night away . . ." *Alton Telegraph*, July 21, 1973

[79] Thompson, Doug. "Roberta gave a show; the crowd gave flak" *Alton Telegraph*, August 6, 1975

[80] Dissett, Jim. "Ten Years After." *Belleville News-Democrat*, July 28, 1991

[81] "Students working for River Festival." *Woodstock Sentinel-Review*. August 17, 1976.

[82] Peters, Frank. "The Day 32,123 People Drove To Edwardsville." *St. Louis Post-Dispatch*, August 22, 1971

[83] Newsom, Thomas B. "Who Draws 34,000? The Who, That's Who." *St. Louis Post-Dispatch*, August 17, 1971

[84] Tighe, Theresa. "Symphony Sales Demon Bowing Out." *St. Louis Post-Dispatch*, April 1, 1994

[85] Thompson, Doug. "Guess Who: 'Where it's at.'" *Alton Telegraph*, August 4, 1970

[86] Ibid

[87] www.stlmusicyesterdays.com

[88] Thompson, Doug. "MRF Moog, blues & upcoming." *Alton Telegraph*, August 11, 1972

[89] Landers, Jim. "Money isn't total story at MRF." *Alton Telegraph*, August 25, 1973

[90] Jost, Mary. "Progressive 'Yes' Mixes Fresh, Original Talents." *Belleville News-Democrat*, August 22, 1972.

[91] Ibid

[92] Landers, Jim. "Money isn't total story at MRF." *Alton Telegraph*, August 25, 1973

[93] Cullinane, John S. "YES Rock Group At River Festival." *St. Louis Post-Dispatch*, July 10, 1975

[94] Jost, Mary. "Beach Boys Songs Have Stale Style at Festival." *Belleville News-Democrat*, August 17, 1972.

[95] Hamilton, Thomas. "Beach Boys Give Concert At The River Festival." *St. Louis Post-Dispatch*, August 17, 1972

[96] Richmond, Dick. "Beach Boys Perform At The River Festival." *St. Louis Post-Dispatch*, August 22, 1977

[97] Dissett, Jim. "Ten Years After." *Belleville News-Democrat*, July 28, 1991

[98] Uetz, Carl. "Dying blues comes to MRF." *Alton Telegraph*, July 17, 1974.

[99] Thompson, Doug. "The music was blues; but the sound was good." *Alton Telegraph*, July 16, 1975

[100] Rosenbaum, Connie. "Revival-Style Rock Moves River Festival Audience." *St. Louis Post-Dispatch*, July 30, 1970

[101] Landers, Jim. "Huge MRF audience lauds Harry Chapin." *Alton Telegraph*, July 18, 1973

[102] Ibid

[103] Baker, Nora. "Chapin: Pragmatic poet." *Alton Telegraph*, August 23, 1975

[104] Richmond, Dick. "Harry Chapin Sings At Festival" *St. Louis Post-Dispatch*. July 1, 1976.

[105] Thompson, Doug. "Story-singer Chapin charms 6,451 at MRF." *Alton Telegraph*, July 1, 1976.

[106] Ibid

[107] Sharp, Walt. "MRF performer bewitches crowd via unique mystique." *Alton Telegraph*, August 11, 1978

[108] Ibid

[109] Ibid

[110] Hemmer, Cheryl. "Harry Chapin: on stage and off stage." *Belleville News-Democrat*, August 13, 1978

[111] Ibid

[112] Richmond, Dick. "Fool's Gold Opens Edwardsville Festival." *St. Louis Post-Dispatch*, June 23, 1977

[113] Baker, Nora. "R.E.O. Speedwagon thrills 15,000 MRF fans." *Alton Telegraph*, August 16, 1975

[114] Thompson, Doug. "Bonnie brings husband, friends to home scene for MRF concert." *Alton Telegraph*, July 30, 1970

[115] Hillig, Terry. "6,000 Brave Heat, Humidity." *Edwardsville Intelligencer*, July 30, 1970

[116] Rosenbaum, Connie. "Revival-Style Rock Moves River Festival Audience." *St. Louis Post-Dispatch*, July 30, 1970

[117] Ibid

[118] Thompson, Doug. "A 'Tina-bit' of soul . . ." *Alton Telegraph*, July 31, 1971

[119] Ibid

[120] Newsom, Thomas B. "River Festival Crowd Applauds Earl Scruggs And His Banjo." *St. Louis Post-Dispatch*, July 28, 1971

[121] Barnes, Harper. "Marching With Different Drummer." *St. Louis Post-Dispatch*, July 30, 1976.

[122] Ibid

[123] Ibid

[124] Thompson, Doug. "MRF fans cheer folk-rock." *Alton Telegraph*, August 2, 1973

[125] Thompson, Doug. "Crosby and Nash end fifth season of MRF on good note." *Alton Telegraph*, August 30, 1973

[126] Landers, Jim. "Money isn't total story at MRF." *Alton Telegraph*, August 25, 1973

[127] Avins, Mimi. "Pop Goes The Sentimental." *St. Louis Post-Dispatch*, September 7, 1973.

[128] Thompson, Doug. "Return of the hack: Joe Walsh at MRF." *Alton Telegraph*, July 18, 1974.

[129] Thompson, Doug. "29,700 hear Eagles' rock as brawls erupt at MRF" Alton Telegraph, July 30, 1975

[130] Ibid

[131] "Rock fans blow it!" *Alton Telegraph*, July 31, 1975

[132] Barnes, Harper. "Program of New Jazz At Mississippi Festival." *St. Louis Post-Dispatch*, July 31, 1974.

[133] Thompson, Doug. "Dixieland fading." *Alton Telegraph*, August 11, 1972

[134] Frohman, Clayton. "Mahavishnu Erupts At Festival." *St. Louis Post-Dispatch*, August 15, 1973.

[135] Thompson, Doug. "SIU's Rendleman happy with new music festival." *Alton Telegraph*, July 3, 1970

[136] Norrish, Dick. "It may be the end for the MRF." *Edwardsville Intelligencer*, September 22, 1974.

[137] Thompson, Doug. "SIUE takes over summer festival; symphony is out." *Alton Telegraph*, November 8, 1974.

[138] Landers, Jim. "MRF greets Miller band with collective sigh of memories." *Alton Telegraph*, July 22, 1972

[139] Thompson, Doug. "Is America losing Hope in Bob?" *Alton Telegraph*, July 26, 1975

[140] Smith, Susan Jay. "Bob Hope: insults and patriotism." *Alton Telegraph*, July 9, 1977

[141] "Hope Couldn't Wait For TV." *St. Louis Post-Dispatch*, July 10, 1977

[142] Thompson, Doug. "Benny Goodman legend in his own time – which was last night at MRF." *Alton Telegraph*, June 25, 1976.

[143] Richmond, Dick. "Cab Calloway Star Performer At Mississippi River Festival." *St. Louis Post-Dispatch*. August 7, 1976.

[144] Viets, Elaine. "Cab Calloway: Hi-De-Ho!" *St. Louis Post-Dispatch*. November 4, 1976.

[145] Archibald, John J. "Buffy Sainte-Marie Performs At Festival." *St. Louis Post-Dispatch*, August 14, 1971

[146] Uetz, Carl. "Arlo Guthrie: still singing his protest songs." *Alton Telegraph*, August 31, 1974.

[147] Ibid

[148] Thompson, Doug. "After 36 years, still singing for change" *Alton Telegraph*, August 9, 1975

[149] Pollack, Joe. "Seeger And Guthrie: Spanning Generations." *St. Louis Post-Dispatch*, August 12, 1977

[150] Pollack, Joe. "Seeger And Guthrie: Spanning Generations." *St. Louis Post-Dispatch*, August 12, 1977

[151] Williams, Jill. "Joni Mitchell returns to MRF." *Alton Telegraph*, August 7, 1974.

[152] Richmond, Dick. "Peter, Paul & Mary: Arrivin' On A Jet Plane." *St. Louis Post-Dispatch*, August 9, 1978

[153] Ibid

[154] Sharp, Walt. "It was a time for old friends." *Alton Telegraph*, August 12, 1978

[155] Thompson, Doug. "Hawkers sell Cassidy stuff." *Alton Telegraph*, August 21, 1972

[156] Ibid

[157] Cullinane, John S. "Osmonds Perform At River Festival." *St. Louis Post-Dispatch*, August 21, 1975

[158] Ibid

[159] Dissett, Jim. "Ten Years After." *Belleville News-Democrat*, July 28, 1991

[160] "Here From The Land of Os . . ." *St. Louis Post-Dispatch*, August 12, 1976.

[161] Dissett, Jim. "Ten Years After." *Belleville News-Democrat*, July 28, 1991

[162] Richmond, Dick. "Festival Audience Screams As Andy Gibb Sings, Plays." *St. Louis Post-Dispatch*, June 16, 1978

[163] "River Festival Draws 225,311; May Break Even." *St. Louis Post-Dispatch*, September 14, 1975

[164] "Festival Recovery." *St. Louis Post-Dispatch*, September 15, 1975

[165] "Mississippi River Festival Cites SIU-E's John Rendleman." *SIUE News Service*, January 23, 1976.

[166] Ingrassia, Paul. "SIU-E President John S. Rendleman Dies at 48." *Southern Illinoisan*, March 4, 1976.

[167] "John Rendleman dead." *Belleville News-Democrat*, March 4, 1976.

[168] Sanford, Robert. "Hal Holbrook Portrays Twain At Festival." *St. Louis Post-Dispatch*, September 17, 1976.

[169] Thompson, Doug. "Shakespearean presentation may be too good for MRF." *Alton Telegraph*, August 19, 1977

[170] Cullen, Cathy. "Speedy artists replace backdrop." *Alton Telegraph*, August 20, 1977

[171] Cullen, Cathy. "Prop artist saves day for MRF." *Alton Telegraph*, August 23, 1977

[172] Ibid

[173] Ibid

[174] "An Evening With Julie Harris." *St. Louis Post-Dispatch*, June 17, 1976.

[175] Ibid

[176] Rice, Patricia. "Julie, In Roles Of Real Women" *St. Louis Post-Dispatch*, July 6, 1976.

[177] "River Festival Food Service Geared Up for Another Season." *Edwardsville Intelligencer*, June 19, 1972

[178] Riordan, Carol Ann. "MRF entertainers get royal treatment when it's mealtime." *Belleville News-Democrat*, July 28, 1976.

[179] Ibid

[180] "River Festival Is Calmer Under Tighter Security." *St. Louis Post-Dispatch*, July 15, 1979

[181] Uetz, Carl. "Huge MRF crowd cheers Tucker's loud rock while lightning flickers above." *Alton Telegraph*, July 8, 1976.

[182] "No way to fight festival problems." *Belleville News-Democrat*, July 9, 1976.

[183] Cullinane, John S. "Tucker Band At River Festival." *St. Louis Post-Dispatch*, June 13, 1979

[184] Thompson, Doug. "MRF to crack down on booze in picnic lunches at concerts." *Alton Telegraph*, February 8. 1973

[185] Brown, Merrill. "River Festival Tries Dry Run." *St. Louis Post-Dispatch*, July 19, 1973.

[186] Ibid

[187] Avins, Mimi. "Rescuing Stoned Fans At Rock Concerts." *St. Louis Post-Dispatch*, October 21, 1973.

[188] "They'll Watch for Drug Crises." *Edwardsville Intelligencer*, June 3, 1974

[189] Heires, Marty. "Festival officials 'Hope' for good season." *Belleville News-Democrat*, April 9, 1975

[190] "Citizen Sound-Off." *Belleville News-Democrat*, July 22, 1976.

[191] Thompson, Doug. "MRF 1977: Where will all the people have gone?" *Alton Telegraph*, March 5, 1977

[192] Thompson, Doug. "An evening of good, honest rock music for 18,000 fans." *Alton Telegraph*, August 9, 1973

[193] Maddox, Teri. "Mississippi River Festival – We'll never forget you." *Belleville News-Democrat*, March 12, 1999

[194] "MRF to study its problems." *Belleville News-Democrat*, October 5, 1976.

[195] Norrish, Dick. "Festival Future Uncertain." *Edwardsville Intelligencer*, October 5, 1976.

[196] Garner, Joe. "Mississippi River Festival" *Southern Illinoisan*, May 22, 1977

[197] Thompson, Doug. "MRF 1977 a festival on a diet" *Alton Telegraph*, April 16, 1977

[198] "Citizen Sound-Off" *Belleville News-Democrat*, April 18, 1977

[199] Thompson, Doug. "Will MRF fold up its tent after another poor season?" *Alton Telegraph*, August 27, 1977

[200] "MRF's newest deficit adds $118,000 to its SIUE debt." *Alton Telegraph*, October 6, 1977

[201] "St. Louis promoter says MRF season still possible." *Alton Telegraph*, February 11, 1978

[202] Ibid

[203] Boul, John. "Promoter to manager Mississippi River Festival." *Belleville News-Democrat*, April 6, 1978

[204] Sharp, Walt. "New York promoters to run MRF." *Alton Telegraph*, April 6, 1978

[205] Ibid

[206] "Serious music abandoned." *Alton Telegraph*, April 7, 1978

[207] Thompson, Doug. "The professionals are coming . . ." *Alton Telegraph*, April 12, 1978

[208] Sharp, Walt. "'Name' acts announced for MRF's ninth year." *Alton Telegraph*, May 5, 1978

[209] Ibid

[210] "The audience was quiet." *Alton Telegraph*, June 5, 1978

[211] Rosenbaum, Connie. "Buck Owens Show Gives Down-Home Air To Festival." *St. Louis Post-Dispatch*, July 18, 1970

[212] Thompson, Doug. "Kristofferson sings – almost." *Alton Telegraph*, July 14, 1972

[213] Ibid

[214] Riley, Marianna. "He wants to move people." *St. Louis Post-Dispatch*, August 28, 1977

[215] Cullinane, John S. "Dolly Parton, Eddie Rabbitt In Show At River Festival." *St. Louis Post-Dispatch*, June 26, 1978

[216] Stankoven, Rick. "Willie, Emmylou please crowd with country rock." *Alton Telegraph*, July 7, 1978

[217] Maddox, Teri. "Willie Nelson is always on his mind." *Belleville News-Democrat*, October 30, 2016

[218] I bid

[219] Richmond, Dick. "Richard Pryor At SIU Festival." *St. Louis Post-Dispatch*, September 11, 1978

[220] Grinstead, Jeanne. "Real 'Hot Stuff.'" *Belleville News-Democrat*, July 17, 1979

[221] Ibid

[222] "Attendance up at MRF." *Belleville News-Democrat*, August 10, 1978

[223] Rice, Patricia. "New Entertainment Wave At SIU-E River Festival." *St. Louis Post-Dispatch*, August 29, 1978

[224] Ibid

[225] Sharp, Walt. "SIUE will be making property deals, including sale of Olin site." *Alton Telegraph*, September 15, 1978

[226] Ibid

[227] Sharp, Walt. "MRF may not survive long enough to mark 10th year." *Alton Telegraph*, January 13, 1979

[228] Ibid

[229] Ibid

[230] "Wrong attractions." *Alton Telegraph*, June 15, 1979

[231] Cullen, Cathy. "MRF promoter castigated." *Alton Telegraph*, July 10, 1979

[232] "Toffant threatens MRF pullout." *Belleville News-Democrat*, July 10, 1979

[233] Ibid

[234] Ibid

[235] "Deputies to continue security at the MRF." *Belleville News-Democrat*, July 12, 1979

[236] "Deputies Cut River Festival Patrols." *St. Louis Post-Dispatch*, July 12, 1979

[237] Thompson, Doug. "Come to MRF: Have yourself a brawl." *Alton Telegraph*, July 11, 1979

[238] "County exec urges Shaw to reappraise MRF lease." *Alton Telegraph*, July 20, 1979

[239] "SIU-E Student Senate Votes To Boycott River Festival." *St. Louis Post-Dispatch*, August 10, 1979

[240] Pollack, Joe. "Silence Shrouds Mississippi River Festival Season." *St. Louis Post-Dispatch*, May 25, 1980

[241] Stroud, Jerri. "Festival At SIU Clouded." *St. Louis Post-Dispatch*, June 8, 1980

[242] Ibid

[243] Sharp, Walt. "MRF promoter defends festival at press parley." *Alton Telegraph*, June 12, 1980

[244] Ibid

[245] Ibid

[246] Stroud, Jerri. "SIU Festival Schedule Is Defended By Promoter." *St. Louis Post-Dispatch*, June 12, 1980

[247] Lesh, Phil (2005). "Searching for the Sound." Little, Brown & Co.; New York, NY. Chapter 19.

[248] Rowland, Mark. "Bring Me The Head Of Jerry Garcia." *St. Louis Post-Dispatch*, August 14, 1980

[249] "MRF promoter hasn't told SIU-E he wants out." *Belleville News-Democrat*, February 25, 1981

[250] "MRF is dead for year." *Alton Telegraph*, May 23, 1981

[251] Bosworth Jr., Charles. "River Festival Down But Not Out, SIU-E Officials Say." *St. Louis Post-Dispatch*, May 24, 1981

[252] "End Of The River Festival?" *St. Louis Post-Dispatch*, May 28, 1981

[253] Richmond, Dick. "Decline And Fall Of River Festival." *St. Louis Post-Dispatch*, June 9, 1980

[254] Gauen, Pat. "River Festival is gone, but memory rises again." *St. Louis Post-Dispatch*, January 21, 2002

[255] Bosworth Jr., Charles. "Problems Of River Festival Make '82 Season Unlikely." *St. Louis Post-Dispatch*, April 5, 1982

[256] Ibid

[257] Clarkin, Carol. "The MRF: shadows of the past." *Alton Telegraph*, August 6, 1983

[258] Ibid

[259] Ahmed, Safir. "Amphitheater Sought For E. St. Louis Riverfront Park." *St. Louis Post-Dispatch*, April 2, 1985

[260] Schlueter, Roger. "Symphony, Mark Russell highlight SIUE Arts & Issues Series." *Belleville News-Democrat*, September 2, 1999

[261] Maddox, Teri. "MRF site to get a historical marker." *Belleville News-Democrat*, April 21, 2009

[262] Dissett, Jim. "Ten Years After." *Belleville News-Democrat*, July 28, 1991

[263] Ibid

[264] Maddox, Teri. "Mississippi River Festival – We'll never forget you." *Belleville News-Democrat*, March 12, 1999

[265] Ibid